German

German phrasebook
2nd edition – April 2003
First published – November 1997

Published by
Lonely Planet Publications Pty Ltd ABN 36 005 607 983
90 Maribyrnong St, Footscray, Victoria 3011, Australia

Lonely Planet Offices
Australia Locked Bag 1, Footscray, Victoria 3011
USA 150 Linden St, Oakland CA 94607
UK 72-82 Rosebery Ave, London, EC1R 4RW

Cover illustration
Beers & V-dubs by Daniel New

ISBN 1 86450 153 7

text © Lonely Planet Publications Pty Ltd 2003
cover illustration © Lonely Planet Publications Pty Ltd 2003

  10 9 8 7 6 5   3 2 1

Printed through Colorcraft Ltd, Hong Kong
Printed in Malaysia

acknowledgments

Lonely Planet Language Products and editor Emma Koch would like to get up on the table and thank the whole, noisy *Bierhalle*:

Publishing manager Jim 'Goethe' Jenkin whose great vision saw the new series develop from the ground up and who generously offered his German language expertise.

Editor Francesca 'Dietrich' Coles for her invaluable assistance on the project and in-house native German speaker Birgit 'Bauhaus' Jordan for answering queries.

Language expert Gunter Muehl for the German translations, the pronunciation guides, for proofing and for excellent advice on all things German. Freelance proofer Adrienne 'Baroque' Costanzo for her sharp eyes and language awareness and the Swiss family Robinson for survival tactics.

Layout designer Daniel 'Love Parade' New for the great illustrations and cover, freelance layout designer Patrick 'Vee Dub' Marris for contributing his layout prowess to the German project, layout designer Sally 'Wunderkind' Morgan for support in layout and input and series designer Yukiyoshi 'Kraftwerk' Kamimura for his input into the project.

Cartographer Natasha 'Zeppelin' Velleley, specialist projects managing cartographer Paul 'Lagerfeld' Piaia and map editor Wayne 'Bismark' Murphy for the language map.

Commissioning editors Karin 'Hingis' Vidstrup Monk and Karina 'Nina' Coates for getting the ball rolling and helping out with layout checks.

Project manager Fabrice 'Kafka' Rocher and managing editor Annelies 'Blue Danube' Mertens who helped bring the project to completion.

And last but not least, Language Products editors Piers 'Lederhosen' Kelly, Ben 'Wagner' Handicott, Meg 'Oom pah pah' Worby and Quentin 'Einstein' Frayne who all contributed to the German cause in various ways.

make the most of this phrasebook ...

Anyone can speak another language! It's all about confidence. Don't worry if you can't remember your school language lessons or if you've never learnt a language before. Even if you learn the very basics (on the inside covers of this book), your travel experience will be the better for it. You have nothing to lose and everything to gain when the locals hear you making an effort.

> finding things in this book

For ease of navigation, this book is in sections. The Tools chapters are the ones you'll thumb through time and again. The Practical section covers basic travel situations like catching transport and finding a bed. The Social section gives you conversational phrases, pick-up lines, the ability to express opinions – so you can get to know people. Food has a section all of its own: gourmets and vegetarians are covered and local dishes feature. Safe Travel equips you with health and police phrases, just in case. Remember the colours of each section and you'll find everything easily; or use the comprehensive Index. Otherwise, check the two-way traveller's Dictionary for the word you need.

> being understood

Throughout this book you'll see coloured phrases on the right-hand side of each page. They're phonetic guides to help you pronounce the language. You don't even need to look at the language itself, but you'll get used to the way we've represented particular sounds. The pronunciation chapter in Tools will explain more, but you can feel confident that if you read the coloured phrase slowly, you'll be understood.

> communication tips

Body language, ways of doing things, sense of humour – all have a role to play in every culture. 'Local talk' boxes show you common ways of saying things, or everyday language to drop into conversation. 'Listen for ...' boxes supply the phrases you may hear. They start with the phonetic guide (because you'll hear it before you know what's being said) and then lead in to the language and the English translation.

introduction 6

tools 9

practical 35

social 87

food 139

safe travel 173

dictionaries 187

index 249

contents

5

Denmark
Copenhagen ○

Berlin ○

Germany

Brussels ○
Belgium
Luxembourg
Luxembourg ○

Prague ○
Czech
Republic

Liechtenstein
Vienna ○
Bern ○
○ *Budapest*
Switzerland *Vaduz*
Austria
Hungary

■ **official language**　■ **widely understood**

For more details see the **introduction**.

Romantic, flowing, literary ... not usually how German is described, but maybe it's time to reconsider. After all, this is a language that has played a major role in the history of Europe and remains one of the most widely spoken languages on the continent. Outside of Europe, it's taught throughout the world and chances are you're already familiar with a number of German words that have entered English – kindergarten, kitsch and waltz are all of German origin.

German is spoken by approximately 100 million people, and is the official language of Germany, Austria and Liechtenstein, and one of the official languages of Belgium, Switzerland and Luxembourg. It's also understood in a number of countries in Eastern Europe. German did not spread across the rest of the world with the same force as English, Spanish and French. This is largely due to the fact that Germany only became a unified nation in 1871 and never established itself as a colonial power.

In recent years, however, the reunification of East and West Germany has seen the language become more important in global politics and economics. Its role in science has long been recognised and German literature lays claim to some of the most famous written works ever printed. Just think of the enormous influence of Goethe, Nietzsche, Freud and Einstein.

at a glance ...

language name: German

name in language:
Deutsch doytsh

language family:
West Germanic

key country: Germany

approximate number of speakers: 100 million

close relatives: Afrikaans, Dutch, English, Frisian, Yiddish

donations to English:
numerous contributions including aspirin, chromosome, eiderdown, hamburger, hamster, plunder, poodle and spanner

introduction

German is commonly divided into two forms – Low German (*Plattdeutsch*) and High German (*Hochdeutsch*). Low German is an umbrella term used for the dialects spoken in Northern Germany. High German is considered the standard form and is understood throughout German-speaking communities: it's the form of German used in this book.

Both German and English belong to the West Germanic language family, along with a number of other languages including Dutch and Yiddish. What this means is that as well as having recognisable words, the grammar of German will also make sense to an English speaker. Don't be put off by the fact that words can have 'different endings' or that there are many ways of saying 'the'. Even with a slight grasp of German grammar, you'll still manage to get your point across.

From the Swiss Alps to the cosy cafes of Vienna, this book gives you the words you need to get by, as well as all the fun, spontaneous phrases that will enrich your experience. Need more encouragement? Remember, the contact you make through using German will make your travels unique. Local knowledge, new relationships and a sense of satisfaction are on the tip of your tongue, so don't just stand there, say something!

> abbreviations used in this book

f	feminine
inf	informal
m	masculine
n	neuter
pl	plural
pol	polite
sg	singular

German is not difficult to pronounce because almost all its sounds are also found in English.

vowel sounds

As in English, vowels can be pronounced short or long with different meanings (compare 'ship' and 'sheep'). Vowels are pronounced crisply and cleanly with your mouth tenser than English, so *Tee* (tea) is pronounced tay not *tay-ee*.

symbol	english equivalent	german example
a	run	*hat*
ah	rather	*habe*
ai	aisle	*mein*
air	hair	*Bär*
aw	saw	*Boot*
ay	say	*leben*
e	red	*Bett/Männer/kaufen*
ee	bee	*fliegen*
er	teacher	*schön*
i	bit	*mit*
o	pot	*Koffer*
oy	boy	*Leute/Häuser*
oo	moon	*Schuhe*
ow	house	*Haus*
ü	(ee with rounded lips, so half-way between ee and oo)	*zurück*
u	foot	*unter*

consonant sounds

All German consonant sounds exist in English except for the kh and r sounds – you might need to spend some time getting familiar with them.

The kh sound is generally like the 'ch' in 'Bach' or the Scottish 'loch', also pronounced at the back of the throat. After the vowels e and i it's pronounced more forward in your mouth, almost like a sh sound. A kh sound, however, will always get you by. In this book we've used one symbol for both sounds to simplify things.

The r sound is pronounced at the back of the throat, almost like saying a g sound, but with some friction, a bit like gargling.

symbol	english equivalent	german example
b	big	*Bett*
ch	chili	*Tschüss*
d	din	*dein*
f	fun	*vier*
g	go	*gehen*
h	hit	*helfen*
k	kick	*kein*
kh	loch	*Sprache/ich*
l	loud	*laut*
m	man	*Mann*
n	no	*nein*
ng	sing	*singen*
p	pig	*Preis*
r	run	*Reise*
s	so	*heiß*
sh	show	*schön*
t	tin	*Tag*
ts	hits	*Zeit*
v	van	*wohnen*
y	yes	*ja*
z	zoo	*sitzen*
zh	pleasure	*Garage*

word stress

Stress in German is straightforward – almost all native German words are pronounced with stress on the first syllable. There are just a couple of things to watch for.

Some prefixes aren't stressed, like *ver-* in the verb *verstehen* fer·*shtay*·en (understand). Also, words borrowed from other languages keep their original stress, like *Organisation* or·ga·ni·sa·*tsyawn* (organisation) and *Student* shtu·*dent* (student) and may have the stress on a different syllable than in English.

While these are handy rules of thumb, you can always rely on the coloured pronunciation guide which shows the stressed syllable in *italics*.

intonation

German intonation is quite similar to English. If you're asking a question, your voice goes up at the end, just like in English: *Bist du fertig?* bist du *fer*·tikh (Are you ready?) or *Tee?* tay (Tea?). If you start with a question word, however, your voice falls, also like in English: *Woher kommst du?* vo·*hair* komst du (Where are you from?).

Note that, like in English, a rise in intonation can indicate that the speaker hasn't finished. For example, if someone asks you where you're from, you can say *Melbourne ... eine Stadt ... in Australien mel*·bawn ... *ai*·ne shtat ... in ow·*stra*·li·en (Melbourne ... a city ... in Australia), rising on the first two parts, and everyone will wait with bated breath!

reading & writing

The relationship between German sounds and the characters that represent them in writing is a regular one, so once you become familiar with them, you should be able to pronounce a new word without a hitch. Also, German doesn't have silent letters – you pronounce the *k* at the start of *Kneipe knai·*pe (pub) and the *e* on the end of *ich verstehe* ikh fair·*shtay·*e (I understand).

The examples in the tables on the previous pages show the correspondence between the sounds (in the first column) and how they're typically spelt (in the third column). However, there are a few features worth noting:

- the letter *ß* stands for *ss* (but the rules for when you can use *ß* or *ss* are confusing to Germans themselves so you can ignore these!)
- the letters *sp* and *st* at the start of a word are pronounced like shp and sht (eg, *Sport* (sport) is pronounced shport)
- final *d*, *g*, and *b* are 'unvoiced', ie, pronounced more like t, k and p (eg, *Geld* (money) *is pronounced* gelt)

Don't be intimidated by the length of some German words. Unlike English, which often uses a number of separate words to express one single idea or notion, German tends to join words together. After a while you'll start to recognise parts of words and you'll find it easy to also understand longer words. For example, *Haupt-* howpt· means 'main', so *Hauptpost* howpt·post means 'main post-office' or 'GPO', and *Hauptstadt* howpt·shtat (literally 'main city') means 'capital'.

This chapter is arranged alphabetically and is designed to help you create your own sentences. If you can't find the exact phrase you need in this book, remember this: there are no rules, only particular ways of saying things. Some grammar, a few gestures, a couple of well-chosen words and you'll generally get the message across.

adjectives see describing things

a/an

Is that a bank or a museum?

Ist das eine Bank oder ein Museum?
(lit: is that a bank or a museum)

ist das *ai*·ne bank *aw*·der ain mu·*zay*·um

German has three words for the articles 'a' or 'an'. The gender of the noun (see **gender**) determines which word you use.

a/an					
masculine	ein	ain	a guide	ein Reiseführer	ain *rai*·ze·fü·rer
neuter	ein	ain	a room	ein Zimmer	ain *tsi*·mer
feminine	eine	*ai*·ne	a ticket	eine Fahrkarte	*ai*·ne *fahr*·kar·te

articles see a/an and the

be

The food is great!
Das Essen ist fantastisch!   das e·sen ist fan·*tas*·tish
(lit: the food is great)

I'm tired.
Ich bin müde.   ikh bin *mü*·de
(lit: I am tired)

Just as in English, the verb 'be' changes depending on who or
what is the subject of the sentence:

to be			sein	
I	am	ich	bin	ikh bin
you sg	are	du	bist	doo bist
he/she/it	is	er/sie/es	ist	er/zee/es ist
we	are	wir	sind	veer zind
you pl	are	ihr	seid	eer zait
they	are	sie	sind	zee zind
you sg&pl pol	are	Sie	sind	zee zind

case see me, myself, I

describing things

My meal is cold.
Mein Essen ist kalt.   main e·sen ist kalt
(lit: my meal is cold)

Adjectives don't change their endings if they come after 'be', as
in the example above. However, if they come before a noun, eg,
das kaltes Essen, you have to add endings which roughly follow
the same pattern as the article 'the' (see **the**). Nevertheless, using
the basic form given in the dictionary, you'll still be understood.

future see planning ahead

gender

The cathedral, the gallery and the museum are on Möhl Street.

*Der Dom, die Galerie
und das Museum sind
in der Möhlstrasse.*
(lit: the cathedral the gallery
  and the museum are
  on the Möhl-street)

dair dawm die ga·le·*ree*
unt das mu·*zay*·um zint
in dair *merl*·shtra·se

All nouns – words that denote a person, place, thing or concept, such as *Claudia*, *Berlin*, *Schlüssel* (key) or *Hunger* (hunger) – in German are assigned a gender. (Nouns are really easy to spot in written German, as they always begin with a capital letter.) They're classified as masculine, feminine or neuter. These distinctions have nothing to do with sex, for example, *Schlüssel* (key) is masculine and *Mädchen* (girl) is neuter even if the girl is obviously female.

Gender affects the appearance of words which accompany the noun, like the articles 'a' and 'the' (as in the example above), 'some', 'none' and adjectives. If you're not sure what gender a word has, don't worry because people will still understand you.

There are no hard and fast rules for predicting the gender of German nouns, but below are some useful generalisations:

- nouns ending in *-er* are generally masculine,
  eg, *der Lehrer* dair *lair*·rer (the male teacher)
- nouns ending in *-in* are feminine,
  eg, *die Lehrerin* dee *lair*·re·rin (the female teacher)
- young people and animals are neuter,
  eg, *das Baby* das *bay*·bi (the baby)

See also **a/an**, **the**, **some**, **none** and **describing things**.

---

m before f

In this book, masculine forms appear before the feminine forms. If letters have been added to the masculine word to form the feminine word (often *in*), these will appear in parentheses. Where the change involves more than the addition of *in*, two words are given, separated by a slash. The neuter form – where applicable – is mentioned last.

have

I have a flat tyre.
Ich habe eine Reifenpanne.   ikh *hah*·be *ai*·ne *rai*·fen·pa·ne
(lit: I have a flat-tyre)

Do you have a quieter room?
Haben Sie ein   *hah*·ben zee ain
ruhigeres Zimmer?   roo·i·ge·res *tsi*·mer
(lit: have you a quieter room)

As with all verbs in German, 'have' changes depending on who or what 'has' something.

have		haben		
I	have	*ich*	*habe*	ikh *hah*·be
you sg	have	*du*	*hast*	doo hast
he/she/it	has	*er/sie/es*	*hat*	er/zee/es hat
we	have	*wir*	*haben*	veer *hah*·ben
you pl	have	*ihr*	*habt*	eer hapt
they	have	*sie*	*haben*	zee *hah*·ben
you sg&pl pol	have	*Sie*	*haben*	zee *hah*·ben

more than one

I'd like two tickets, please.
Ich möchte zwei   ikh *merkh*·te tsvai
Fahrkarten, bitte.   *fahr*·kar·ten *bi*·te
(lit: I would-like two tickets please)

There are a number of ways of forming plurals in German. It can be difficult to predict plural endings, but the most common ones are:

- *-n* for words ending in *-e*, or *-en* for some words ending in a consonant,
  eg, *Fahrkarte* 'ticket' becomes *Fahrkarten* 'tickets' and *Fink* 'finch' becomes *Finken* 'finches'

TOOLS

- -e for some words ending in a consonant,
  eg, *Tag* 'day' becomes *Tage* 'days'
- -e + umlaut (two dots) over the vowel for some words
  ending in a consonant, eg, *Zug* 'train' becomes *Züge* 'trains'

If in doubt, just put a number in front of a singular noun and
you will be understood. For more on numbers, see **numbers &
amounts**, page 27.

me, myself, I

In English you use the subject, eg, 'I', before a verb, but the
object, eg, 'me', after a verb. You would say, for example, 'She
likes me' and not 'She likes I'. German is similar and uses the
following forms:

subject			object		
I	ich	ikh	me	mich	mikh
you sg	du	du	you sg	dich	dikh
he	er	air	him	ihn	een
she	sie	zee	her	sie	zee
it	es	es	it	es	es
we	wir	veer	us	uns	uns
you pl	ihr	eer	you pl	euch	oykh
they	sie	zee	them	sie	zee
you sg&pl pol	Sie	zee	you sg&pl pol	Sie	zee

German does this with other words too. For example, the
masculine word for the article 'the', *der* dair, changes to *den* dayn
after a verb:

The tour guide is handsome.
Der Reiseführer ist schön. dair *rai*·ze·fü·rer ist shern
(lit: the tour-guide is handsome)

I love the tour guide.
Ich liebe den Reiseführer. ikh *lee*·be dayn *rai*·ze·fü·rer
(lit: I love the tour-guide)

There are other forms like this, which are beyond the scope of this book, but if you come across an unfamiliar short word (like *dem* or *des*) it's likely to be a variation on the word for 'the'.

my & your

You room is on the second floor.
Ihr Zimmer ist im   eer *tsi*·mer ist im
zweiten Stock.   *tsvait*·en shtok
(lit: your room is on-the second floor)

Here is my passport.
Hier ist mein Pass.   heer ist main pas
(lit: here is my passport)

The possessive pronouns like 'my' and 'your' in English follow the same pattern as the article 'a/an' – they change depending on the gender or number of the nouns they refer to.

	masculine		neuter		feminine	
my	*mein*	main	*mein*	main	*meine*	mai·ne
your sg	*dein*	dain	*dein*	dain	*deine*	dai·ne
his	*sein*	sain	*sein*	sein	*seine*	sai·ne
her	*ihr*	eer	*ihr*	eer	*ihre*	ee·re
its	*sein*	sain	*sein*	sain	*seine*	sai·ne
our	*unser*	un·zer	*unser*	un·zer	*unsere*	un·ze·re
your pl	*euer*	oy·er	*euer*	oy·er	*eure*	oy·re
their	*ihr*	eer	*ihr*	eer	*ihre*	ee·re
your sg&pl pol	*Ihr*	eer	*Ihr*	eer	*Ihre*	ee·re

negative   see not

not

I don't smoke.
> *Ich rauche nicht.*   ikh *row*·khe nikht
> (lit: I smoke not)

Saying you don't do something is much easier in German than in English – just add *nicht* nikht (not) after the verb. You don't need to add 'don't' like you often do in English.

planning ahead

Tomorrow I'm travelling to Berlin.
> *Ich fahre Morgen*   ikh *fah*·re mor·gen
> *nach Berlin.*   nakh ber·*leen*
> (lit: I travel tomorrow to Berlin)

The easiest way to talk about future events or plans is to use a word like 'tomorrow', or a phrase like 'next week', 'at 3 o'clock' and so on. If you want to talk about future plans but don't have a specific time in mind, you can use the constructions below. This equates to the English construction 'going to'.

I'm going to travel to Berlin.
> *Ich werde nach*   ikh *ver*·de nakh
> *Berlin fahren.*   ber·*leen fah*·ren
> (lit: I am-going-to to
> Berlin travel)

We're going to take a day trip.
> *Wir werden einen*   veer *ver*·den *ai*·nen
> *Tagesausflug machen.*   *tah*·ges·ows·flookh *ma*·khen
> (lit: we are-going-to a
> day-trip make)

The verb *werden* changes depending on who or what is going to do something. People will understand if you just use *werden* in all cases, but the correct forms of the verb are given on the next page in case you want to give them a try:

going to		werden		
I	am going to	*ich*	*werde*	ikh ver·de
you sg	are going to	*du*	*wirst*	doo veerst
he/she/it	is going to	*er/sie/es*	*wird*	er/zee/es veert
we	are going to	*wir*	*werden*	veer ver·den
you pl	are going to	*ihr*	*werdet*	eer ver·det
they	are going to	*sie*	*werden*	zee ver·den
you sg & pl pol	are going to	*Sie*	*werden*	zee ver·den

plural see more than one

pointing something out

That's my bag and those are her suitcases.

Das ist meine Tasche und   das ist *mai*·ne *ta*·she unt
das sind ihre Koffer.   das zint *ee*·re *ko*·fer
(lit: that is my bag and
   that are her suitcases)

It's very easy to point something out in German. Use *das ist* (that is) and *das sind* (that are) no matter what the gender. The only thing you have to think about is whether you're pointing out one or more things.

possession see have and my & your

question words

An easy way to form a question is by using a question word. These are as follows:

question words

who?	*Wer?*	vair
Who is that?	*Wer ist das?* (lit: who is that)	vair ist das
what?	*Was?*	vas
What is that?	*Was ist das?* (lit: what is that)	vas ist das
which?	*Welcher?*	*vel·*kher
Which station is this?	*Welcher Bahnhof ist das?* (lit: which station is that)	*vel·*kher *bahn·*hawf ist das
when?	*Wann?*	van
When does it open?	*Wann öffnet es?* (lit: when opens it)	van *erf·*net es
here?	*Wo?*	vaw
Where is the station?	*Wo ist der Bahnhof?* (lit: where is the station)	vaw ist dair *bahn·*hawf
how?	*Wie?*	vee
How do you say it in German?	*Wie sagt man das auf deutsch?* (lit: how says one that in German)	vee zagt man das owf doytsh
how much?	*Wieviel?*	vee·*feel*
how many?	*Wie viele?*	vee *fee·*le
How much is it?	*Wieviel kostet es?* (lit: how much costs it)	vee·*feel kos·*tet es
why?	*Warum?*	va·*rum*
Why is it shut?	*Warum ist es geschlossen?* (lit: why is it shut)	va·*rum* ist es ge·*shlo·*sen

some

I'd like some ham, please.
> *Ich möchte etwas*   ikh *mer*·khte *et*·vas
> *Schinken bitte.*   *shin*·ken *bi*·te
> (lit: I would-like some ham please)

To ask for 'some' is really simple – just use *etwas* (some), in the same way you'd say 'some' in English.

the

The cathedral, the gallery and the museum are on Möhl Street.
> *Der Dom, die Galerie*   dair dawm die ga·le·*ree*
> *und das Museum sind*   unt das mu·*zay*·um zint
> *in der Möhlstrasse.*   in dair *merl*·shtra·se
> (lit: the cathedral the gallery
>   and the museum are
>   on the Möhl-street)

Unlike English, where there's only one form of the article 'the', German has a number of words which would all be translated in English as 'the'. Which word you use depends on the word it refers to and the way that word fits into the rest of the sentence. It can get a bit complicated, but if you use the simplest forms of 'the', as outlined below, you'll get your message across.

the					
masculine	*der*	der	**the guide**	*der Reiseführer*	dair *rai*·ze·fü·rer
neuter	*das*	das	**the room**	*das Zimmer*	das *tsi*·mer
feminine	*die*	dee	**a ticket**	*die Fahrkarte*	dee *fahr*·kar·te
plural	*die*	dee	**the trains**	*die Züge*	dee *tsü*·ge

See also **a/an** and **gender**.

this/these

This dish is fantastic!
Dieses Gericht ist fantastisch!   dee·zes ge·*rikht* ist fan·*tas*·tish
(lit: this dish is fantastic)

The word *dieser* (this/these) follows the same pattern as 'the':

this/these					
masculine	*dieser*	dee·zer	**this guide**	*dieser Führer*	dee·zer fü·rer
neuter	*dieses*	dee·zes	**this room**	*dieses Zimmer*	dee·zes tsi·mer
feminine	*diese*	dee·ze	**this ticket**	*diese Fahrkarte*	dee·ze fahr·kar·te
plural	*diese*	dee·ze	**these trains**	*diese Züge*	dee·ze tsü·ge

yes/no questions

The hotel is on Potsdamer Square?
Das Hotel ist am Potsdamerplatz?   das *haw*·tel ist am *pots*·dah·mer·plats
(lit: the hotel is on-the Potsdamer-square)

There are three main ways of forming yes/no questions. The one which requires least effort is to make a statement, but to say it like a question, rising in intonation towards the end of the sentence, as illustrated above.

The hotel is on Potsdamer Square, isn't it?
> *Das Hotel ist am*　　　　　das *haw*·tel ist am
> *Potsdamerplatz, nicht wahr?*　pots·dah·mer·plats nikht var
> (lit: the hotel is on
>   Potsdamer-square not true)

The second example shows that you can also add *nicht wahr* (not true) to the end of a statement. This is much easier than in English, where you'd use a variety of question tags, such as 'isn't it?', 'aren't you?' and 'doesn't it?'.

Is the hotel on Potsdamer Square?
> *Ist das Hotel am*　　　　ist das *haw*·tel am
> *Potsdamerplatz?*　　　　pots·dah·mer·plats
> (lit: is the hotel on-the
>   Potsdamer-square)

Finally, the third example shows you can turn a statement into a question by reversing the order of the subject and the verb.

Also see **word order**.

word order

I'm travelling to Berlin.
> *Ich fahre nach Berlin.*　ikh *fah*·re nakh ber·*leen*
> (lit: I travel to Berlin)

Tomorrow I'm travelling to Berlin.
> *Morgen fahre ich*　　　*mor*·gen *fah*·re ikh
> *nach Berlin.*　　　　　nakh ber·*leen*
> (lit: tomorrow travel I to Berlin)

In a straightforward German statement, the verb is the second element (note that this does not necessarily mean it's the second word as the first element can contain more than one word).
　　The verb would usually follow the subject, ie, the concept or thing you're talking about. So if you start the sentence with a word like 'tomorrow', you have to reverse the order of the subject and verb to keep the verb in second spot, as illustrated above. To turn a statement into a question, you can reverse the order of the subject and the verb: the verb comes first – see the example at the top of this page.

language difficulties

There are two forms of the second person singular pronoun 'you'. Use the polite form *Sie* with anyone you don't know well. You should only use the informal form *du* with people you know very well. All the phrases in this chapter use *Sie* – use your intuition to work out when to use formal and informal forms.

Do you speak English?
Sprechen Sie Englisch?   shpre·khen zee eng·lish

Does anyone speak English?
Spricht hier jemand   shprikht heer yay·mant
Englisch?   eng·lish

Do you understand (me)?
Verstehen Sie (mich)?   fer·shtay·en zee (mikh)

Yes, I understand (you).
Ja, ich verstehe (Sie).   yah ikh fer·shtay·e (zee)

No, I don't understand (you).
Nein, ich verstehe (Sie) nicht.   nain ikh fer·shtay·e (zee) nikht

I (don't) understand.
Ich verstehe (nicht).   ikh fer·shtay·e (nikht)

I speak a little German.
Ich spreche ein   ikh shpre·khe ain
bisschen Deutsch.   bis·khen doytsh

How do you ...?	*Wie ...?*	vee ...
pronounce this	*spricht man*	shprikht man
	dieses Wort aus	dee·zes vort ows
say 'ticket' in	*sagt man 'ticket'*	zagt man ti·ket
German	*auf Deutsch*	owf doytsh
write 'Schweiz'	*schreibt man*	shraipt man
	'Schweiz'	shvaits

What does _'Kugel'_ mean?
Was bedeutet 'Kugel'?   vas be·_doy_·tet _koo_·gel

Could you please ...?	_Könnten Sie ...?_	_kern_·ten zee ...
repeat that	_das bitte wiederholen_	das _bi_·te vee·der·_haw_·len
speak more slowly	_bitte langsamer sprechen_	_bi_·te _lang_·za·mer _shpre_·khen
write it down	_das bitte aufschreiben_	das _bi_·te _owf_·shrai·ben

false friends

Many German words look like English words but have a completely different meaning, so be careful! Here are a few examples:

blank   blank   shiny
not 'blank', which is _leer_, leer

Chef   shef   boss
not 'chef', which is _Koch_, kokh

komisch   _kaw_·mish   strange
not 'comical', which is _lustig_, _lus_·tikh

Konfektion   kon·fekt·_tsyawn_ ready-made clothes
not 'confectionary', which is _Konfekt_, kon·_fekt_

sensibel   zen·_zee_·bel   sensitive
not 'sensible', which is _vernünftig_, fer·_nünf_·tikh

Tip   tip   advance information
not 'tip', which is _Trinkgeld_, _trink_·gelt

cardinal numbers

kardinalzahlen

1	*eins*	aints
2	*zwei*	tsvai
3	*drei*	drai
4	*vier*	feer
5	*fünf*	fünf
6	*sechs*	zeks
7	*sieben*	*zee*·ben
8	*acht*	akht
9	*neun*	noyn
10	*zehn*	tsayn
11	*elf*	elf
12	*zwölf*	zverlf
13	*dreizehn*	*drai*·tsayn
14	*vierzehn*	*feer*·tsayn
15	*fünfzehn*	*fünf*·tsayn
16	*sechzehn*	*zeks*·tsayn
17	*siebzehn*	*zeep*·tsayn
18	*achtzehn*	*akht*·tsayn
19	*neunzehn*	*noyn*·tsayn
20	*zwanzig*	*tsvan*·tsikh
21	*einundzwanzig*	*ain*·unt·tsvan·tsikh
22	*zweiundzwanzig*	*tsvai*·unt·tsvan·tsikh
30	*dreißig*	*drai*·tsikh
40	*vierzig*	*feer*·tsikh
50	*fünfzig*	*fünf*·tsikh
60	*sechzig*	*zekh*·tsikh
70	*siebzig*	*zeep*·tsikh
80	*achtzig*	*akht*·tsikh
90	*neunzig*	*noyn*·tsikh
100	*hundert*	*hun*·dert
1,000	*tausend*	*tow*·sent
1,000,000	*eine Million*	*ai*·ne mil·*yawn*

ordinal numbers

1st	*erste*	ers·te
2nd	*zweite*	tsvai·te
3rd	*dritte*	dri·te
4th	*vierte*	feer·te
5th	*fünfte*	fünf·te

fractions

a quarter	*ein Viertel*	ain fir·tel
a third	*ein Drittel*	ain dri·tel
a half	*eine Hälfte*	ai·ne helf·te
three-quarters	*drei Viertel*	drai fir·tel
all	*alles*	a·les
none	*nichts*	nikhts

amounts

How much?	*Wieviel?*	vee·feel
How many?	*Wie viele?*	vee fee·le
(100) grams	*(100) Gramm*	(hun·dert) gram
half a dozen	*ein halbes Dutzend*	ain hal·bes du·tsent
a kilo	*ein Kilo*	ain kee·lo
a packet	*eine Packung*	ai·ne pa·kung
a slice	*eine Scheibe*	ai·ne shai·be
a tin	*eine Dose*	ai·ne daw·ze
less	*weniger*	vay·ni·ger
(just) a little	*(nur) ein bisschen*	(noor) ain bis·khen
much/a lot	*viel*	feel
many	*viele*	fee·le
more	*mehr*	mair
some	*einige*	ai·ni·ge

telling the time

What time is it?	*Wie spät ist es?*	vee shpayt ist es
It's (ten) o'clock.	*Es ist (zehn) Uhr.*	es ist (tsayn) oor
Quarter past one.	*Viertel nach eins.*	fir·tel nahkh ains
Twenty past one.	*Zwanzig nach eins.*	tsvan·tsikh nahkh ains
Half past one.	*Halb zwei.* (lit: half two)	halp tsvai
Twenty to one.	*Zwanzig vor eins.*	tsvan·tsikh fawr ains
Quarter to one.	*Viertel vor eins.*	fir·tel fawr ains
It's 2.12 pm.	*Es ist 14:12.*	es ist feer·tsayn oor tsverlf
am	*vormittags*	fawr·mi·tahks
pm	*nachmittags/ abends*	nahkh·mi·tahks/ ah·bents

the time of your life

English uses 'pm' to denote any time between midday and midnight, but German is a bit more specific. Use *nachmittags* for times between midday and six in the evening, and *abends* between six and midnight.

days of the week

Monday	*Montag*	mawn·tahk
Tuesday	*Dienstag*	deens·tahk
Wednesday	*Mittwoch*	mit·vokh
Thursday	*Donnerstag*	do·ners·tahk
Friday	*Freitag*	frai·tahk
Saturday	*Samstag*	zams·tahk
Sunday	*Sonntag*	zon·tahk

months

die monate

English	German	Pronunciation
January	Januar	yan·u·ahr
February	Februar	fay·bru·ahr
March	März	merts
April	April	a·pril
May	Mai	mai
June	Juni	yoo·ni
July	Juli	yoo·li
August	August	ow·gust
September	September	zep·tem·ber
October	Oktober	ok·taw·ber
November	November	no·vem·ber
December	Dezember	de·tsem·ber

seasons

die jahreszeiten

English	German	Pronunciation
summer	Sommer	zo·mer
autumn	Herbst	herpst
winter	Winter	vin·ter
spring	Frühling	frü·ling

dates

das datum

What date?
Welches Datum? vel·khes dah·tum

What date it is today?
Der Wievielte ist heute? dair vee·feel·te ist hoy·te

It's 18 October.
Heute ist der hoy·te ist dair
18. Oktober. akh·tsayn·te ok·taw·ber

present

die gegenwart

now	*jetzt*	yetst
right now	*jetzt gerade*	yetst ge·*rah*·de
this ...		
afternoon	*heute*	*hoy*·te
	Nachmittag	*nahkh*·mi·tahk
month	*diesen Monat*	*dee*·zen *maw*·nat
morning	*heute Morgen*	*hoy*·te *mor*·gen
week	*diese Woche*	*dee*·ze vo·khe
year	*dieses Jahr*	*dee*·zes yahr
today	*heute*	*hoy*·te
tonight	*heute Abend*	*hoy*·te *ah*·bent

past

die vergangenheit

day before yesterday	*vorgestern*	*fawr*·ges·tern
last month	*letzten Monat*	*lets*·ten *maw*·nat
last night	*vergangene Nacht*	fer·*gang*·e·ne nakht
last week	*letzte Woche*	*lets*·te vo·khe
last year	*letztes Jahr*	*lets*·tes yahr
since (May)	*seit (Mai)*	zait (mai)
a while ago	*vor einer Weile*	fawr *ai*·ner *vai*·le
(three) days ago	*vor (drei) Tagen*	fawr (drai) *tah*·gen
(half an) hour ago	*vor (einer halben) Stunde*	fawr (*ai*·ner *hal*·ben) *shtun*·de
(five) years ago	*vor (fünf) Jahren*	fawr (fünf) *yah*·ren
yesterday ...	*gestern ...*	*ges*·tern ...
afternoon	*Nachmittag*	*nahkh*·mi·tahk
evening	*Abend*	*ah*·bent
morning	*Morgen*	*mor*·gen

future

day after tomorrow	übermorgen	ü·ber·mor·gen
in (six) days	in (sechs) Tagen	in (zeks) tah·gen
in (five) minutes	in (fünf) Minuten	in (fünf) mi·noo·ten
next month	nächsten Monat	naykhs·ten maw·nat
next week	nächste Woche	naykhs·te vo·khe
next year	nächstes Jahr	naykhs·tes yahr
tomorrow ...	morgen ...	mor·gen ...
afternoon	Nachmittag	nahkh·mi·tahk
evening	Abend	ah·bent
morning	früh	frü
until (June)	bis (Juni)	bis (yoo·ni)
within a month	in einem Monat	in ai·nem maw·nat
within an hour	in einer Stunde	in ai·ner shtun·de

during the day

It's early.	Es ist früh.	es ist frü
It's late.	Es ist spät.	es ist shpayt
afternoon	Nachmittag m	nahkh·mi·tahk
dawn	Dämmerung f	de·me·rung
day	Tag m	tahk
evening	Abend m	ah·bent
midday	Mittag m	mi·tahk
midnight	Mitternacht f	mi·ter·nakht
morning	Morgen m	mor·gen
night	Nacht f	nakht
noon	Mittag m	mi·tahk
sunrise	Sonnenaufgang m	zo·nen·owf·gang
sunset	Sonnenunter-gang m	zo·nen·un·ter-gang

How much is it?
  Wie viel kostet es?   vee feel *kos*·tet es

Can you write down the price?
  Können Sie den Preis   ker·nen zee dayn prais
  aufschreiben?   owf·shrai·ben

Do you accept …?	*Nehmen Sie …?*	nay·men zee …
credit cards	*Kreditkarten*	kre·*deet*·kar·ten
debit cards	*Debitkarten*	day·bit·kar·ten
travellers cheques	*Reiseschecks*	rai·ze·sheks
I'd like to …	*Ich möchte …*	ikh *merkh*·te …
cash a cheque	*einen Scheck*	ai·nen shek
	einlösen	ain·ler·zen
change money	*Geld umtauschen*	gelt *um*·tow·shen
change some	*Reiseschecks*	rai·ze·sheks
travellers cheques	*einlösen*	ain·ler·zen
get a cash	*eine*	ai·ne
advance	*Barauszahlung*	bahr·ows·tsah·lung
withdraw money	*Geld abheben*	gelt *ap*·hay·ben
Where's	*Wo ist der/die*	vaw ist dair/dee
the nearest …?	*nächste …?* m/f	*naykhs*·te …
automatic teller	*Geldautomat* m	gelt·ow·to·maht
machine		
foreign exchange	*Geldwechsel-*	gelt·vek·sel·
office	*stube* f	shtoo·be

What's the ...?	Wie ...?	vee ...
charge for that	*hoch sind die*	hawkh zint dee
	Gebühren dafür	ge·*bü*·ren da·*für*
commission	*hoch ist die*	hawkh ist dee
	Kommission	ko·mi·*syawn*
exchange rate	*ist der*	ist dair
	Wechselkurs	*vek*·sel·kurs

It's free.
    Das ist umsonst.   das ist um·*zonst*
It costs (30) euros.
    Das kostet (30) Euro.   das *kos*·tet (*drai*·tsikh) *oy*·ro

money talks

Talking about prices is really easy in German because you
don't need to add a plural ending to the currency. Twenty
dollars is simply *zwanzig Dollar.* Below are a few currencies
translated into German to get you started:

cent	*Cent*	sent
dollar	*Dollar*	*do*·lahr
euro	*Euro*	*oy*·ro
franc	*Franc*	frank
pence	*Pence*	pens
pound	*Pfund*	pfunt
rouble	*Rubel*	*roo*·bel
yen	*Yen*	yen

getting around

What time does the ... leave?	*Wann fährt ... ab?*	van fairt ... ap
boat	*das Boot*	das bawt
bus	*der Bus*	dair bus
train	*der Zug*	dair tsook

What time does the plane leave?
Wann fliegt das Flugzeug ab?   van fleekt das *flook*·tsoyk ap

What time's the ... bus?	*Wann fährt der ... Bus?*	van fairt dair ... bus
first	*erste*	*ers*·te
last	*letzte*	*lets*·te
next	*nächste*	*naykhs*·te

I'd like a/an ... seat.	*Ich hätte gern einen ...*	ikh *he*·te gern *ai*·nen ...
aisle	*Platz am Gang*	plats am gang
non-smoking	*Nichtraucherplatz*	*nikht*·row·kher·plats
smoking	*Raucherplatz*	*row*·kher·plats
window	*Fensterplatz*	*fens*·ter·plats

How long will it be delayed?
Wie viel Verspätung wird es haben?   vee feel fer·*shpay*·tung virt es *hah*·ben

---

listen for ...

... ist ge·*shtri*·khen *... ist gestrichen.*	**The ... is cancelled.**
... hat fer·*shpay*·tung *... hat Verspätung.*	**The ... is delayed.**

Is this seat free?
Ist dieser Platz frei?   ist *dee*·zer plats frai

That's my seat.
Dieses ist mein Platz.   *dee*·zes ist main plats

Can you tell me when we get to (Kiel)?
Könnten Sie mir bitte   *kern*·ten zee meer *bi*·te
sagen, wann wir in   *zah*·gen van veer in
(Kiel) ankommen?   (keel) *an*·ko·men

I want to get off here.
Ich möchte hier   ikh *merkh*·te heer
aussteigen.   *ows*·shtai·gen

buying tickets

fahrkarten kaufen

Where can I buy a ticket?
Wo kann ich eine   vaw kan ikh *ai*·ne
Fahrkarte kaufen?   *fahr*·kar·te *kow*·fen

Do I need to book?
Muss ich einen Platz   mus ikh *ai*·nen plats
reservieren lassen?   re·zer·*vee*·ren *la*·sen

A ... ticket to (Berlin).	*Einen ... nach (Berlin).*	*ai*·nen ... nahkh (ber·*leen*)
1st-class	*Fahrkarte erster Klasse*	*fahr*·kar·te *ers*·ter *kla*·se
2nd-class	*Fahrkarte zweiter Klasse*	*fahr*·kar·te *tsvai*·ter *kla*·se
child's	*Kinderfahrkarte*	*kin*·der·fahr·kar·te
one-way	*einfache Fahrkarte*	*ain*·fa·khe *fahr*·kar·te
return	*Rückfahrkarte*	*rük*·fahr·kar·te
student's	*Studenten-fahrkarte*	shtu·*den*·ten·fahr·kar·te

Two (return tickets), please.
Zwei (Rückfahrkarten) bitte.   tsvai (*rük*·fahr·kar·ten) *bi*·te

How much is it?
Was kostet das?   vas *kos*·tet das

It's full.
Es ist ausgebucht.   es ist *ows*·ge·bookht

How long does the trip take?
Wie lange dauert die Fahrt?   vee *lang*·e *dow*·ert dee fahrt

Is it a direct route?
Ist es eine direkte   ist es *ai*·ne di·*rek*·te
Verbindung?   fer·*bin*·dung

Can I get a stand-by ticket?
Kann ich ein Standby-Ticket   kan ikh ain stend·*bai*·ti·ket
bekommen?   be·*ko*·men

I'd like to ...	*Ich möchte meine*	ikh *merkh*·te *mai*·ne
my ticket, please.	*Fahrkarte bitte ...*	*fahr*·kar·te *bi*·te ...
cancel	*zurückgeben*	tsu·*rük*·gay·ben
change	*ändern lassen*	*en*·dern *la*·sen
confirm	*bestätigen*	be·*shtay*·ti·gen
	lassen	*la*·sen

getting there

German distinguishes between different types of journeys, depending on the transport used:

| *Fahrt* f | fahrt | **journey by road or rail** |
| *Flug* m | flook | **journey by plane** |

This distinction is reflected in the names of the tickets used for these journeys:

| *Fahrkarte* f | *fahr*·kar·te | **train/bus/underground ticket** |
| *Flugticket* n | *flook*·ti·ket | **plane ticket** |

This chapter mostly uses *Fahrkarte*, except in the plane section, so make sure you use the appropriate word when you're buying tickets.

luggage

My luggage has been ...	*Mein Gepäck ist ...*	main ge·*pek* ist ...
damaged	*beschädigt*	be·*shay*·dikht
lost	*verloren*	fer·*law*·ren
	gegangen	ge·*gang*·en
stolen	*gestohlen*	ge·*shtaw*·len
	worden	*vor*·den

My luggage hasn't arrived.
*Mein Gepäck ist
nicht angekommen.*
main ge·*pek* ist
nikht *an*·ge·ko·men

I'd like a luggage locker.
*Ich hätte gern ein
Gepäckschließfach.*
ikh *he*·te gern ain
ge·*pek*·shlees·fakh

Can I have some coins/tokens?
*Können Sie mir
ein paar Münzen/
Wertmarken geben?*
ker·nen zee meer
ain pahr *mün*·tsen/
vert·mar·ken gay·ben

plane

When's the next flight to ...?
*Wann ist der nächste
Flug nach ...?*
van ist dair *naykhs*·te
flook nahkh ...

What time do I have to check in?
*Wann muss ich
einchecken?*
van mus ikh
ain·che·ken

For phrases about getting through customs, see **border crossing**, page 48.

bus

Which bus	*Welcher Bus*	*vel·*kher bus
goes to ...?	*fährt ...?*	fairt ...
Cologne	*nach Köln*	nakh kerln
the station	*zum Bahnhof*	tsum *bahn·*hawf
the youth hostel	*zur Jugend-herberge*	tsur *yoo·*gent·her·ber·ge
the city centre	*zum Stadt-zentrum*	tsum *shtat·*tsen·trum

This one.	*Dieser hier.*	*dee·*zer heer
That one.	*Der da.*	dair dah
Bus number ...	*Bus Nummer ...*	bus *nu·*mer ...

See **numbers & amounts** page 27.

where to?

German uses two different words for the English word 'to'. With place names, use *nach*:

| to Germany | *nach Deutschland* | nakh *doytsh·*lant |
| to Salzburg | *nach Salzburg* | nakh *zalts·*boorg |

For all other destinations, use *zum/zur/zum* m/f/n:

to the station	*zum Bahnhof* m	tsum *bahn·*hawf
to the youth hostel	*zur Jugend-herberge* f	tsur *yoo·*gent·her·ber·ge
to the city centre	*zum Stadt-zentrum* n	tsum *shtat·*tsen·trum

transport

train

What station is this?
Welcher Bahnhof ist das?   vel·kher *bahn*·hawf ist das

What's the next station?
Welches ist der   vel·khes ist dair
nächste Halt?   *naykhs*·te halt

Does this train stop at (Freiburg)?
Hält dieser Zug in   helt *dee*·zer tsook in
(Freiburg)?   (*frai*·boorg)

Do I need to change trains?
Muss ich umsteigen?   mus ikh *um*·shtai·gen

Which carriage	*Welcher*	vel·kher
is (for) ...?	*Wagen ...?*	*vah*·gen ...
dining	*ist der*	ist dair
	Speisewagen	shpai·ze·vah·gen
Munich	*geht nach*	gayt nahkh
	München	*mün*·khen
1st class	*ist erste Klasse*	ist *ers*·te *kla*·se

40

boat

Are there life jackets?
Gibt es Schwimmwesten?   gipt es *shvim*·ves·ten

What's the sea like today?
Wie ist das Meer heute?   vee ist das mair *hoy*·te

I feel seasick.
Ich bin seekrank.   ikh bin zay·krangk

taxi

taxi

I'd like a taxi ...	*Ich hätte gern ein Taxi für ...*	ikh *he*·te gern ain *tak*·si für ...
now	*sofort*	zo·*fort*
tomorrow	*morgen*	*mor*·gen
at (9am)	*(9 Uhr)*	(noyn oor)

Are you free?
Sind Sie frei?   zint zee frai

Please put the meter on.
Schalten Sie bitte den Taxameter ein.   *shal*·ten zee *bi*·te dayn tak·sa·*may*·ter ain

How much is it to ...?
Was kostet es bis ...?   vas *kos*·tet es bis ...

Please take me to (this address).
Bitte bringen Sie mich zu (dieser Adresse).   *bi*·te *bring*·en zee mikh tsoo (*dee*·zer a·*dre*·se)

I'm really late.
Ich bin wirklich spät dran.   ikh bin *virk*·likh shpayt dran

Please slow down.
Fahren Sie bitte langsamer.   *fah*·ren zee *bi*·te *lang*·za·mer

Please wait here.
Bitte warten Sie hier.   *bi*·te *var*·ten zee heer

Stop ...	*Halten Sie ...*	*hal*·ten zee ...
at the corner	*an der Ecke*	an dair *e*·ke
here	*hier*	heer

car & motorbike

> car & motorbike hire

Where can I hire a/an ...?	Wo kann ich ... mieten?	vaw kan ikh ... mee·ten
I'd like to hire a/an ...	Ich möchte ... mieten.	ikh merkh·te ... mee·ten
automatic	ein Fahrzeug mit Automatik	ain fahr·tsoyk mit ow·to·mah·tik
car	ein Auto	ain ow·to
4WD	ein Allradfahr-zeug	ain al·raht·fahr·tsoyk
manual	ein Fahrzeug mit Schaltung	ain fahr·tsoyk mit shal·tung
motorbike	ein Motorrad	ain maw·tor·raht

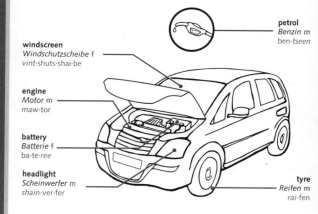

petrol
Benzin m
ben·*tseen*

windscreen
Windschutzscheibe f
vint·shuts·shai·be

engine
Motor m
maw·tor

battery
Batterie f
ba·te·ree

headlight
Scheinwerfer m
shain·ver·fer

tyre
Reifen m
rai·fen

PRACTICAL

42

How much	Wie viel kostet	vee feel kos·tet
is it per ...?	es pro ...?	es praw ...
day	Tag	tahk
hour	Stunde	shtun·de
week	Woche	vo·khe

> on the road

Does this road go to ...?

Führt diese Straße nach ...? fürt dee·ze shtrah·se nahkh ...

What's the ...	Was ist die Höchst-	vas ist dee herkhst·
speed limit?	geschwindigkeit ...?	ge·shvin·dikh·kait ...
city	in der Stadt	in dair shtat
country	auf dem Land	owf daym lant
motorway	auf der	owf dair
	Autobahn	ow·to·bahn

road signs

Ausfahrt	ows·fahrt	**Exit**
Ausfahrt	ows·fahrt	**Keep Clear**
Freihalten	frai·hal·ten	
Baustelle	bow·shte·le	**Roadworks**
Einbahnstraße	ain·bahn·shtrah·se	**One-way**
Einfahrt	ain·fahrt	**Entrance**
Einfahrt	ain·fahrt	**No Entry**
Verboten	fer·baw·ten	
Gefahr	ge·fahr	**Danger**
Halteverbot	hal·te·fer·bawt	**No Stopping**
Mautstelle	mowt·shte·le	**Toll**
Parkverbot	park·fer·bawt	**No Parking**
Radweg	raht·vayk	**Cycle Path**
Sackgasse	zak·ga·se	**No Through Road**
Stopp	shtop	**Stop**
Überholverbot	ü·ber·hawl·fer·bawt	**No Overtaking**
Umleitung	um·lai·tung	**Detour**

(How long) Can I park here?
(Wie lange) Kann ich   (vee *lang*·e) kan ikh
hier parken?   heer *par*·ken

Where do I pay?
Wo muss ich bezahlen?   vaw mus ikh be·*tsah*·len

Where's a petrol station?
Wo ist eine Tankstelle?   vaw ist *ai*·ne *tangk*·shte·le

diesel	*Diesel* m	*dee*·zel
leaded	*verbleites Benzin* n	fer·*blai*·tes ben·*tseen*
LPG	*Autogas* n	*ow*·to·gahs
petrol (gas)	*Benzin* n	ben·*tseen*
regular	*Normalbenzin* n	nor·*mahl*·ben·tseen
unleaded	*bleifreies Benzin* n	*blai*·frai·es ben·*tseen*

> problems

I need a mechanic.
Ich brauche einen   ikh *brow*·khe *ai*·nen
Mechaniker.   me·*khah*·ni·ker

My car/motorbike has broken down (at ...).
Ich habe (in ...) eine   ikh *hah*·be (in ...) *ai*·ne
Panne mit meinem   *pa*·ne mit *mai*·nem
Auto/Motorrad.   *ow*·to/*maw*·tor·raht

I had an accident.
Ich hatte einen Unfall.   ikh *ha*·te *ai*·nen *un*·fal

The car/motorbike won't start.
Das Auto/Motorrad   das *ow*·to/*maw*·tor·raht
springt nicht an.   shpringkt nikht an

I have a flat tyre.
Ich habe eine Reifenpanne.   ikh *hah*·be *ai*·ne *rai*·fen·pa·ne

---

listen for ...

vel·khes fa·bri·*kaht*/mo·*del* ist es
Welches Fabrikat/   **What make/model is it?**
Modell ist es?

I've lost my car keys.
Ich habe meine   ikh *hah*·be *mai*·ne
Autoschlüssel verloren. *ow*·to·*shlü*·sel fer·*law*·ren

I've locked my keys inside the car.
Ich habe meine Schlüssel ikh *hah*·be *mai*·ne *shlü*·sel
im Wagen eingeschlossen. im *vah*·gen *ain*·ge·shlo·sen

I've run out of petrol.
Ich habe kein Benzin mehr. ikh *hah*·be kain ben·*tseen* mair

Can you fix it (today)?
Können Sie es (heute) *ker*·nen zee es (*hoy*·te)
reparieren? re·pa·*ree*·ren

When will it be ready?
Wann ist es fertig? van ist es *fer*·tikh

bicycle

Where can I ...?	*Wo kann ich ...?*	vaw kan ikh ...
buy a second-hand bike	*ein gebrauchtes Fahrrad kaufen*	ain ge·*browkh*·tes *fahr*·raht *kow*·fen
hire a bicycle	*ein Fahrrad mieten*	ain *fahr*·raht *mee*·ten
How much is it per ...?	*Wie viel kostet es für ...?*	vee feel *kos*·tet es für ...
afternoon	*einen Nachmittag*	*ai*·nen *nahkh*·mi·tahk
day	*einen Tag*	*ai*·nen tahk
hour	*eine Stunde*	*ai*·ne *shtun*·de
morning	*einen Vormittag*	*ai*·nen *fawr*·mi·tahk

I have a puncture.
Ich habe einen Platten. ikh *hah*·be *ai*·nen *pla*·ten

local transport

Where's the nearest metro station?
Wo ist der nächste   vaw ist dair *naykhs*·te
U-Bahnhof?   oo·bahn·hawf

Which line goes to (Potsdamer Platz)?
Welche Linie geht zum   *vel*·khe *lee*·ni·e gayt tsum
(Potsdamer Platz)?   (pots·*dah*·mer plats)

day ticket	*Tageskarte* f	*tah*·ges·kar·te
ticket for	*Mehrfach-*	*mair*·fakh·
multiple trips	*fahrkarte* f	fahr·kar·te
tram	*Straßenbahn* f	*shtrah*·sen·bahn
tram stop	*Straßenbahn-*	*shtrah*·sen·bahn·
	haltestelle f	hal·te·shte·le
underground	*U-Bahn* f	*oo*·bahn
underground station	*U-Bahnhof* m	*oo*·bahn·hawf
urban railway	*S-Bahn* f	*es*·bahn
weekly ticket	*Wochenkarte* f	*vo*·khen·kar·te

ticket machines

Buying tickets from machines is very common in Germany, Austria and Switzerland. Some common terms you'll need to know are:

Automat Gibt Rückgeld	**Change Given**
Bitte Wählen	**Please Choose**
Kennzahl Eingeben	**Enter Code**
Korrektur	**Correction**
Taste Drücken	**Press Button**
Zahlbar mit …	**Pay with …**

If you can't get the machine to work, you can always try asking someone:

Wie funktioniert das?
  vee foonk·tsywa·*neert* das   **How does this work?**

passport control

passkontrolle

I'm here ...	Ich bin hier ...	ikh bin heer ...
in transit	auf der Durchreise	owf dair durkh·rai·ze
on business	auf Geschäftsreise	owf ge·shefts·rai·ze
on holiday	im Urlaub	im oor·lowp
I'm here for ...	Ich bin hier für ...	ikh bin heer für ...
(four) days	(vier) Tage	(feer) tah·ge
(three) weeks	(drei) Wochen	(drai) vo·khen
(two) months	(zwei) Monate	(tsvai) maw·na·te

listen for ...

... bi·te	..., bitte.	Your ..., please.
ee·ren	Ihren	
rai·ze·pas	Reisepass	passport
eer vee·zum	Ihr Visum	visa
rai·zen zee ...	Reisen Sie ...?	Are you travelling ...?
a·lain	allein	on your own
in ai·ner gru·pe	in einer Gruppe	in a group
mit ee·rer	mit Ihrer	with your
fa·mee·li·e	Familie	family

at customs

I have nothing to declare.
*Ich habe nichts
zu verzollen.*

ikh *hah*·be nikhts
tsoo fer·*tso*·len

I have something to declare.
*Ich habe etwas
zu verzollen.*

ikh *hah*·be *et*·vas
tsoo fer·*tso*·len

I didn't know I had to declare it.
*Ich wusste nicht, dass ich
das verzollen muss.*

ikh *vus*·te nikht das ikh
das fer·*tso*·len mus

bureaucabulary

Although Germany has a reputation for being a well-organised country, you may find your spontaneity as a traveller hampered by endless red tape. Learning some of these words can help you get on your way:

Abschrift	*ahb*·shrift	**copy/extract**
Abstammungs-urkunde	*ahb·shta*·mungs·ur·kun·de	**birth certificate**
Bekenntnis	be·*kent*·nis	**religion**
Familienname	fa·*mee*·li·en·nah·me	**surname**
Familienstand	fa·*mee*·li·en·shtant	**marital status**
geborene	ge·*baw*·re·ne	**maiden name**
geboren am	ge·*baw*·ren am	**born on**
Geburtsdatum	ge·*burts*·da·tum	**date of birth**
Heirats-urkunde	*hai*·rahts·ur·kun·de	**marriage certificate**
Staatsange-hörigkeit	*shtahts*·an·ge·her·rikh·kait	**citizenship/nationality**
Urkunde	*ur*·kun·de	**document**
Vorname	*for*·nah·me	**first name**
Wohnort	*vawn*·ort	**place of residence**

finding accommodation

eine unterkunft finden

Where's a/an ...?	Wo ist ...?	vaw ist ...
bed & breakfast	eine Pension	ai·ne pahng·zyawn
camping ground	ein Campingplatz	ain kem·ping·plats
guesthouse	eine Pension	ai·ne pahng·zyawn
hotel	ein Hotel	ain ho·tel
inn	ein Gasthof	ain gast·hawf
room in a private home	ein Privatzimmer	ain pri·vaht·tsi·mer
youth hostel	eine Jugendherberge	ai·ne yoo·gent·her·ber·ge

Can you	Können Sie	ker·nen zee
recommend	etwas ...	et·vas ...
somewhere ...?	empfehlen?	emp·fay·len
cheap	Billiges	bi·li·ges
good	Gutes	goo·tes
luxurious	Luxuriöses	luk·su·ri·er·ses
nearby	in der Nähe	in dair nay·e
romantic	Romantisches	ro·man·ti·shes

What's the address?
Wie ist die Adresse?   vee ist dee a·dre·se

For responses, see **directions**, page 59.

> booking ahead & checking in

I'd like to book a room, please.
Ich möchte bitte ein   ikh merkh·te bi·te ain
Zimmer reservieren.   tsi·mer re·zer·vee·ren

I have a reservation.
Ich habe eine   ikh hah·be ai·ne
Reservierung.   re·zer·vee·rung

My name's ...
Mein Name ist ...   main *nah*·me ist ...

For (three) nights/weeks.
Für (drei) Nächte/Wochen.   für (drai) *nekh*·te/*vo*·khen

From (July 2) to (July 6).
Vom (2. Juli) bis   vom (*tsvai*·ten *yoo*·li) bis
zum (6. Juli).   tsum (*zeks*·ten *yoo*·li)

How much	*Wie viel kostet*	vee feel *kos*·tet
is it per ...?	*es pro ...?*	es praw ...
night	*Nacht*	nakht
person	*Person*	per·*zawn*
week	*Woche*	*vo*·khe

Do you have	*Haben Sie ein ...?*	*hah*·ben zee ain ...
a ... room?		
double	*Doppelzimmer*	*do*·pel·tsi·mer
	mit einem	mit *ai*·nem
	Doppelbett	*do*·pel·bet
single	*Einzelzimmer*	*ain*·tsel·tsi·mer
twin	*Doppelzimmer*	*do*·pel·tsi·mer
	mit zwei	mit tsvai
	Einzelbetten	*ain*·tsel·be·ten

listen for ...

dair *shlü*·sel ist an dair re·tsep·*tsyawn*
Der Schlüssel ist   **The key is at reception.**
an der Rezeption.

ee·ren pas *bi*·te
Ihren Pass, bitte.   **Your passport, please.**

es toot meer lait veer *hah*·ben *kai*·ne *tsi*·mer frai
Es tut mir Leid, wir   **I'm sorry, we're full.**
haben keine Zimmer frei.

für vee *fee*·le *nekh*·te
Für wie viele Nächte?   **For how many nights?**

Can I see it?
Kann ich es sehen? kan ikh es *zay*·en

Is there hot water all day?
Gibt es den ganzen gipt es dayn *gan*·tsen
Tag warmes Wasser? tahk *var*·mes *va*·ser

It's fine. I'll take it.
Es ist gut, ich nehme es. es ist goot ikh *nay*·me es

Do I need to pay upfront?
Muss ich im Voraus mus ikh im *faw*·rows
bezahlen? be·*tsah*·len

Can I pay by ...?	*Nehmen Sie ...?*	*nay*·men zee ...
credit card	*Kreditkarten*	kre·*deet*·kar·ten
travellers cheque	*Reiseschecks*	*rai*·ze·sheks

For other methods of payment see **shopping**, page 61.

> requests & queries

When's/Where's breakfast served?
Wann/Wo gibt es Frühstück? van/vaw gipt es *frü*·shtük

Please wake me at (seven).
Bitte wecken Sie mich *bi*·te ve·ken zee mikh
um (sieben) Uhr. um (*zee*·ben) oor

Can I use the ...?	*Kann ich ...*	kan ikh ...
	benutzen?	be·*nu*·tsen
kitchen	*die Küche*	dee *kü*·khe
laundry	*eine*	*ai*·ne
	Waschmaschine	*vash*·ma·shee·ne
telephone	*das Telefon*	das te·le·*fawn*

Do you have a ...?	*Haben Sie ...?*	*hah*·ben zee ...
lift (elevator)	*einen Aufzug*	*ai*·nen *owf*·tsook
laundry service	*einen*	*ai*·nen
	Wäscheservice	*ve*·she·ser·vis
message board	*ein Nachrichten-*	ain *nahkh*·rikh·ten·
	brett	bret
safe	*einen Safe*	*ai*·nen sayf
swimming pool	*ein Schwimmbad*	ain *shvim*·baht

Do you arrange tours here?
*Arrangieren Sie
hier Touren?*
a·rang·zhee·ren zee
heer *too*·ren

Do you change money here?
Wechseln Sie hier Geld?
vek·seln zee heer gelt

Can I leave a message for someone?
*Kann ich eine Nachricht
für jemanden
hinterlassen?*
kan ikh *ai*·ne *nahkh*·rikht
für *yay*·man·den
hin·ter·*la*·sen

Is there a message for me?
*Haben Sie eine
Nachricht für mich?*
hah·ben zee *ai*·ne
nahkh·rikht für mikh

I'm locked out of my room.
*Ich habe mich aus
meinem Zimmer ausgesperrt.*
ikh *hah*·be mikh ows
mai·nem *tsi*·mer ows·ge·shpert

signs

Aufzug	*owf*·tsook	**Lift/Elevator**
Fahrstuhl	*fahr*·shtool	**Lift/Elevator**
Fernsehzimmer	*fern*·zay·tsi·mer	**TV Room**
Frühstücksraum	*frü*·shtüks·rowm	**Breakfast Room**
Notausgang	*nawt*·ows·gang	**Emergency Exit**

Could I have	*Könnte ich bitte*	*kern*·te ikh *bi*·te
... please?	*... haben?*	*... hah*·ben
my key	*meinen Schlüssel*	*mai*·nen *shlü*·sel
a receipt	*eine Quittung*	*ai*·ne *kvi*·tung

It's too ...	*Es ist zu ...*	es ist tsoo ...
cold	*kalt*	kalt
dark	*dunkel*	*dung*·kel
expensive	*teuer*	*toy*·er
light/bright	*hell*	hel
noisy	*laut*	lowt
small	*klein*	klain

The ... doesn't work.   *... funktioniert nicht.*   ... fungk·tsyo·*neert* nikht

  air-conditioning   *Die Klima-anlage*   dee klee·ma·an·lah·ge

  fan   *Der Ventilator*   dair ven·ti·*lah*·tor

  toilet   *Die Toilette*   dee to·a·*le*·te

The (bathroom) door is locked.

Die (Badezimmer)Tür ist abgeschlossen.   dee (*bah*·de·tsi·mer·)tür ist *ap*·ge·shlo·sen

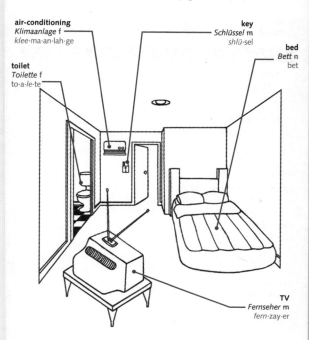

air-conditioning
Klimaanlage f
klee·ma·an·lah·ge

key
Schlüssel m
shlü·sel

bed
Bett n
bet

toilet
Toilette f
to·a·*le*·te

TV
Fernseher m
fern·zay·er

accommodation

53

The window won't open/close.

Das Fenster lässt sich		das *fens*·ter lest zikh
nicht öffnen/schließen.		nikht *erf*·nen/*shlee*·sen

Can I get | *Kann ich noch* | kan ikh nokh
another ...? | *einen/eine/ein ...* | *ai*·nen/*ai*·ne/ain ...
| *bekommen?* m/f/n | be·*ko*·men
blanket | *Decke* f | *de*·ke
duvet cover | *Bettbezug* m | *bet*·be·tsook
pillow | *Kopfkissen* n | *kopf*·ki·sen
pillowcase | *Kopfkissen-* | *kopf*·ki·sen·
| *bezug* m | be·tsook
sheet | *Bettlaken* n | *bet*·lah·ken
towel | *Handtuch* n | *hant*·tookh

a knock at the door

Who is it?	*Wer ist da?*	vair ist dah
Just a moment.	*Einen Augenblick,*	*ai*·nen ow·gen·*blik*
	bitte!	*bi*·te
Come in.	*Herein!*	he·*rain*
Come back	*Kommen Sie*	*ko*·men zee
later, please.	*bitte später*	*bi*·te shpay·ter
	noch einmal.	nokh *ain*·mahl

> checking out

What time is checkout?

Wann muss ich	van mus ikh
auschecken?	*ows*·che·ken

How much extra to stay until (6 o'clock)?

Was kostet es extra, wenn	vas *kos*·tet es *eks*·tra ven
ich bis (6 Uhr) bleiben	ikh bis (zeks oor) *blai*·ben
möchte?	*merkh*·te

I'm leaving now.

Ich reise jetzt ab.	ikh *rai*·ze yetst ap

Can you call a taxi for me (for 11 o'clock)?

Können Sie mir (für 11 Uhr)	*ker*·nen zee meer (für elf oor)
ein Taxi rufen?	ain *tak*·si *roo*·fen

Can I leave my bags here until ...?	Kann ich meine Taschen bis ... hier lassen?	kan ikh *mai*·ne *ta*·shen bis ... heer *la*·sen
next week	nächste Woche	*naykhs*·te *vo*·khe
tonight	heute Abend	*hoy*·te *ah*·bent
Wednesday	Mittwoch	*mit*·vokh

Could I have my ... please?	Könnte ich bitte ... haben?	*kern*·te ikh *bi*·te ... *hah*·ben
deposit	meine Anzahlung	*mai*·ne *an*·tsah·lung
passport	meinen Pass	*mai*·nen pas
valuables	meine Wertsachen	*mai*·ne *vert*·za·khen

There's a mistake in the bill.
Da ist ein Fehler in der Rechnung.
dah ist ain *fay*·ler in dair *rekh*·nung

I had a great stay, thank you.
Es hat mir hier sehr gut gefallen.
es hat meer heer zair goot ge·*fa*·len

I'll recommend it to my friends.
Ich werde Sie weiterempfehlen.
ikh *ver*·de zee *vai*·ter·emp·fay·len

camping

Where's the nearest ...?	Wo ist der nächste ...?	vaw ist dair *naykhs*·te ...
camp site	Zeltplatz	*tselt*·plats
shop	Laden	*lah*·den
shower facility	Duschraum	*doosh*·rowm
toilet block	Toilettenblock	to·a·*le*·ten·blok

Do you have ...?	Haben Sie ...?	*hah*·ben zee ...
electricity	Strom	shtrawm
shower facilities	Duschen	*doo*·shen
a site	einen Stellplatz	*ai*·nen *shtel*·plats
tents for hire	Zelte zu vermieten	*tsel*·te tsoo fer·*mee*·ten

Is it coin-operated?
Braucht man dafür Münzen?   browkht man da·*für* mün·tsen

Is the water drinkable?
Kann man das Wasser trinken?   kan man das va·ser *tring*·ken

Who do I ask to stay here?
Wen muss ich fragen,   vayn mus ikh *frah*·gen
wenn ich hier zelten   ven ikh heer *tsel*·ten
möchte?   *merkh*·te

How much do you charge ...?	*Wie viel berechnen Sie ...?*	vee feel be·*rekh*·nen zee ...
for a car	*für ein Auto*	für ain *ow*·to
for a caravan	*für einen Wohnwagen*	für *ai*·nen *vawn*·vah·gen
for a tent	*für ein Zelt*	für ain tselt
per person	*pro Person*	praw per·*zawn*
Can I ...?	*Kann ich ...?*	kan ikh ...
camp here	*hier zelten*	heer *tsel*·ten
park next to my tent	*neben meinem Zelt parken*	*nay*·ben *mai*·nem tselt *par*·ken

gas cylinder	*Gasflasche* f	*gahs*·fla·she
mallet	*Holzhammer* m	*holts*·ha·mer
peg	*Hering* m	*hay*·ring
rope	*Seil* n	zail
shower token	*Duschmünze* f	*doosh*·mün·tse
sleeping bag	*Schlafsack* m	*shlahf*·zak
spade	*Spaten* m	*shpah*·ten
tent	*Zelt* n	tselt
torch (flashlight)	*Taschenlampe* f	*ta*·shen·lam·pe

renting

| I'm here about the ... for rent. | *Ich komme wegen des/der/des zu vermietenden ... m/f/n* | ikh ko·me vay·gen des/dair/des tsoo fer·mee·ten·den ... |

apartment	*Appartement n*	a·part·ment
cabin	*Hütte f*	hü·te
holiday apartment	*Ferienwohnung f*	fay·ri·en·vaw·nung
house	*Haus n*	hows
room	*Zimmer n*	tsi·mer
villa	*Villa f*	vi·la

furnished	*möbliert*	mer·bleert
partly furnished	*teilmöbliert*	tail·mer·bleert
unfurnished	*unmöbliert*	un·mer·bleert

Do you have a/an ... for rent?
Haben Sie ... zu vermieten?
hah·ben zee ...
tsoo fer·mee·ten

How many rooms does it have?
Wie viele Zimmer hat es?
vee fee·le
tsi·mer hat es

I want something near the ...	*Ich möchte etwas in der Nähe ...*	ikh merkh·te et·vas in dair nay·e ...
beach	*des Strandes*	des shtran·des
city centre	*des Stadtzentrums*	des shtat·tsen·trums
shops	*der Geschäfte*	dair ge·shef·te

How much is it for ...?	*Was kostet es für ...?*	vas kos·tet es für ...
(one) week	*(eine) Woche*	(ai·ne) vo·khe
(two) months	*(zwei) Monate*	(tsvai) maw·na·te

Who is my ...?	*Wer ist ...?*	vair ist ...
agent	*mein Makler*	main mahk·ler
contact person	*meine Kontaktperson*	mai·ne kon·takt·per·zawn

I want to rent it from (July 2) to (July 6).
Ich möchte es vom
(2. Juli) bis zum
(6. Juli) mieten.

ikh *merkh*·te es fom
(tsvai·ten *yoo*·li) bis tsum
(zeks·ten *yoo*·li) *mee*·ten

Is there a bond?
Gibt es eine Kaution?

gipt es *ai*·ne kow·*tsyawn*

Are bills extra?
Kommen noch
Nebenkosten dazu?

ko·men nokh
nay·ben·kos·ten da·*tsoo*

staying with locals

bei einheimischen übernachten

Can I stay at your place?
Kann ich bei Ihnen/dir
übernachten? pol/inf

kan ikh bai *ee*·nen/deer
ü·ber·*nakh*·ten

Is there anything I can do to help?
Kann ich Ihnen/dir
irgendwie helfen? pol/inf

kan ikh *ee*·nen/deer
ir·gent·vee *hel*·fen

I have my own ...	*Ich habe ...*	ikh *hah*·be ...
mattress	*meine eigene*	*mai*·ne *ai*·ge·ne
	Matratze	ma·*tra*·tse
sleeping bag	*meinen eigenen*	*mai*·nen *ai*·ge·nen
	Schlafsack	*shlahf*·zak

Can I ...?	*Kann ich ...?*	kan ikh ...
bring anything	*etwas für das*	et·vas für das
for the meal	*Essen mitbringen*	*e*·sen *mit*·bring·en
do the dishes	*abwaschen*	*ap*·va·shen
set/clear	*den Tisch decken/*	dayn tish *de*·ken/
the table	*abräumen*	*ap*·roy·men
take out the	*den Müll*	dayn mül
rubbish	*rausbringen*	*rows*·bring·en

Thanks for your hospitality.
Vielen Dank für Ihre/deine
Gastfreundschaft. pol/inf

fee·len dangk für *ee*·re/*dai*·ne
gast·froynt·shaft

See also expressions in **food**, pages 143 & 155.

PRACTICAL

Where's (a bank)?
Wo ist (eine Bank)?   vaw ist (*ai*·ne bangk)

I'm looking for (the cathedral).
Ich suche (den Dom).   ikh *zoo*·khe (dayn dawm)

Which way is (a public toilet)?
In welcher Richtung ist   in *vel*·kher *rikh*·tung ist
(eine öffentliche Toilette)? (*ai*·ne *er*·fent·li·khe to·a·*le*·te)

listen for ...

es ist ...	*Es ist ...*	It's ...
an dair *e*·ke	*an der Ecke*	on the corner
dort	*dort*	there
fawr ...	*vor ...*	in front of ...
gay·gen·*ü*·ber ...	*gegenüber ...*	opposite ...
ge·rah·de·*ows*	*geradeaus*	straight ahead
heer	*hier*	here
hin·ter ...	*hinter ...*	behind ...
lingks	*links*	left
nah·e	*nahe*	near
nay·ben ...	*neben ...*	next to ...
rekhts	*rechts*	right
vait vek	*weit weg*	far away
bee·gen zee ... ap	*Biegen Sie ... ab.*	Turn ...
an dair *e*·ke	*an der Ecke*	at the corner
bai dair *am*·pel	*bei der Ampel*	at the traffic lights
lingks/rekhts	*links/rechts*	left/right
es ist ... ent·*fernt*	*Es ist ... entfernt.*	It's ...
(*hun*·dert) *may*·ter	*(100) Meter*	(100) metres
(fünf) mi·*noo*·ten	*(5) Minuten*	(five) minutes
nor·den	*Norden* m	north
zü·den	*Süden* m	south
os·ten	*Osten* m	east
ves·ten	*Westen* m	west

How can I get there?
Wie kann ich da hinkommen?   vee kan ikh dah *hin*·ko·men

Can you show me (on the map)?
Können Sie es mir   *ker*·nen zee es meer
(auf der Karte) zeigen?   (owf dair *kar*·te) *tsai*·gen

What's the address?
Wie ist die Adresse?   vee ist dee a·*dre*·se

How far is it?
Wie weit ist es?   vee *vait* ist es

by ...	*mit ...*	mit ...
bus	*dem Bus*	daym *bus*
taxi	*dem Taxi*	daym *tak*·si
train	*dem Zug*	daym *tsook*

on foot	*zu Fuß*	tsoo *foos*

avenue	*Allee* f	a·*lay*
lane	*Gasse* f	*ga*·se
square	*Platz* m	*plats*
street	*Straße/Weg* f/m	*shtrah*·se/vayk

traffic light
Ampel f
am·pel

bus
Bus m
bus

shop
Geschäft m
ge·*sheft*

intersection
Kreuzung f
kroy·zung

pedestrian crossing
Fußgänger-überweg m
foos·*genger*·*über*·vek

corner
Ecke f
e·ke

taxi
Taxi n
tak·see

looking for ...

Where's (a/the supermarket)?
Wo ist (ein/der   vaw ist (ain/dair
Supermarkt)?   zoo·per·markt)

Where can I buy ...?
Wo kann ich ... kaufen?   vaw kan ikh ... kow·fen

For phrases on directions, see **directions**, page 59, and for additional shops and services, see the **dictionary**.

making a purchase

I'd like to buy ...
Ich möchte ... kaufen.   ikh *merkh*·te ... kow·fen

I'm just looking.
Ich schaue mich nur um.   ikh *show*·e mikh noor um

How much is this?
Wie viel kostet das?   vee feel *kos*·tet das

Can you write down the price?
Können Sie den Preis   *ker*·nen zee dayn prais
aufschreiben?   *owf*·shrai·ben

Do you have any others?
Haben Sie noch andere?   *hah*·ben zee nokh *an*·de·re

Can I look at it?
Können Sie es   *ker*·nen zee es
mir zeigen?   meer *tsai*·gen

Do you accept ...?   *Nehmen Sie ...?*   *nay*·men zee ...
    credit cards   *Kreditkarten*   kre·*deet*·kar·ten
    debit cards   *Debitkarten*   *day*·bit·kar·ten
    travellers cheques   *Reiseschecks*   *rai*·ze·sheks

Could I have ... please?	Könnte ich ... bekommen?	kern·te ikh ... be·ko·men
a bag	eine Tüte	ai·ne tü·te
a receipt	eine Quittung	ai·ne kvi·tung
it wrapped	es eingepackt	es ain·ge·pakt

Does it have a guarantee?
Gibt es darauf Garantie?   gipt es da·rowf ga·ran·tee

Can I have it sent overseas?
Kann ich es ins Ausland   kan ikh es ins ows·lant
verschicken lassen?   fer·shi·ken la·sen

Can you order it for me?
Können Sie es für   ker·nen zee es für
mich bestellen?   mikh be·shte·len

Can I pick it up later?
Kann ich es später   kan ikh es shpay·ter
abholen?   ap·haw·len

It's faulty/broken.
Es ist fehlerhaft/kaputt.   es ist fay·ler·haft/ka·put

I'd like ... please.	Ich möchte bitte ...	ikh merkh·te bi·te ...
my change	mein Wechselgeld	main vek·sel·gelt
my money back	mein Geld	main gelt
	zurückhaben	tsu·rük·hah·ben
to return this	dieses	dee·zes
	zurückgeben	tsu·rük·gay·ben

bargaining

That's too expensive.
Das ist zu teuer.   das ist tsoo *toy*·er

Can you lower the price?
Können Sie mit dem   *ker*·nen zee mit dem
Preis heruntergehen?   prais he·*run*·ter·gay·en

Do you have something cheaper?
Haben Sie etwas   *hah*·ben zee *et*·vas
Billigeres?   *bi*·li·ge·res

I'll give you ...
Ich gebe Ihnen ...   ikh *gay*·be *ee*·nen ...

clothes

Can I try it on?
Kann ich es anprobieren?   kan ikh es *an*·pro·bee·ren

My size is ...
Ich habe Größe ...   ikh *hah*·be *grer*·se ...

It doesn't fit.
Es passt nicht.   es past nikht

repairs

Can I have my ... repaired here?
Kann ich hier mein ...   kan ikh heer main ...
reparieren lassen?   re·pa·*ree*·ren *la*·sen

When will my shoes be ready?
Wann sind meine   van zint *mai*·ne
Schuhe fertig?   *shoo*·e *fer*·tikh

When will my ... be ready?	Wann ist mein/ meine/mein ... fertig? m/f/n	van ist main/ mai·ne/main ... fer·tikh
backpack	Rucksack m	ruk·zak
camera	Kamera f	ka·me·ra
(sun)glasses	(Sonnen)Brille f	(zo·nen·)bri·le

darn holes

buttons	Knöpfe m pl	knerp·fe
needle	Nadel f	nah·del
scissors	Schere f	shair·re
thread	Faden m	fah·den

hairdressing

beim friseur

I'd like (a) ...	Ich möchte ...	ikh merkh·te ...
blow wave	eine Fönwelle	ai·ne fern·ve·le
colour	mir die Haare färben lassen	meer dee hah·re fer·ben la·sen
foils	Folien	faw·li·en
haircut	mir die Haare schneiden lassen	meer dee hah·re shnai·den la·sen
my beard trimmed	mir den Bart stutzen lassen	meer dayn bart shtu·tsen la·sen
shave	mich rasieren lassen	mikh ra·zee·ren la·sen
streaks	Strähnchen	shtrayn·khen
trim	mir die Haare nachschneiden lassen	meer dee hah·re nahkh·shnai·den la·sen

Please use a new blade.

Benutzen Sie bitte
eine neue Klinge.

be·nu·tsen zee bi·te
ai·ne noy·e kling·e

Don't cut it too short.

Schneiden Sie es
nicht zu kurz.

shnai·den zee es
nikht tsoo kurts

Shave it all off!
Rasieren Sie alles ab!   ra·*zee*·ren zee *a*·les ap

I should never have let you near me!
Ich hätte Sie nie an mein   ikh *he*·te zee nee an main
Haar lassen dürfen!   hahr *la*·sen *dür*·fen

For colours, see the **dictionary**.

books & reading

bücher und lesen

Is there a/an (English-language) ...?	*Gibt es ...?*	gipt es ...
bookshop	*einen Buch-laden (für englische Bücher)*	*ai*·nen *bookh*·lah·den (für *eng*·li·she *bü*·kher)
section	*eine Abteilung (für englische Bücher)*	*ai*·ne ap·*tai*·lung (für *eng*·li·she *bü*·kher)

Do you have Lonely Planet guidebooks?
Haben Sie Lonely-Planet-   hah·ben zee *lohn*·li·*ple*·net·
Reiseführer?   rai·ze·fü·rer

Do you have a better phrasebook than this?
Haben Sie einen besseren   hah·ben zee *ai*·nen be·se·ren
Sprachführer als diesen?   *shprahkh*·fü·rer als *dee*·zen

---

listen for ...

nain (*hah*·ben veer) *lai*·der nikht
Nein, (haben wir)   **No, we don't have any.**
leider nicht.

shopping

65

music

I'd like (a) ...	*Ich hätte gern ...*	ikh *he*·te gern ...
CD	*eine CD*	*ai*·ne tsay·*day*
blank tape	*eine leere Kassette*	*ai*·ne *lair*·re ka·*se*·te
headphones	*Kopfhörer*	*kopf*·her·rer

I heard a band called ...
Ich habe eine Band mit — ikh *hah*·be *ai*·ne bent mit
dem Namen ... gehört. — daym *nah*·men ... ge·hert

I heard a singer called ...
Ich habe einen Sänger mit — ikh *hah*·be *ai*·nen *zeng*·er mit
dem Namen ... gehört. — daym *nah*·men ... ge·hert

What's his/her best recording?
Was ist seine/ihre — vas ist *zai*·ne/*ee*·re
beste CD? — *bes*·te tsay·*day*

Can I listen to this?
Kann ich mir das anhören? — kan ikh meer das *an*·her·ren

Is this a pirated copy?
Ist das eine Raubkopie? — ist das *ai*·ne *rowp*·ko·pee

photography

I need a ... film for this camera.	*Ich brauche einen ... für diese Kamera.*	ikh *brow*·khe *ai*·nen ... für *dee*·ze *ka*·me·ra
APS	*APS-Film*	ah·*pay*·es·film
B&W	*Schwarzweißfilm*	shvarts·*vais*·film
colour	*Farbfilm*	*farp*·film
slide	*Diafilm*	*dee*·a·film
(200) speed	*(200)-ASA-Film*	(*tsvai*·hun·dert)·*ah*·za·film

Can you ...?	Können Sie ...?	ker·nen zee ...
develop this film	*diesen Film entwickeln*	*dee·*zen film ent·*vi·*keln
load my film	*mir den Film einlegen*	meer dayn film *ain·*lay·gen

How much is it to develop this film?
Was kostet es, diesen Film entwickeln zu lassen?
vas *kos·*tet es *dee·*zen film ent·*vi·*keln tsoo *la·*sen

When will it be ready?
Wann ist er fertig?
van ist air *fer·*tikh

I need a passport photo taken.
Ich möchte ein Passfoto machen lassen.
ikh *merkh·*te ain *pas·*faw·to *ma·*khen *la·*sen

I'm not happy with these photos.
Mit diesen Fotos bin ich nicht zufrieden.
mit *dee·*zen *faw·*tos bin ikh nikht tsu·*free·*den

I don't want to pay the full price.
Ich möchte nicht den vollen Preis bezahlen.
ikh *merkh·*te nikht dayn *fo·*len prais be·*tsah·*len

cheers for beers & souvenirs

Here's a list of some of the most common souvenirs from Germany, Austria and Switzerland, displayed by region:

Aachen: *Aachener Printen* (gingerbread)

All over Germany: beer steins

Austria: chocolates like *Mozartkugeln* (chocolates filled with marzipan, hazelnuts and nougat) and fruit brandies

Bavarian Forest: crystal glassware

Harz Mountains: puppets and marionettes, especially of witches; also famous for glassware

Lübeck: marzipan

Meissen: modern and antique porcelain

cheers for beers & souvenirs

Nuremberg: toys, especially wooden figures and tin toys; also *Lebkuchen* (gingerbread)

Rhine and Moselle Rivers: renowned for their white wines

Rothenburg ob der Tauber: wooden toys and Christmas decorations

Switzerland: typical souvenirs include cuckoo clocks, chocolate and cow bells – also famous for all kinds of timepieces

The Black Forest: cuckoo clocks, dolls and fruit brandies

Thuringia: wooden figures and Christmas decorations

beer stein	*Bierkrug* m	beer·krook
chocolate	*Schokolade* f	sho·ko·*lah*·de
chocolates	*Pralinen* n pl	pra·*lee*·nen
Christmas decorations	*Weihnachts-schmuck* m	*vai*·nakhts·shmuk
clock	*Uhr* f	oor
cow bell	*Kuhglocke* f	*koo*·glo·ke
crystal glassware	*Kristallglas* n	kris·*tal*·glahs
cuckoo clock	*Kuckucksuhr* f	*ku*·kuks·oor
doll	*Puppe* f	*pu*·p e
fruit brandy	*Obstler* m	*awpst*·ler
glassware	*Glaswaren* pl	*glahs*·vah·ren
gingerbread	*Lebkuchen* m	*layp*·koo·khen
marionette	*Marionette* f	ma·ri·o·*ne*·te
marzipan	*Marzipan* n	*mar*·tsi·pahn
porcelain	*Porzellan* n	por·tse·*lahn*
puppet	*Puppe* f	*pu*·pe
tin toys	*Blechspielzeug* n	*blekh*·shpeel·tsoyk
white wine	*Weißwein* m	*vais*·vain
witch	*Hexe* f	*hek*·se
wooden figure	*Holzfigur* f	*holts*·fi·goor
wooden toys	*Holzspielzeug* n	*holts*·shpeel·tsoyk

post office

post

I want to send a ...	Ich möchte ... senden.	ikh *merkh*·te ... *zen*·den
fax	ein Fax	ain faks
parcel	ein Paket	ain pa·*kayt*
postcard	eine Postkarte	*ai*·ne *post*·kar·te
I want to buy a/an...	Ich möchte ... kaufen.	ikh *merkh*·te ... *kow*·fen
aerogram	ein Aerogramm	ain air·ro·*gram*
envelope	einen Umschlag	*ai*·nen *um*·shlahk
stamp	eine Briefmarke	*ai*·ne *breef*·mar·ke

airmail	Luftpost n	*luft*·post
customs declaration	Zollerklärung f	*tsol*·er·klair·rung
domestic	Inlands-	*in*·lants·
express mail	Expresspost f	eks·*pres*·post
fragile	zerbrechlich	tser·*brekh*·likh
international	international	in·ter·na·tsyo·*nahl*
mail box	Briefkasten m	*breef*·kas·ten
postcode	Postleitzahl f	*post*·lait·tsahl
registered mail	Einschreiben n	*ain*·shrai·ben
surface mail	Landbeförderung f	*lant*·be·fer·de·rung

Please send it by air/surface mail to ...

Bitte schicken Sie das per
Luftpost/Landbeförderung
nach ...

bi·te shi·ken zee das per
luft·post/lant·be·fer·de·rung
nahkh ...

It contains ...

Es enthält ...

es ent·helt ...

Where's the poste restante section?

Wo ist der Schalter für
postlagernde Briefe?

vaw ist dair shal·ter für
post·lah·gern·de bree·fe

Is there any mail for me?

Ist Post für mich da?

ist post für mikh dah

listen for ...

merkh·ten zee das per eks·pres·post aw·der
nor·mahl·post shi·ken
Möchten Sie das per   **Would you like to send it**
Expresspost oder   **express or regular post?**
Normalpost schicken?

vas ist dah drin
Was ist da drin?   **What does it contain?**

vaw·hin merkh·ten zee das shi·ken
Wohin möchten   **Where are you**
Sie das schicken?   **sending it?**

phone

telefon

I want to make a ... (to Singapore).	*Ich möchte ...*	ikh merkh·te ...
call	*(nach Singapur)* *telefonieren*	*(nahkh zing·a·poor)* te·le·fo·nee·ren
reverse-charge/ collect call	*ein R-Gespräch* *(nach Singapur)* *führen*	ain air·ge·shpraykh *(nahkh zing·a·poor)* fü·ren

PRACTICAL

70

What's your phone number?
*Wie ist Ihre/deine
Telefonnummer?* pol/inf

vee ist ee·re/*dai*·ne
te·le·*fawn*·nu·mer

Where's the nearest public phone?
*Wo ist das nächste
öffentliche Telefon?*

vaw ist das *naykhs*·te
er·fent·li·khe te·le·*fawn*

I want to buy a phone card.
*Ich möchte eine
Telefonkarte kaufen.*

ikh *merkh*·te *ai*·ne
te·le·*fawn*·kar·te *kow*·fen

The number is ...
Die Nummer ist ...

dee *nu*·mer ist ...

What's the area/country code for ...?
Was ist die Vorwahl für ...?

vas ist dee *fawr*·vahl für ...

It's engaged.
Es ist besetzt.

es ist be·*zetst*

I've been cut off.
Ich bin unterbrochen worden.

ikh bin un·ter·*bro*·khen *vor*·den

The connection's bad.
Die Verbindung ist schlecht.

dee fer·*bin*·dung ist shlekht

Hello.
Hallo!

ha·lo

Can I speak to ...?
Kann ich mit ... sprechen?

kan ikh mit ... *shpre*·khen

It's ...
Hier ist ...

heer ist ...

Can I leave a message?
*Kann ich eine Nachricht
hinterlassen?*

kan ikh *ai*·ne *nahkh*·rikht
hin·ter·*la*·sen

phone numbers

To avoid confusion with *drei*, three, on the phone,
Germans use *zwo* instead of *zwei*, for two.

Please tell him/her I called.
> *Bitte sagen Sie*
> *ihm/ihr, dass ich*
> *angerufen habe.*

bi·te zah·gen zee
eem/eer das ikh
an·ge·roo·fen hah·be

I'll call back later.
> *Ich rufe später*
> *nochmal an.*

ikh roo·fe shpay·ter
nokh·mahl an

What time should I call?
> *Wann kann ich am*
> *besten anrufen?*

van kan ikh am
bes·ten an·roo·fen

My number is ...
> *Meine Nummer ist ...*

mai·ne nu·mer ist ...

I don't have a contact number.
> *Ich habe keine Nummer,*
> *unter der Sie mich*
> *erreichen können.*

ikh hah·be kai·ne nu·mer
un·ter dair zee mikh
er·rai·khen ker·nen

---

listen for ...

ai·nen ow·gen·blik bi·te
> *Einen Augenblick, bitte.* **One moment, please.**

es toot meer lait (air/zee) ist nikht heer
> *Es tut mir Leid, (er/sie)* **I'm sorry, (he/she)**
> *ist nicht hier.* **is not here.**

mit vaym *merkh·ten* zee *shpre·khen*
> *Mit wem möchten* **Who do you want**
> *Sie sprechen?* **to speak to?**

toot meer lait zee *hah·ben* dee *fal·she nu·mer*
> *Tut mir Leid, Sie haben* **Sorry, wrong number.**
> *die falsche Nummer.*

vair ist am a·pa·*raht*
> *Wer ist am Apparat?* **Who's calling?**

yah (air/zee) ist heer
> *Ja, (er/sie) ist hier.* **Yes, (he/she) is here.**

> mobile/cell phone

Where can I find a/an ...?	Wo kann ich ... finden?	vaw kan ikh ... fin·den
I'd like a/an ...	Ich hätte gern ...	ikh he·te gern ...
adaptor plug	einen Adapter für die Steckdose	ai·nen a·dap·ter für dee shtek·daw·ze
charger for my phone	ein Ladegerät für mein Handy	ain lah·de·ge·rayt für main hen·di
mobile/cell phone for hire	ein Miethandy	ain meet·hen·di
prepaid mobile/ cell phone	ein Handy mit Prepaidkarte	ain hen·di mit pree·payd·kar·te
SIM card for your network	eine SIM-Karte für Ihr Netz	ai·ne zim·kar·te für eer nets

What are the rates?
Wie hoch sind   vee hawkh zint
die Gebühren?   dee ge·bü·ren

(30c) per (30) seconds.
(30 Cent) für   (drai·sikh sent) für
(30) Sekunden.   (drai·sikh) ze·kun·den

the internet

das internet

Where's the local Internet cafe?
Wo ist hier ein   vaw ist heer ain
Internet-Café?   in·ter·net·ka·fay

I'd like to ...	Ich möchte ...	ikh *merkh*·te ...
check my email	meine E-Mails checken	*mai*·ne *ee*·mayls *che*·ken
get Internet access	Internetzugang haben	*in*·ter·net·tsoo·gang *hah*·ben
use a printer	einen Drucker benutzen	*ai*·nen *dru*·ker be·*nu*·tsen
use a scanner	einen Scanner benutzen	*ai*·nen *ske*·ner be·*nu*·tsen

How much per ...?	Was kostet es ...?	vas *kos*·tet es ...
(five) minutes	für (fünf) Minuten	für (fünf) mi·*noo*·ten
hour	pro Stunde	praw *shtun*·de
page	pro Seite	praw *zai*·te

Do you have ...?	Haben Sie ...?	*hah*·ben zee ...
PCs	PCs	pay·*tsays*
Macs	Macs	meks
a Zip drive	ein Zip-Laufwerk	ain *tsip*·lowf·verk

I'm attending a ...   *Ich nehme an ... teil.*   ikh *nay*·me an ... tail
    conference   *einer Konferenz*   *ai*·ner kon·fe·*rents*
    course   *einem Kurs*   *ai*·nem kurs
    meeting   *einem Meeting*   *ai*·nem *mee*·ting

I'm visiting a trade fair
    Ich besuche eine Messe.   ikh be·*zoo*·khe *ai*·ne *me*·se

I'm with ...   *Ich bin ...*   ikh bin ...
    (company ...)   *bei (Firma ...)*   bai (*fir*·ma ...)
    my colleague   *mit meinem*   mit *mai*·nem
       Kollegen hier m   ko·*lay*·gen heer
       mit meiner   mit *mai*·ner
       Kollegin hier f   ko·*lay*·gin heer
    my colleagues   *mit meinen*   mit *mai*·nen
       Kollegen hier m pl   ko·*lay*·gen heer
       mit meinen   mit *mai*·nen
       Kolleginnen   ko·*lay*·gi·nen
       hier f pl   heer
    (two) others   *mit (zwei)*   mit (tsvai)
       anderen hier   *an*·de·ren heer

I'm alone.
    Ich bin allein.   ikh bin a·*lain*

I'm staying at ..., room ...
    Ich wohne im ..., Zimmer ...   ikh *vaw*·ne im ... *tsi*·mer ...

I'm here for (three) days/weeks.
    Ich bin für (drei)   ikh bin für (drai)
    Tage/Wochen hier.   *tah*·ge/*vo*·khen heer

Here's my business card.
    Hier ist meine Karte.   heer ist *mai*·ne *kar*·te

Where's the ...?	Wo ist ...?	vaw ist ...
business centre	das Tagungs-zentrum	das *tah*·gungks·tsen·trum
conference	die Konferenz	dee kon·fe·*rents*
meeting	das Meeting	das *mee*·ting

I have an appointment with ...
Ich habe einen
Termin bei ...
ikh *hah*·be *ai*·nen
ter·*meen* bai ...

That went very well.
Das war sehr gut.
das vahr zair goot

Shall we go for a drink/meal?
Sollen wir noch etwas
trinken/essen gehen?
zo·len veer nokh *et*·vas
tring·ken/e·sen *gay*·en

It's on me.
Ich lade Sie ein.
ikh *lah*·de zee ain

body language

Shaking hands is customary for both men and women in Germany, Austria and Switzerland. Always give a firm handshake and look people in the eye. Never keep your other hand in your pocket, as this is considered impolite.

Where can I ...?	Wo kann ich ...?	vaw kan ikh ...
I'd like to ...	Ich möchte ...	ikh merkh·te ...
cash a cheque	einen Scheck einlösen	ai·nen shek ain·ler·zen
change money	Geld umtauschen	gelt um·tow·shen
change some travellers cheques	Reiseschecks einlösen	rai·ze·sheks ain·ler·zen
get a cash advance	eine Barauszahlung	ai·ne bahr·ows·tsah·lung
withdraw money	Geld abheben	gelt ap·hay·ben
Where's the nearest ...?	Wo ist der/die nächste ...? m/f	vaw ist dair/dee naykhs·te ...
automatic teller machine	Geldautomat m	gelt·ow·to·maht
foreign exchange office	Geldwechsel- stube f	gelt·vek·sel· shtoo·be

What time does the bank open?

Wann macht die Bank auf?   van makht dee bangk owf

The automatic teller machine took my card.

Der Geldautomat hat   dair gelt·ow·to·maht hat
meine Karte einbehalten.   mai·ne kar·te ain·be·hal·ten

I've forgotten my PIN.

Ich habe meine   ikh hah·be mai·ne
Geheimnummer vergessen.   ge·haim·nu·mer fer·ge·sen

Can I use my credit card to withdraw money?

Kann ich mit meiner   kan ikh mit mai·ner
Kreditkarte Geld abheben?   kre·deet·kar·te gelt ap·hay·ben

What's the ...?	Wie ...?	vee ...
charge for that	*hoch sind die Gebühren dafür*	hawkh zint dee ge·bü·ren da·für
commission	*hoch ist die Kommission*	hawkh ist dee ko·mi·syawn
exchange rate	*ist der Wechselkurs*	ist dair vek·sel·kurs

Has my money arrived yet?

Ist mein Geld schon angekommen?

ist main gelt shawn an·ge·ko·men

How long will it take to arrive?

Wie lange dauert es, bis es da ist?

vee lang·e dow·ert es bis es dah ist

---

listen for ...

bi·te *shrai*·ben zee es owf
Bitte schreiben Sie es auf. **Please write it down.**

bi·te un·ter·*shrai*·ben zee heer
Bitte unterschreiben Sie hier. **Please sign here.**

das *ker*·nen veer nikht *ma*·khen
Das können wir nicht machen. **We can't do that.**

es gipt dah ain pro·*blaym* mit ee·rem *kon*·to
Es gibt da ein Problem mit Ihrem Konto. **There's a problem with your account.**

eer *kon*·to ist ü·ber·*tsaw*·gen
Ihr Konto ist überzogen. **You're overdrawn.**

in *ai*·ner *vo*·khe
In einer Woche. **In one week.**

in (feer) *ar*·baits·tah·gen
In (vier) Arbeitstagen. **In (four) working days.**

kan ikh *bi*·te *ai*·nen *ows*·vais zay·en
Kann ich bitte einen Ausweis sehen? **Can I see some ID please?**

I'd like a/an ...	Ich hätte gern ...	ikh *he*·te gern ...
audio set	einen Audioführer	*ai*·nen ow·di·o·fü·rer
catalogue	einen Katalog	*ai*·nen ka·ta·*lawg*
guide	einen Reiseführer	*ai*·nen rai·ze·fü·rer
guidebook in English	einen Reiseführer auf Englisch	*ai*·nen rai·ze·fü·rer owf *eng*·lish
(local) map	eine Karte (von hier)	*ai*·ne *kar*·te (fon heer)

Do you have information on ... sights?	Haben Sie Informationen über ... Sehenswürdigkeiten?	*hah*·ben zee in·for·ma·*tsyaw*·nen *ü*·ber ... *zay*·ens·vür·dikh·kai·ten
cultural	kulturelle	kul·tu·*re*·le
local	örtliche	*ert*·li·khe
religious	religiöse	re·li·*gyer*·ze
unique	einzigartige	*ain*·tsikh·ar·ti·ge

We only have (one day).
Wir haben nur (einen Tag).
veer *hah*·ben noor (*ai*·nen tahk)

I'd like to see ...
Ich möchte ... sehen.
ikh *merkh*·te ... *zay*·en

What's that?
Was ist das?
vas ist das

Who made it?
Wer hat das gemacht?   vair hat das ge·*makht*

How old is it?
Wie alt ist es?   vee alt ist es

Could you take a photograph of me?
Könnten Sie ein Foto   *kern*·ten zee ain *faw*·to
von mir machen?   fon meer ma·khen

Can I take photographs (of you)?
Kann ich (Sie) fotografieren?   kan ikh (zee) fo·to·gra·*fee*·ren

I'll send you the photograph.
Ich schicke Ihnen das Foto.   ikh *shi*·ke ee·nen das *faw*·to

getting in

What time does it open/close?
Wann macht es auf/zu?   van makht es owf/tsoo

What's the admission charge?
Was kostet der Eintritt?   vas *kos*·tet dair *ain*·trit

It costs ...
Er kostet ...   air *kos*·tet ...

Is there a	*Gibt es eine*	gipt es *ai*·ne
discount for ...?	*Ermäßigung für ...?*	er·*may*·si·gung für ...
children	*Kinder*	*kin*·der
families	*Familien*	fa·*mee*·li·en
groups	*Gruppen*	*gru*·pen
pensioners	*Rentner*	*rent*·ner
students	*Studenten*	shtu·*den*·ten

tours

When's the next ...?	*Wann ist der/die nächste ...?* m/f	van ist dair/dee naykhs·te ...
boat-trip	*Bootsrundfahrt* f	bawts·runt·fahrt
daytrip	*Tagesausflug* m	tah·ges·ows·flook
excursion	*Ausflug* m	ows·flook
tour	*Tour* f	toor
Is ... included?	*Ist ... inbegriffen?*	ist ... in·be·gri·fen
accommodation	*die Unterkunft*	dee un·ter·kunft
equipment	*die Ausrüstung*	dee ows·rüs·tung
food	*das Essen*	das e·sen
transport	*die Beförderung*	dee be·fer·de·rung

Can you recommend a ...?
Können Sie ein ... empfehlen?   ker·nen zee ain ... emp·fay·len

Do I need to take ... with me?
Muss ich ... mitnehmen?   mus ikh ... mit·nay·men

The guide will pay.
   Der Reiseleiter bezahlt.   dair *rai*·ze·lai·ter be·*tsahlt*

The guide has paid.
   Der Reiseleiter hat bezahlt.   dair *rai*·ze·lai·ter hat be·*tsahlt*

How long is the tour?
   Wie lange dauert   vee *lang*·e *dow*·ert
   die Führung?   dee *fü*·rung

What time should we be back?
   Wann sollen wir   van *zo*·len veer
   zurück sein?   tsu·*rük* zain

Be back here at (ten) o'clock.
   Seien Sie um (zehn) Uhr zurück.   *zai*·en zee um (tsayn) oor tsu·*rük*

I'm with them.
   Ich gehöre zu ihnen.   ikh ge·*her*·re tsoo *ee*·nen

I've lost my group.
   Ich habe meine   ikh *hah*·be *mai*·ne
   Gruppe verloren.   *gru*·pe fer·*law*·ren

Have you seen a group of (Australians)?
   Haben Sie eine Gruppe   *hah*·ben zee *ai*·ne *gru*·pe
   (Australier) gesehen?   (ows·*trah*·li·er) ge·*zay*·en

signs

Eingang	*ain*·gang	**Entrance**
Ausgang	*ows*·gang	**Exit**
Offen	*o*·fen	**Open**
Geschlossen	ge·*shlo*·sen	**Closed**
Heiß	hais	**Hot**
Kalt	kalt	**Cold**
Kein Zutritt	kain *tsu*·trit	**No Entry**
Rauchen	*row*·khen	**No Smoking**
Verboten	fer·*baw*·ten	
Verboten	fer·*baw*·ten	**Prohibited**
Toiletten (WC)	to·a·*le*·ten (vee·*tsee*)	**Toilets**
Herren	*hair*·en	**Men**
Damen	*dah*·men	**Women**

I'm disabled.
Ich bin behindert. — ikh bin be·*hin*·dert

I need assistance.
Ich brauche Hilfe. — ikh *brow*·khe *hil*·fe

What services do you have for disabled people?
Was für Leistungen gibt — vas für *lais*·tung·en gipt
es für behinderte Reisende? — es für be·*hin*·der·te *rai*·zen·de

Are there any toilets for the disabled?
Gibt es Toiletten für — gipt es to·a·*le*·ten für
Behinderte? — be·*hin*·der·te

Is there wheelchair access?
Gibt es eine Rollstuhlrampe? — gipt es *ai*·ne *rol*·shtool·ram·pe

How wide are the doors?
Wie breit sind die Türen? — vee brait sind dee *tü*·ren

How many steps are there?
Wieviele Stufen sind es? — vee·*fee*·le *shtoo*·fen sind es

Is there a lift?
Gibt es einen Aufzug? — gipt es *ai*·nen owf·*tsook*

Is there an induction loop for the hard of hearing?
Gibt es eine Induktions- — gipt es *ai*·ne in·duk·*tsyawns*·
schleife für Schwerhörige? — shlai·fe für shver·*her*·ri·ge

I have a hearing aid. Speak more loudly, please.
Ich habe ein Hörgerät. — ikh *hah*·be ain *her*·ge·rayt
Sprechen Sie bitte lauter. — *shpre*·khen zee *bi*·te *low*·ter

I'm deaf.
Ich bin taub.　　　　　　　　　ikh bin towp

Are guide dogs permitted?
Sind Blindenhunde erlaubt?　　zint *blin*·den·hun·de er·*lowpt*

Could you help me cross this street safely?
Könnten Sie mich sicher　　　*kern*·ten zee mikh *zi*·kher
über diese Straße bringen?　　*ü*·ber *dee*·ze *shtrah*·se *bring*·en

Braille library	*Blindenbibliothek* f	*blin*·den·bi·bli·o·tayk
disabled man	*Behinderter* m	be·*hin*·der·ter
disabled woman	*Behinderte* f	be·*hin*·der·te
guide dog	*Blindenhund* m	*blin*·den·hunt
wheelchair	*Rollstuhl* m	*rol*·shtool
wheelchair ramp	*Rollstuhlrampe* f	*rol*·shtool·ram·pe
wheelchair space	*Rollstuhlplatz* m	*rol*·shtool·plats

Is there a/an...?	*Gibt es ...?*	gipt es ...
baby change room	*einen Wickelraum*	*ai*·nen *vi*·kel·rowm
child-minding service	*einen Babysitter-Service*	*ai*·nen *bay*·bi·si·ter·*ser*·vis
children's menu	*eine Kinderkarte*	*ai*·ne *kin*·der·kar·te
(English-speaking) babysitter	*einen (englischsprachigen) Babysitter*	*ai*·nen (*eng*·lish·shprah·khi·gen) *bay*·bi·si·ter
family discount	*eine Familienermäßigung*	*ai*·ne fa·*mee*·li·en·er·may·si·gung
highchair	*einen Kinderstuhl*	*ai*·nen *kin*·der·shtool
park	*einen Park*	*ai*·nen park
playground nearby	*einen Spielplatz in der Nähe*	*ai*·nen *shpeel*·plats in dair *nay*·e
theme park	*einen Freizeitpark*	*ai*·nen *frai*·tsait·park

I need a ...	*Ich brauche ...*	ikh *brow*·khe ...
baby seat	*einen Babysitz*	*ai*·nen *bay*·bi·zits
booster seat	*einen Kindersitz*	*ai*·nen *kin*·der·zits
potty	*ein Kindertöpfchen*	ain *kin*·der·terpf·khen
stroller	*einen Kinderwagen*	*ai*·nen *kin*·der·vah·gen

Can I breast-feed here?
    Kann ich meinem Kind   kan ikh *mai*·nem kint
    hier die Brust geben?   heer dee brust *gay*·ben

Are children allowed?
    Sind Kinder erlaubt?   zint *kin*·der er·*lowpt*

Is this suitable for (three) year old children?
    Ist das für (drei) Jahre alte   ist das für (drai) *yah*·re *al*·te
    Kinder geeignet?   *kin*·der ge·*aig*·net

For children's sicknesses, see **symptoms & conditions**, page 180, and the **dictionary**.

---

signs

When travelling with children, keep an eye out for the following signs:

Junioren bis 5 Jahre frei	**Children up to the age of 5 free**
Junioren bis 15 Jahre halber Preis	**Children up to the age of 15 half price**
Wickeltisch	**Change Room**
Spielplatz	**Playground**

basics

grundlagen

Yes.	*Ja.*	yah
No.	*Nein.*	nain
Please.	*Bitte.*	*bi·*te
Thank you.	*Danke.*	*dang·*ke
Thank you very much.	*Vielen Dank.*	*fee·*len dangk
You're (very) welcome.	*Bitte (sehr).*	*bi·*te (zair)
Excuse me.	*Entschuldigung.*	ent·*shul·*di·gung
Sorry.	*Entschuldigung.*	ent·*shul·*di·gung
Don't worry.	*Macht nichts.*	makht nikhts

greetings

grüsse

Hello.		
(all over Germany)	*Guten Tag.*	*goo·*ten tahk
(in southern Germany)	*Grüß Gott.*	grüs got
(in Switzerland)	*Grüezi.*	*grü·*e·tsi
(in Austria)	*Servus.*	*zer·*vus
Hi.	*Hallo.*	*ha·*lo
Good ...	*Guten ...*	*goo·*ten ...
afternoon	*Tag*	tahk
day	*Tag*	tahk
evening	*Abend*	*ah·*bent
morning	*Morgen*	*mor·*gen
See you later.	*Bis später.*	bis *shpay·*ter
Goodbye.	*Auf Wiedersehen.*	owf *vee·*der·zay·en
Bye.	*Tschüss/Tschau.*	chüs/chow

How are you?
Wie geht es
Ihnen/dir? pol/inf

vee gayt es
ee·nen/deer

Fine. And you?
Danke, gut.
Und Ihnen/dir? pol/inf

dang·ke goot
unt ee·nen/deer

What's your name?
Wie ist Ihr Name? pol
Wie heißt du? inf

vee ist eer nah·me
vee haist doo

My name is ...
Mein Name ist ... pol
Ich heiße ... inf

main nah·me ist ...
ikh hai·se ...

I'd like to introduce you to ...
Darf ich Ihnen/dir
... vorstellen? pol/inf

darf ikh ee·nen/dir
... fawr·shte·len

I'm pleased to meet you.
Angenehm.

an·ge·naym

titles & addressing people

In the past, *Fräulein* was used to address all unmarried women regardless of age but today the term is only used to address girls (and sometimes female waiters). All other women should be addressed using *Frau*. There's no equivalent of the English 'Ms' – use *Frau*. The equivalents of Sir and Madam, *Mein Herr* and *Meine Dame*, are very old-fashioned.

If you want to include academic titles when addressing somebody, these are combined with *Herr* and *Frau*, eg, *Frau Professor* or *Herr Doktor*.

Mr	Herr	her
Mrs	Frau	frow
Miss	Frau/Fräulein	frow/froy·lain

SOCIAL

making conversation

Do you live here?
Wohnen Sie hier? pol   vaw·nen zee heer
Wohnst du hier? inf   vawnst doo heer

Where are you going?
Wohin fahren Sie? pol   vaw·hin *fah*·ren zee
Wohin fährst du? inf   vaw·hin fairst doo

What are you doing?
Was machen Sie? pol   vas *ma*·khen zee
Was machst du? inf   vas makhst doo

Are you waiting (for a bus)?
Warten Sie   var·ten zee
(auf einen Bus)? pol   (owf *ai*·nen bus)
Wartest du   var·test doo
(auf einen Bus)? inf   (owf *ai*·nen bus)

Are you also travelling (on this train)?
Fahren Sie auch   *fah*·ren zee owkh
(mit diesem Zug)? pol   (mit *dee*·zem tsook)
Fährst du auch   fairst doo owkh
(mit diesem Zug)? inf   (mit *dee*·zem tsook)

Can I have a light?
Haben Sie Feuer? pol   *hah*·ben zee *foy*·er
Hast du Feuer? inf   hast doo *foy*·er

Nice day, isn't it?
Schönes Wetter heute!   *sher*·nes *we*·ter *hoy*·te

Terrible weather today!
Furchtbares Wetter heute!   furkht·bah·res *we*·ter *hoy*·te

Just joking!
Das war nur ein Scherz!   das vahr noor ain sherts

This is my ...	Das ist mein/meine/ mein ... m/f/n	das ist main/mai·ne/ main ...
child	Kind n	kint
colleague	Kollege/ Kollegin m/f	ko·lay·ge/ ko·lay·gin
friend	Freund(in) m/f	froynt/froyn·din
husband	Mann m	man
partner (intimate)	Partner(in) m/f	part·ner/part·ne·rin
wife	meine Frau f	frow

Do you like it here?
Gefällt es Ihnen/ dir hier? pol/inf — ge·felt es ee·nen/ deer heer

I love it here.
Mir gefällt es hier sehr gut. — meer ge·felt es heer zair goot

What do you think (about ...)?
Was denken Sie (über ...)? pol — vas deng·ken zee (ü·ber ...)
Was denkst du (über ...)? inf — vas dengkst doo (ü·ber ...)

What's this called?
Wie heißt das? — vee haist das

What a beautiful baby!
Was für ein schönes Baby! — vas für ain sher·nes bay·bi

Can I take a photo (of you)?
Kann ich ein Foto (von Ihnen/dir) machen? pol/inf — kan ikh ain faw·to (fon ee·nen/deer) ma·khen

That's (beautiful), isn't it?
Ist das nicht (schön)? — ist das nikht (shern)

Are you here on holiday?
Sind Sie hier im Urlaub? pol — zint zee heer im oor·lowp
Bist du hier im Urlaub? inf — bist doo heer im oor·lowp

I'm here ...	*Ich bin hier ...*	ikh bin heer ...
for a holiday	*im Urlaub*	im *oor*·lowp
on business	*auf Geschäfts-*	owf ge·*shefts*·
	reise	rai·ze
to study	*zum Studieren*	tsum shtu·*dee*·ren
with my family	*mit meiner*	mit *mai*·ner
	Familie	fa·*mee*·li·e
with my partner	*mit meinem*	mit *mai*·nem
	Partner m	*part*·ner
	mit meiner	mit *mai*·ner
	Partnerin f	*part*·ne·rin

How long are you here for?

Für wie lange sind	für vee *lang*·e zint
Sie hier? pol	zee heer
Für wie lange bist	für vee *lang*·e bist
du hier? inf	doo heer

I'm here for (four) weeks/days.

| *Ich bin für (vier)* | ikh bin für (feer) |
| *Tage/Wochen hier.* | *tah*·ge/*vo*·khen heer |

---

local talk

Hey!	*Hi/Hey!*	hai/hei
Great!	*Toll/Geil!/*	tol/gail/
	Super!/Spitze!	zoo·per/*shpi*·tse
No problem.	*Kein Problem.*	kain pro·*blaym*
Sure.	*Klar!*	klahr
Maybe.	*Vielleicht.*	fi·*laikht*
No way!	*Auf keinen Fall!*	owf *kai*·nen fal
It's OK.	*Das ist OK.*	das ist o·*kay*
I'm OK.	*Alles klar.*	*a*·les klahr
Look!	*Guck mal!*	guk mahl
Listen!	*Hör mal!*	her mahl
Listen to this!	*Hör dir das an!*	her deer das an
I'm ready.	*Ich bin so weit.*	ikh bin zaw vait
Are you ready?	*Bist du so weit?*	bist doo zaw vait
Just a minute.	*Einen Augenblick.*	*ai*·nen ow·gen·*blik*

nationalities

Where are you from?
   Woher kommen Sie? pol   *vaw*·hair *ko*·men zee
   Woher kommst du? inf   *vaw*·hair komst doo

I'm from ...	*Ich komme aus ...*	ikh *ko*·me ows ...
Australia	*Australien*	ows·*trah*·li·en
the US	*den USA*	dayn oo·es·*ah*
Wales	*Wales*	waylz

For more countries, see the **dictionary**.

age

How old ...?	*Wie alt ...?*	vee alt ...
are you	*sind Sie* pol	zint zee
	bist du inf	bist doo
is your daughter	*ist Ihre/deine*	ist *ee*·re/*dai*·ne
	Tochter pol/inf	*tokh*·ter
is your son	*ist Ihr/dein*	ist eer/dain
	Sohn pol/inf	zawn

I'm ... years old.
   Ich bin ... Jahre alt.   ikh bin ... *yah*·re alt

He's/She's ... years old.
   Er/Sie ist ... Jahre alt.   air/zee ist ... *yah*·re alt

Too old!
   Zu alt!   tsoo alt

I'm younger than I look.
   Ich bin jünger als   ikh bin *yüng*·er als
   ich aussehe.   ikh *ows*·zay·e

For your age, see **numbers & amounts**, page 27.

occupations & studies

What's your occupation?

Als was arbeiten Sie? pol		als vas *ar*·bai·ten zee
Als was arbeitest du? inf		als vas *ar*·bai·test doo

I'm a ...	*Ich bin ein/*	ikh bin ain/
	eine ... m/f	*ain*·e ...
drag queen	*Drag Queen* f	dreg kween
farmer	*Bauer/*	*bow*·er/
	Bäuerin m/f	*boy*·e·rin
writer	*Schriftsteller/*	*shrift*·shte·ler/
	Schriftstellerin m/f	*shrift*·shte·le·rin

I work in ...	*Ich arbeite ...*	ikh *ar*·bai·te ...
administration	*in der Verwaltung*	in dair fer·*val*·tung
IT	*in der*	in dair
	IT-Branche	ai·*tee*·brang·she
sales &	*im Verkauf*	im fer·*kowf*
marketing	*und Marketing*	unt *mar*·ke·ting

I'm ...	*Ich bin ...*	ikh bin ...
retired	*Rentner/*	*rent*·ner/
	Rentnerin m/f	*rent*·ne·rin
self-employed	*selbstständig*	*zelpst*·shten·dikh
unemployed	*arbeitslos*	*ar*·baits·laws

What are you studying?

Was studieren Sie? pol		vas shtu·*dee*·ren zee
Was studierst du? inf		vas shtu·*deerst* doo

I'm studying ...	*Ich studiere ...*	ikh shtu·*dee*·re ...
engineering	*Ingenieurwesen*	in·zhe·*nyer*·vay·zen
German	*Deutsch*	doytsh
medicine	*Medizin*	me·di·*tseen*

For more occupations and fields of study, see the **dictionary**.

family

Do you have a ...?
Haben Sie einen/eine ...? m/f pol   hah·ben zee *ai*·nen/*ai*·ne ...
Hast du einen/eine ...? m/f inf   hast doo *ai*·nen/*ai*·ne ...

I (don't) have a ...
Ich habe (k)einen/   ikh *hah*·be (k)*ai*·nen/
(k)eine ... m/f   (k)*ai*·ne ...

Do you live with (your parents)?
Leben Sie bei   *lay*·ben zee bai
(Ihren Eltern)? pol   (ee·ren el·tern)
Lebst du bei   laypst doo bai
(deinen Eltern)? inf   (dai·nen el·tern)

I live with my ...
Ich lebe bei meinem/   ikh *lay*·be bai *mai*·nem/
meiner/meinen ... m/f/pl   *mai*·ner/*mai*·nen ...

This is my ...
Das ist mein/meine ... m/f   das ist main/*mai*·ne ...

Are you married?
Sind Sie verheiratet? pol   zint zee fer·*hai*·ra·tet
Bist du verheiratet? inf   bist doo fer·*hai*·ra·tet

I live with someone.
Ich lebe mit jemandem   ikh *lay*·be mit *yay*·man·dem
zusammen.   tsu·*za*·men

I'm ...   *Ich bin ...*   ikh bin ...
  married   *verheiratet*   fer·*hai*·ra·tet
  separated   *getrennt*   ge·*trent*
  single   *ledig*   *lay*·dikh

children

When's your birthday?
Wann hast du Geburtstag?   van hast doo ge·*burts*·tahk

Do you go to school or kindergarten?
Gehst du in die Schule   gayst doo in dee *shoo*·le
oder in den Kindergarten?   *aw*·der in dayn *kin*·der·gar·ten

What grade are you in?
In welcher Klasse bist du?   in *vel*·kher *kla*·se bist doo

What do you do after school?
Was machst du   vas makhst doo
nach der Schule?   nahkh dair *shoo*·le

Do you learn English?
Lernst du Englisch?   lernst doo *eng*·lish

I come from very far away.
Ich komme von sehr weit her.   ikh *ko*·me fon zair vait hair

Are you lost?
Hast du dich verlaufen?   hast doo dikh fer·*low*·fen

farewells

Tomorrow is my last day here.
Morgen ist mein   *mor*·gen ist main
letzter Tag hier.   *lets*·ter tahk heer

Here's my ...	*Hier ist meine ...*	heer ist *mai*·ne ...
What's your...?	*Wie ist Ihre/*	vee ist *ee*·re/
	deine ...? pol/inf	*dai*·ne ...
address	*Adresse*	a·*dre*·se
email address	*E-mail-Adresse*	ee·mayl·a·dre·se
fax number	*Faxnummer*	faks·nu·mer
mobile number	*Handynummer*	hen·di·nu·mer
pager number	*Pagernummer*	*pay*·dzher·nu·mer
work number	*Nummer bei*	nu·mer bai
	der Arbeit	dair *ar*·bait

For addresses, see **directions**, page 59.

meeting people

95

If you ever visit (Scotland), come and visit us.

Wenn Sie jemals nach	ven zee *yay*·mahls nahkh
(Schottland) kommen,	(*shot*·lant) *ko*·men
besuchen Sie uns	be·*zoo*·khen zee uns
doch mal. pol	dokh mahl
Wenn du jemals nach	ven doo *yay*·mahls nahkh
(Schottland) kommst,	(*shot*·lant) komst
besuche uns doch mal. inf	be·*zoo*·khe uns dokh mahl

Keep in touch!

Melden Sie sich	*mel*·den zee zikh
doch mal! pol	dokh mahl
Melde dich mal! inf	*mel*·de dikh mahl

It's been great meeting you.

Es war schön, Sie/dich	es vahr shern zee/dikh
kennen zu lernen. pol/inf	*ke*·nen tsoo *ler*·nen

---

local talk

Bless you! (when sneezing)	*Gesundheit!*	ge·*zunt*·hait
Bon voyage!	*Gute Reise!*	*goo*·te *rai*·ze
Cheers!	*Prost!*	prawst
Good luck!	*Viel Glück!*	feel glük
Happy birthday!	*Herzlichen*	*herts*·li·khen
	Glückwunsch	*glük*·vunsh
	zum Geburtstag!	tsum ge·*burts*·tahk
What a pity!	*Schade!*	*shah*·de

common interests

What do you do in your spare time?

Was machen Sie in
Ihrer Freizeit? pol
vas *ma*·khen zee in
ee·rer *frai*·tsait

Was machst du in
deiner Freizeit? inf
vas makhst doo in
dai·ner *frai*·tsait

Do you like ...?	*Mögen Sie ...?* pol	*mer*·gen zee ...
	Magst du ...? inf	mahkst doo ...
I (don't) like ...	*Ich mag (keine/*	ikh mahk (*kai*·ne/
	keinen) ... m/f	*kai*·nen) ...
music	*Musik* f	mu·*zeek*
sport	*Sport* m	shport

I (don't) like ...	*Ich ... (nicht) gern.*	ikh ... (nikht) gern
dancing	*tanze*	*tan*·tse
drawing	*zeichne*	*tsaikh*·ne
hiking	*wandere*	*van*·de·re
painting	*male*	*mah*·le
photography	*fotografiere*	fo·to·gra·*fee*·re
reading	*lese*	*lay*·ze
travelling	*reise*	*rai*·ze

I (don't) like ...	*Ich ... (nicht) gern ...*	ikh ... (nikht) gern ...
films	*sehe ... Filme*	*zay*·e ... *fil*·me
gardening	*arbeite ...*	*ar*·bai·te ...
	im Garten	im *gar*·ten
shopping	*kaufe ... ein*	*kow*·fe ... ain
socialising	*gehe ... aus*	*gay*·e ... ows
And you?	*Und Sie/du?* pol/inf	unt zee/doo

For types of sport, see **sports**, page 123 and the **dictionary**.

music

Do you like to …?

listen to music	*Hören Sie gern Musik?* pol	*her*·ren zee gern mu·*zeek*
	Hörst du gern Musik? inf	herst doo gern mu·*zeek*
dance	*Tanzen Sie gern?* pol	*tan*·tsen zee gern
	Tanzt du gern? inf	tantst doo gern
go to concerts	*Gehen Sie gern in Konzerte?* pol	*gay*·en zee gern in kon·*tser*·te
	Gehst du gern in Konzerte? inf	gayst doo gern in kon·*tser*·te
sing	*Singen Sie gern?* pol	*zing*·en zee gern
	Singst du gern? inf	zingkst doo gern

Do you play an instrument?

Spielen Sie ein Instrument? pol	*shpee*·len zee ain in·stru·*ment*
Spielst du ein Instrument? inf	shpeelst doo ain in·stru·*ment*

What … do you like?	*Welche … mögen Sie?* pol	*vel*·khe … *mer*·gen zee
	Welche … magst du? inf	*vel*·khe … mahkst doo
bands	*Bands*	bents
music	*Art von Musik*	art fon mu·*zeek*

classical music	*klassische Musik* f	*kla·si·she mu·zeek*
electronic music	*elektronische Musik* f	*e·lek·traw·ni·she mu·zeek*
jazz	*Jazz* m	*dzhez*
metal	*Metal* m	*me·tel*
pop	*Popmusik* f	*pop·mu·zeek*
punk	*Punk* m	*pangk*
rock	*Rockmusik* f	*rok·mu·zeek*
R & B	*Rhythm'n'Blues* m	*rithm·n·blooz*
traditional music	*traditionelle Musik* f	*tra·di·tsyo·ne·le mu·zeek*
world music	*Weltmusik* f	*velt·mu·zeek*

Planning to go to a concert? See **going out**, page 108.

cinema & theatre

kino und theater

I feel like going to a ...	*Ich hätte Lust, ... zu gehen.*	*ikh he·te lust ... tsoo gay·en*
film	*ins Kino*	*ins kee·no*
play	*ins Theater*	*ins te·ah·ter*

Did you like it?
Hat es Ihnen/dir gefallen? pol/inf
hat es ee·nen/deer ge·fa·len

What's showing at the cinema/theatre tonight?
Was gibt es heute im Kino/Theater?
vas gipt es hoy·te im kee·no/te·ah·ter

Is it in English?
Ist es auf Englisch?
ist es owf eng·lish

Does it have subtitles?
Hat es Untertitel?
hat es un·ter·tee·tel

Are those seats taken?
Sind diese Plätze besetzt?
zint dee·ze ple·tse be·zetst

Have you seen ...?
Haben Sie ... gesehen? pol
hah·ben zee ... ge·zay·en
Hast du ... gesehen? inf
hast doo ... ge·zay·en

interests

99

Who's in it?
Wer spielt da mit? vair shpeelt dah mit

It stars ...
Es ist mit ... es ist mit ...

I thought	*Ich fand es ...*	ikh fant es ...
it was ...		
excellent	*ausgezeichnet*	ows·ge·*tsaikh*·net
long	*lang*	lang
OK	*okay*	o·*kay*

I (don't) like ...	*Ich mag ...*	ikh mahk ...
action movies	*(keine)*	*(kai*·ne)
	Actionfilme	*ek*·shen·fil·me
animated films	*(keine)*	*(kai*·ne)
	Zeichentrickfilme	*tsai*·khen·trik·fil·me
classical theatre	*(kein) klassisches*	*(kain) kla*·si·shes
	Theater	te·*ah*·ter
comedies	*(keine)*	*(kai*·ne)
	Komödien	ko·*mer*·di·en
documentaries	*(keine)*	*(kai*·ne)
	Dokumentarfilme	do·ku·men·*tahr*·fil·me
drama	*(keine)*	*(kai*·ne)
	Schauspiele	*show*·shpee·le
German cinema	*(keine) deutsche(n)*	*(kai*·ne) *doyt*·she(n)
	Filme	*fil*·me
horror movies	*(keine)*	*(kai*·ne)
	Horrorfilme	*ho*·ror·fil·me
period dramas	*(keine)*	*(kai*·ne)
	Historienfilme	his·*taw*·ri·en·fil·me
realism	*(keinen) Realismus*	*(kai*·nen) re·a·*lis*·mus
sci-fi	*(keinen)*	*(kai*·nen)
	Sciencefiction	sai·ens·*fik*·shen
short films	*(keine) Kurzfilme*	*(kai*·ne) *kurts*·fil·me
war movies	*(keine) Kriegsfilme*	*(kai*·ne) *kreeks*·fil·me

feelings & opinions
gefühle und meinungen

feelings

I'm (not) ...	*Ich bin (nicht) ...*	ikh bin (nikht) ...
Are you ...?	*Sind Sie ...?* pol	zint zee ...
	Bist du ...? inf	bist doo ...
annoyed	*verärgert*	fer·er·gert
disappointed	*enttäuscht*	en·toysht
in a hurry	*in Eile*	in ai·le
sad	*traurig*	trow·rikh
tired	*müde*	mü·de
I'm (not) ...	*Ich habe (kein) ...*	ikh hah·be (kain) ...
Are you ...?	*Haben Sie ...?* pol	hah·ben zee ...
	Hast du ...? inf	hast doo ...
hungry	*Hunger*	hung·er
thirsty	*Durst*	durst

I'm (not) ...	*Mir ist (nicht) ....*	meer ist (nikht) ...
Are you ...?	*Ist Ihnen/*	ist ee·nen/
	dir ...? pol/inf	deer ...
cold	*kalt*	kalt
hot	*heiß*	hais
I'm (not) ...		
embarrassed	*Das ist mir*	das ist meer
	(nicht) peinlich.	(nikht) pain·likh
worried	*Ich mache mir*	ikh ma·khe meer
	(keine) Sorgen.	(kai·ne) zor·gen

Are you ...?

embarrassed	*Ist Ihnen/dir das peinlich?* pol/inf	ist ee·nen/deer das *pain*·likh
worried	*Machen Sie sich Sorgen?* pol	ma·khen zee zikh zor·gen
	Machst du dir Sorgen? inf	makhst doo deer zor·gen

---

intense feelings

a little	*ein bisschen*	ain *bis*·khen
I'm a little sad.	*Ich bin ein bisschen traurig.*	ikh bin ain *bis*·khen *trow*·rikh
terribly	*furchtbar*	*furkht*·bahr
I'm terribly sorry.	*Es tut mir furchtbar Leid.*	es toot meer *furkht*·bahr lait
very	*sehr*	zair
I feel very lucky.	*Ich schätze mich sehr glücklich.*	ikh *she*·tse mikh zair *glük*·likh
completely	*völlig*	*fer*·likh
not at all	*überhaupt nicht*	ü·ber·*howpt* nikht
profoundly	*abgrundtief*	*ap*·grun·teef
quite	*ziemlich*	*tseem*·likh
totally	*total*	to·*tahl*

---

opinions

meinungen

Did you like it?

Hat es Ihnen/dir gefallen? pol/inf

hat es ee·nen/deer ge·*fa*·len

What did you think of it?

Wie hat es Ihnen/dir gefallen? pol/inf

vee hat es ee·nen/deer ge·*fa*·len

It is/was ...	Es ist/war ...	es ist/vahr ...
awful	schrecklich	shrek·likh
beautiful	schön	shern
boring	langweilig	lang·vai·likh
great	toll	tol
interesting	interessant	in·tre·sant
OK	okay	o·kay
too expensive	zu teuer	tsoo toy·er

politics & social issues

politische und soziale fragen

I support the ... party.	Ich unterstütze die ... Partei.	ikh un·ter·shtü·tse dee ... par·tai
communist	kommunistische	ko·mu·nis·ti·she
conservative	konservative	kon·zer·va·tee·ve
democratic	demokratische	de·mo·krah·tish·e
green	grüne	grün·e
liberal	liberale	li·be·rahl·e
social democratic	sozial-demokratische	zo·tsyahl·de·mo·krah·tish·e
socialist	sozialistische	zo·tsya·lis·tish·e

I support the labour party.
Ich unterstütze die Arbeiterpartei. — ikh un·ter·shtü·tse dee ar·bai·ter·par·tai

Who do you vote for?
Wen wählen Sie? pol — vayn vay·len zee
Wen wählst du? inf — vayn vaylst doo

Did you hear about ...?
Haben Sie von ... gehört? pol — hah·ben zee fon ... ge·hert
Hast du von ... gehört? inf — hast doo fon ... ge·hert

Do you agree with it?
Sind Sie damit einverstanden? pol — zint zee dah·mit ain·fer·shtan·den
Bist du damit einverstanden? inf — bist doo dah·mit ain·fer·shtan·den

I (don't) agree with that.
   Ich bin damit (nicht)   ikh bin dah·*mit* (nikht)
   einverstanden.   *ain*·fer·shtan·den

Are you against ... ?
   Sind Sie gegen ...? pol   zint zee *gay*·gen ...
   Bist du gegen ...? inf   bist doo *gay*·gen ...

Are you in favour of ...?
   Sind Sie für ...? pol   zint zee für ...
   Bist du für ...? inf   bist doo für ...

How do people feel about ...?
   Was denken die   vas *deng*·ken dee
   Leute über ...?   *loy*·te ü·ber ...

abortion	*Abtreibung* f	*ap*·trai·bung
animal rights	*Tierschutz* m	*teer*·shuts
discrimination	*Diskriminierung* f	dis·kri·mi·*nee*·rung
drugs	*Drogen* f pl	*draw*·gen
the economy	*die Wirtschaft* f	dee *virt*·shaft
education	*Bildung* f	*bil*·dung
the environment	*die Umwelt* f	dee *um*·velt
equal opportunity	*Gleichberech-* *tigung* f	*glaikh*·be·rekh· ti·gung
euthanasia	*Euthanasie* f	oy·ta·na·*zee*
globalisation	*Globalisierung* f	glaw·ba·li·*zee*·rung
human rights	*Menschenrechte* n pl	*men*·shen·rekh·te
immigration	*Einwanderung* f	*ain*·van·de·rung
racism	*Rassismus* m	ra·*sis*·mus
sexism	*Sexismus* m	sek·*sis*·mus
social welfare	*Wohlfahrtsstaat* m	*vawl*·fahrts·shtaht
unemployment	*Arbeitslosigkeit* f	ar·baits·law·zikh·kait

the environment

Is there a ... problem here?
Gibt es hier ein   gipt es heer ain
Problem mit ...?   pro·*blaym* mit ...

What should be done about ...?
Was sollte man   vas *zol*·te man
gegen ... tun?   gay·gen ... toon

biodegradable	*biologisch*	bi·o·*law*·gish
	abbaubar	*ap*·bow·bahr
conservation	*Schutz* m	shuts
deforestation	*Abholzung* f	*ap*·hol·tsung
drought	*Trockenheit* f	*tro*·ken·hait
ecosystem	*Ökosystem* n	*er*·ko·züs·taym
endangered species	*gefährdete Arten* f pl	ge·*fair*·de·te *ar*·ten
floods	*Überschwem-*	ü·ber·*shve*·
	mungen f pl	mung·en
genetically	*genmanipuliertes*	*gayn*·ma·ni·pu·leer·tes
modified food/	*Essen/Getreide* n/n	e·sen/ge·*trai*·de
crops		
hunting	*Jagd* f	yahkt
hydroelectricity	*Strom* m	shtrawm
	aus Wasserkraft	ows va·ser·kraft
nuclear energy	*Atomenergie* f	a·*tawm*·e·ner·gee
nuclear testing	*Atomtests* m pl	a·*tawm*·tests
nuclear waste	*Atommüll* m	a·*tawm*·mül
ozone layer	*Ozonschicht* f	o·*tsawn*·shikht
pesticides	*Pestizide* n pl	pes·ti·*tsee*·de
pollution	*Umweltver-*	*um*·velt·fer·
	schmutzung f	shmu·tsung
recycling	*Recycling-*	ri·*sai*·kling·
programme	*programm* n	pro·gram
toxic waste	*Giftmüll* m	*gift*·mül
water supply	*Wasserver-*	va·ser·fer·
	sorgung f	zor·gung

Is this a protected ...?	Ist das ...?	ist das ...
forest	ein geschützter Wald	ain ge·shüts·ter valt
species	eine geschützte Art	ai·ne ge·shüts·te art

the final say

If you'd like to underline your opinions with some colourful language and impress your new German-speaking acquaintances, try your hand at these sayings:

That goes without saying.
Das versteht sich von selbst.
das ver·*shtet* zikh fon zelbst

That cuts no ice with me.
Damit können Sie bei mir nicht landen.
da·mit *ker*·nen zee bai meer nikht *lan*·den

Nobody cares two hoots about it.
Danach kräht kein Hahn.
da·*nakh* krayt kain han

There's the rub.
Da liegt der Hund begraben.
da leegt dair hunt be·*grab*·en

Stick to the facts!
Bleiben Sie sachlich!
blai·ben zee *zakh*·likh

That will get you nowhere.
Das führt zu nichts.
das fürt tsu nikhts

Tell us another one!
Das können Sie uns nicht erzählen!
das *kern*·en zee uns nikht er·*tsay*·len

to have the final say
das letzte Wort haben
das *lets*·te vort *hab*·en

where to go

wohin ausgehen?

What's there to do in the evenings?
Was kann man abends   vas kan man *ah*·bents
unternehmen?   un·ter·*nay*·men

What's on ...?	*Was ist ... los?*	vas ist ... laws
locally	*hier*	heer
this weekend	*dieses*	*dee*·zes
	Wochenende	*vo*·khen·en·de
today	*heute*	*hoy*·te
tonight	*heute Abend*	*hoy*·te *ah*·bent

Where are the ...?	*Wo sind die ...?*	vaw zint dee ...
clubs	*Klubs*	klups
gay venues	*Schwulen- und*	*shvoo*·len unt
	Lesbenkneipen	*les*·ben·knai·pen
places to eat	*Restaurants*	res·to·*rangs*
pubs	*Kneipen*	*knai*·pen

Is there a local entertainment guide?
Gibt es einen   gipt es *ai*·nen
Veranstaltungskalender?   fer·*an*·shtal·tungks·ka·len·der

Is there a local gay guide?
Gibt es einen Führer für die   gipt es *ai*·nen *fü*·rer für dee
Schwulen- und Lesbenszene?   *shvoo*·len unt *les*·bens·tsay·ne

I feel like going to a/the ...	*Ich hätte Lust, ... zu gehen.*	ikh *he*·te lust ... tsoo *gay*·en
ballet	*zum Ballett*	tsum ba·*let*
bar/pub	*in eine Kneipe*	in *ai*·ne *knai*·pe
cafe	*in ein Café*	in ain ka·*fay*
concert	*in ein Konzert*	in ain kon·*tsert*
movies	*ins Kino*	ins *kee*·no
nightclub	*in einen Nachtklub*	in *ai*·nen *nakht*·klup
opera	*in die Oper*	in dee *aw*·per
restaurant	*in ein Restaurant*	in ain res·to·*rang*
theatre	*ins Theater*	ins te·*ah*·ter

I feel like going out somewhere.
Ich hätte Lust, auszugehen.   ikh *he*·te lust ows·tsu·*gay*·en

invitations

What are you doing (...)?	*Was machst du (...)?*	vas makhst doo (...)
right now	*jetzt gerade*	jetst ge·*rah*·de
this evening	*heute Abend*	*hoy*·te *ah*·bent
this weekend	*am Wochenende*	am *vo*·khen·en·de

Would you like to go (for a) ...?	*Möchtest du ... gehen?*	*merkh*·test doo ... *gay*·en
coffee	*einen Kaffee trinken*	*ai*·nen ka·*fay tring*·ken
dancing	*tanzen*	*tan*·tsen
drink	*etwas trinken*	*et*·vas *tring*·ken
meal	*essen*	*e*·sen

Do you want to come to the ... concert with me?
Möchtest du mit mir   *merkh*·test doo mit meer
zum ...-konzert gehen?   tsum ...·kon·*tsert gay*·en

We're having a party.
Wir machen eine Party.   veer *ma*·khen *ai*·ne *par*·ti

Would you like to come?
Hättest du Lust zu kommen?   *he*·test doo lust tsoo *ko*·men

responding to invitations

Sure!	*Klar!*	klahr
Yes, I'd love to.	*Ja, gerne.*	yah *ger*·ne
That's very kind of you.	*Das ist sehr nett von dir/euch.* sg/pl	das ist zair net fon deer/oykh
Where shall we go?	*Wo sollen wir hingehen?*	vaw *zo*·len veer *hin*·gay·en
No, I'm afraid I can't.	*Nein, es tut mir Leid, aber ich kann nicht.*	nain es toot meer lait *ah*·ber ikh kan nikht
What about tomorrow?	*Wie wäre es mit morgen?*	vee *vair*·re es mit *mor*·gen

local talk

There's nothing going on there.
Da ist nichts los. — dah ist nikhts laws

It's a hole.
Da ist tote Hose. — dah ist *taw*·te *haw*·ze
(lit: there is dead trousers)

It's all happening there.
Da ist die Sau los. — da ist dee zow laws
(lit: there is the sow loose)
Da boxt der Papst. — dah bokst dair pahpst
(lit: there boxes the pope)

arranging to meet

Where/When shall we meet?
Wo/Wann sollen wir uns treffen? — vaw/van *zo*·len veer uns *tre*·fen

Let's meet at ...	*Wir treffen uns ...*	veer *tre*·fen uns ...
(eight) o'clock	*um (acht) Uhr*	um (akht) oor
the (entrance)	*am (Eingang)*	am (*ain*·gang)

OK!
 Okay!   o·*kay*

I'll see you then.
 Bis dann!   bis dan

I'll pick you up.
 Ich hole dich ab.   ikh *haw*·le dikh ap

I'll be coming later. Where will you be?
 Ich komme später.   ikh *ko*·me *shpay*·ter
 Wo wirst du sein?   vaw virst doo zain

If I'm not there by (nine), don't wait for me.
 Wenn ich bis (neun)   ven ikh bis (noyn)
 Uhr nicht da bin,   oor nikht dah bin
 warte nicht auf mich.   *var*·te nikht owf mikh

See you later/tomorrow.
 Bis später/morgen.   bis *shpay*·ter/*mor*·gen

I'm looking forward to it.
 Ich freue mich darauf.   ikh *froy*·e mikh da·*rowf*

Sorry I'm late.
 Es tut mir Leid, dass   es toot meer lait das
 ich zu spät komme.   ikh tsoo shpayt *ko*·me

Never mind.
 Macht nichts.   makht nikhts

drugs

                                          drogen

I don't take drugs.
 Ich nehme keine Drogen.   ikh *nay*·me *kai*·ne *draw*·gen

I take ... occasionally.
 Ich nehme ab und zu ...   ikh *nay*·me ap unt tsoo ...

Do you want to have a smoke?
 Wollen wir einen   *vo*·len veer *ai*·nen
 Joint rauchen?   dzhoynt *row*·khen

I'm high.
 Ich bin high.   ikh bin hai

SOCIAL

asking someone out

sich verabreden

Would you like to do something ...?	*Hättest du Lust, ... was zu unternehmen?*	he·test doo lust ... vas tsoo un·ter·nay·men
Where would you like to go ...?	*Wo würdest du ... gerne hingehen?*	vaw vür·dest doo ... ger·ne hin·gay·en
tomorrow	*morgen*	mor·gen
tonight	*heute Abend*	hoy·te ah·bent
on the weekend	*am Wochenende*	am vo·khen·en·de

Yes, I'd love to.
 Ja, gerne.   yah ger·ne
Sure, thanks.
 Klar! Das wäre nett.   klahr das vair·re net
I'm busy.
 Ich habe keine Zeit.   ikh hah·be kai·ne tsait
Forget it!
 Vergiss es!   fer·gis es

local talk

He's/She's a ...	*Er/Sie ist ...*	air/zee ist ...
babe	*eine Schönheit*	ai·ne shern·hait
bitch	*eine Zicke*	ai·ne tsi·ke
hot guy	*ein heißer Typ*	ain hai·ser tüp
hot girl	*eine heiße Frau*	ai·ne hai·se frow
prick	*ein Depp*	ain dep

He/She looks really great.
 Er/Sie sieht echt geil aus.   air/zee zeet ekht gail ows

He/She gets around.
 Er/Sie lässt nichts anbrennen. air/zee lest nikhts an·bre·nen
 (lit: he/she lets nothing burn)

pick-up lines

Haven't we met before?
Kennen wir uns nicht von irgendwoher? — ke·nen veer uns nikht fon ir·gent·vo·hair

Would you like a drink?
Möchtest du etwas trinken? — merkh·test doo et·vas tring·ken

What star sign are you?
Was für ein Sternzeichen bist du? — vas für ain shtern·tsai·khen bist doo

Shall we get some fresh air?
Sollen wir ein bisschen an die frische Luft gehen? — zo·len veer ain bis·khen an dee fri·she luft gay·en

You have a beautiful personality.
Du hast eine wundervolle Persönlichkeit. — doo hast ai·ne vun·der·vo·ler per·zern·likh·kait

You have (a) beautiful ...	Du hast ...	doo hast ...
body	einen schönen Körper	ai·nen sher·nen ker·per
eyes	schöne Augen	sher·ne ow·gen
hands	schöne Hände	sher·ne hen·de
laugh	ein schönes Lachen	ain sher·nes la·khen

rejections

I'm here with ...	Ich bin mit ... hier.	ikh bin mit ... heer
my boyfriend	meinem Freund	mai·nem froynt
my girlfriend	meiner Freundin	mai·ner froyn·din

Excuse me, I have to go now.
Tut mir Leid, ich muss jetzt gehen. — toot meer lait ikh mus yetst gay·en

No, thank you.
   Nein, danke.   nain *dang*·ke

I'd rather not.
   Lieber nicht.   *lee*·ber nikht

Perhaps some other time.
   Vielleicht ein andermal.   fi·*laikht* ain *an*·der·mahl

Before this goes any further, I must be upfront. I'm (an accountant).
   Bevor wir uns näher   be·*fawr* veer uns *nay*·er
   kennen lernen, muss   *ke*·nen *ler*·nen mus
   ich etwas klarstellen.   ikh *et*·vas *klahr*·shte·len
   Ich bin (Buchhalter/   ikh bin (*bookh*·hal·ter/
   Buchhalterin). m/f   *bookh*·hal·te·rin)

Your ego is out of control.
   Du leidest wohl unter   doo *lai*·dest vawl *un*·ter
   Größenwahn.   *grer*·sen·wahn

romance

getting closer

Will you take me home?
*Kannst du mich nach
Hause bringen?*
kanst doo mikh nahkh
how·ze *bring*·en

Do you want to come inside for a while?
*Möchtest du noch
kurz mit reinkommen?*
merkh·test doo nokh
kurts mit *rain*·ko·men

You're very nice.
Du bist sehr nett.
doo bist zair net

I like you very much.
Ich mag dich sehr.
ikh mahk dikh zair

Do you like me too?
Magst du mich auch?
mahkst doo mikh owkh

You're very attractive.
Du bist sehr attraktiv.
doo bist zair a·trak·*teef*

I'm interested in you.
Ich interessiere mich für dich.
ikh in·tre·*see*·re mikh für dikh

You're great.
Du bist toll.
doo bist tol

sex

Kiss me.	*Küss mich.*	küs mikh
I want you.	*Ich will dich.*	ikh vil dikh
I want to make love to you.	*Ich möchte mit dir schlafen.*	ikh *merkh*·te mit deer *shlah*·fen
Take this off.	*Zieh das aus!*	tsee das ows
Touch me here.	*Berühr mich hier!*	be·*rür* mikh heer
Do you like this?	*Magst du das?*	mahkst doo das

Let's go to bed!
Gehen wir ins Bett!   gay·en veer ins bet

Do you have (a condom)?
Hast du (ein Kondom)?   hast doo (ain kon·*dawm*)

Let's use a (condom).
Lass uns (ein Kondom)   las uns (ain kon·*dawm*)
benutzen.   be·*nu*·tsen

I won't do it without protection.
Ohne Kondom mache   *aw*·ne kon·*dawm ma*·khe
ich es nicht.   ikh es nikht

I (don't) like that.
Das mag ich (nicht).   das mahk ikh (nikht)

Please (don't) stop!
Bitte hör (nicht) auf.   *bi*·te her (nikht) owf

I think we should stop now.
Ich denke, wir sollten   ikh *deng*·ke veer *zol*·ten
jetzt aufhören.   yetst owf·*her*·ren

I can't get it up – sorry.
Ich krieg ihn nicht   ikh kreek een nikht
hoch – tut mir Leid!   hawkh toot meer lait

Fuck me ...	*Fick mich ...*	*fik* mikh ...
harder	*härter*	*her*·ter
faster	*schneller*	*shne*·ler
softer	*sanfter*	*zanf*·ter
slower	*langsamer*	*lang*·zah·mer

Oh yeah!	*Oh ja!*	aw yah
That's great.	*Das ist geil.*	das ist gail
Easy tiger!	*Sachte!*	*zakh*·te
It's my first time.	*Das ist mein*	das ist main
	erstes Mal.	*ers*·tes mahl
Don't worry,	*Gib dir keine*	geep deer *kai*·ne
I'll do it myself.	*Mühe, ich mach*	*mü*·e ikh makh
	es mir selbst.	es meer zelpst

It helps to have a sense of humour.
Mit Humor geht   mit hu·*mawr* gayt
alles besser.   *a*·les *be*·ser

AIDS	*AIDS* n	aydz
contraception	*Empfängnis-verhütung* f	emp·*feng*·nis·fer·hü·tung
dental dam	*Dental Dam* m	*den*·tel dem
HIV	*HIV* n	hah·ee·*fow*
IUD	*Intrauterin-pessar* m	in·tra·u·te·*reen*·pe·sahr
the Pill	*die Pille* f	dee *pi*·le
spermicide	*Spermizid* n	shper·mi·*tseet*

> afterwards

That was ...	*Das war ...*	das vahr ...
amazing	*fantastisch*	fan·*tas*·tish
weird	*seltsam*	*zelt*·zahm
Can I ...?	*Kann ich ...?*	kan ikh ...
call you	*dich anrufen*	dikh *an*·roo·fen
meet you tomorrow	*dich morgen treffen*	dikh *mor*·gen *tre*·fen
see you again	*dich wiedersehen*	dikh *vee*·der·zay·en
stay over	*hier übernachten*	heer ü·ber·*nakh*·ten
I'll ...	*Ich ...*	ikh ...
call you tomorrow	*rufe dich morgen an*	*roo*·fe dikh *mor*·gen an
see you tomorrow	*sehe dich morgen*	*zay*·e dikh *mor*·gen
never forget	*werde das nie vergessen*	*ver*·de das nee fer·*ge*·sen

love

I love you.
Ich liebe dich.   ikh *lee*·be dikh

I think we're good together.
Ich glaube, wir passen   ikh *glow*·be veer *pa*·sen
gut zueinander.   goot tsu·ai·*nan*·der

Will you ...?	*Willst du ...?*	vilst doo ...
go out with me	*mit mir gehen*	mit meer *gay*·en
live with me	*mit mir*	mit meer
	zusammenleben	tsu·*za*·men·lay·ben
marry me	*mich heiraten*	mikh *hai*·ra·ten

problems

Are you seeing someone else?
Gibt es da einen   gipt es dah *ai*·nen
anderen/eine andere? m/f   *an*·de·ren/*ai*·ne *an*·de·re

I never want to see you again.
Ich will dich nie   ikh vil dikh nee
mehr wiedersehen.   mair *vee*·der·zay·en

We'll work it out.
Wir finden schon   veer *fin*·den shawn
eine Lösung.   *ai*·ne *ler*·zung

He's/She's just a friend.
Er/Sie ist nur ein   air/zee ist noor ain
Freund/eine   froynt/*ai*·ne
Freundin. m/f   *froyn*·din

I want to ...	*Ich möchte ...*	ikh *merkh*·te ...
end the	*Schluss*	shlus
relationship	*machen*	*ma*·khen
stay friends	*dass wir Freunde*	das veer *froyn*·de
	bleiben	*blai*·ben

leaving

I have to leave tomorrow.
Ich muss morgen los.   ikh mus *mor*·gen laws

I'll ...	Ich ...	ikh ...
come and	*komme dich*	*ko*·me dikh
visit you	*besuchen*	be·*zoo*·khen
miss you	*werde dich*	*ver*·de dikh
	vermissen	fer·*mi*·sen

on heat

Some German expressions might seem similar to English expressions, but have a very different meaning – beware of the following:

Ich bin heiss.   ikh bin hais
(lit: I am hot)
    I'm feeling sexy.

Ich bin kalt.   ikh bin kalt
(lit: I am cold)
    I'm frigid/I have an unfriendly personality.

To say you're feeling physically hot or cold, use:

Mir ist heiss.   mir ist hais
(lit: to me is hot)
    I'm hot.

Mir ist kalt.   mir ist kalt
(lit: to me is cold)
    I'm cold.

Similarly, be careful not to mix up these:

Ich bin voll.   ikh bin fol
(lit: I am full)
    I'm drunk.

Ich bin satt.   ikh bin zat.
(lit: I am full)
    I've had enough to eat.

religion

religion

What's your religion?
Was ist Ihre/deine   vas ist *ee*·re/*dai*·ne
Religion? pol/inf   re·li·*gyawn*

I'm (not) religious.
Ich bin (nicht) religiös.   ikh bin (nikht) re·li·*gyers*

I'm (not) ...	*Ich bin (kein/ keine) ... m/f*	ikh bin (kain/ *kai*·ne) ...
agnostic	*Agnostiker(in) m/f*	a·*gnos*·ti·ker/ a·*gnos*·ti·ke·rin
Buddhist	*Buddhist(in) m/f*	bu·*dist*/bu·*dis*·tin
Catholic	*Katholik(in) m/f*	ka·to·*leek*/ ka·to·*lee*·kin
Christian	*Christ(in) m/f*	krist/*kris*·tin
Hindu	*Hindu m&f*	*hin*·du
Jewish	*Jude/Jüdin m/f*	*yoo*·de/*yü*·din
Muslim	*Moslem/ Moslime m/f*	*mos*·lem/ mos·*lee*·me
practising	*praktizierender/ praktizierende m/f*	prak·ti·*tsee*·ren·der/ prak·ti·*tsee*·ren·de
Protestant	*Protestant(in) m/f*	pro·tes·*tant*/ pro·tes·*tan*·tin

I (don't) believe in ...	*Ich glaube (nicht) an ...*	ikh *glow*·be (nikht) an ...
God	*Gott*	got
destiny/fate	*das Schicksal*	das *shik*·zahl

Where can I ...?	Wo kann ich ...?	vaw kan ikh ...
attend mass	eine Messe besuchen	ai·ne me·se be·zoo·khen
attend service	einen Gottesdienst besuchen	ai·nen go·tes·deenst be·zoo·khen
make confession (in English)	(auf Englisch) beichten	(owf eng·lish) baikh·ten
pray	beten	bay·ten
receive communion	das Abendmahl empfangen	das ah·bent·mahl emp·fang·en
worship	meine Andacht verrichten	mai·ne an·dakht fer·rikh·ten

cultural differences

kulturelle unterschiede

Is this a local or national custom?
Ist das ein örtlicher oder landesweiter Brauch?
ist das ain ert·li·kher aw·der lan·des·vai·ter browkh

I'm not used to this.
Das ist ganz ungewohnt für mich.
das ist gants un·ge·vawnt für mikh

I don't mind watching, but I'd rather not join in.
Ich sehe gerne zu, würde aber lieber nicht selbst mitmachen.
ikh zay·e ger·ne tsoo vür·de ah·ber lee·ber nikht zelpst mit·ma·khen

I'll try it.
Ich versuche es.
ikh fer·zoo·khe es

I'm sorry, I didn't mean to do anything wrong.
Es tut mir Leid, ich wollte nichts Falsches tun.
es toot meer lait ikh vol·te nikhts fal·shes toon

I'm sorry, it's against my ...	Es tut mir Leid, das ist gegen meine ...	es toot meer lait das ist gay·gen mai·ne ...
beliefs	Anschauungen	an·show·ung·en
culture	Kultur	kul·toor
religion	Religion	re·li·gyawn

Where's (the museum)?
Wo ist (das Museum)? vaw ist (das mu·*zay*·um)

When's (the gallery) open?
Wann hat (die Galerie) van hat (dee ga·le·*ree*)
geöffnet? ge·*erf*·net

What kind of art are you interested in?
Für welche Art von Kunst für *vel*·khe art fon kunst
interessieren Sie sich? pol in·tre·*see*·ren zee zikh
Für welche Art von Kunst für *vel*·khe art fon kunst
interessierst du dich? inf in·tre·*seerst* doo dikh

What's in the collection?
Was gibt es in der vas gipt es in dair
Sammlung? *zam*·lung

What do you think of ...?
Was halten Sie von ...? pol vas *hal*·ten zee fon ...
Was hältst du von ...? inf vas heltst doo fon ...

artistic styles

art nouveau	*Jugendstil*	yoo·*gent*·shteel
baroque art	*barocke Kunst*	ba·*ro*·ke kunst
Bauhaus art	*Bauhaus-Kunst*	*bow*·hows·kunst
expressionist art	*expressionistische Kunst*	eks·pre·syo·*nis*·ti·she kunst
Gothic art	*gotische Kunst*	*gaw*·ti·she kunst
impressionist art	*impressionistische Kunst*	im·pre·syo·*nis*·ti·she kunst
modernist art	*moderne Kunst*	mo·*der*·ne kunst
performance art	*Performance Art*	pe·*faw*·mens aht
Renaissance art	*Renaissance-Kunst*	re·ne·*sangs*·kunst
Romanesque art	*romanische Kunst*	ro·*mah*·ni·she kunst

It's a/an ... exhibition.
Es ist eine ...-Ausstellung.   es ist *ai*·ne ...·ows·shte·lung

I'm interested in ...
Ich interessiere mich für ...   ikh in·tre·*see*·re mikh für ...

I like the works of ...
Ich mag die Arbeiten von ...   ikh mahk dee *ar*·bai·ten fon ...

It reminds me of ...
Es erinnert mich an ...   es er·*i*·nert mikh an ...

tongue twisters

If you're feeling pretty comfortable with the language and want to impress the locals, try these tongue twisters:

Blaukraut bleibt Blaukraut und Brautkleid bleibt Brautkleid.
blow·krowt blaipt *blow*·krowt unt *browt*·klait blaipt *browt*·klait
('Red cabbage remains red cabbage and a wedding dress remains a wedding dress.')

Der Potsdamer Postkutscher putzt den Potsdamer Postkutschkasten.
dair *pots*·dah·mer *post*·ku·cher putst dayn *pots*·dah·mer *post*·kuch·kah·sten
('The Potsdam mailcoach driver cleans the Potsdam mailcoach postboxes.')

Der Dachdecker deckt dein Dach, drum dank dem Dachdecker, der dein Dach deckt.
dair *dakh*·de·ker dekt dain dakh drum dank daym *dakh*·de·ker dair dain dakh dekt
('The roofer roofs your roof, for that thank the roofer, who roofs your roof.')

sporting interests

sportarten

What sport do you play?

Was für Sport treiben Sie? pol — vas für shport *trai*·ben zee

Was für Sport treibst du? inf — vas für shport traipst doo

What sport do you follow?

Für welche Sportarten — für *vel*·khe *shport*·ar·ten

interessieren Sie sich? pol — in·tre·*see*·ren zee zikh

Für welche Sportarten — für *vel*·khe *shport*·ar·ten

interessierst du dich? inf — in·tre·*seerst* doo dikh

I play ...	*Ich spiele ...*	ikh *shpee*·le ...
I do ...	*Ich mache ...*	ikh *ma*·khe ...
I follow ...	*Ich interessiere*	ikh in·tre·*see*·re
	mich für ...	mikh für ...
athletics	*Leichtathletik*	*laikht*·at·lay·tik
basketball	*Basketball*	*bahs*·ket·bal
football (soccer)	*Fußball*	*foos*·bal
handball	*Handball*	*hant*·bal
ice hockey	*Eishockey*	*ais*·ho·ki
skiing	*Skifahren*	*shee*·fah·ren
tennis	*Tennis*	*te*·nis

For more types of sport, see the **dictionary**.

Do you like (sport)?

Mögen Sie (Sport)? pol — *mer*·gen zee (shport)

Magst du (Sport)? inf — mahkst doo (shport)

Yes, very much.

Ja, sehr. — yah zair

Not really.

Nicht besonders. — nikht be·*zon*·ders

I like watching it.

Ich sehe es mir gerne an. — ikh *zay*·e es meer *ger*·ne an

Only as a spectator.
Nur als Zuschauer.　　　　　　noor als *tsoo*·show·er

Who's your favourite sportsperson?
Wer ist Ihr/dein　　　　　　　vair ist eer/dain
Lieblingssportler? pol/inf　　　*leep*·lingks·shport·ler

Who's your favourite team?
Was ist Ihre/deine　　　　　　vas ist ee·re/*dai*·ne
Lieblingsmannschaft? pol/inf　*leep*·lingks·man·shaft

Can you play (soccer)?
Spielen Sie (Fußball)? pol　　shpee·len zee (*foos*·bal)
Spielst du (Fußball)? inf　　　shpeelst doo (*foos*·bal)

going to a game

zu einem spiel gehen

Would you like to go to a game?
Möchten Sie zu einem　　　　*merkh*·ten zee tsoo *ai*·nem
Spiel gehen? pol　　　　　　shpeel *gay*·en
Möchtest du zu einem　　　　*merkh*·test doo tsoo *ai*·nem
Spiel gehen? inf　　　　　　shpeel *gay*·en

Who are you supporting?
Wen unterstützen Sie? pol　　vayn un·ter·*shtü*·tsen zee
Wen unterstützt du? inf　　　vayn un·ter·*shtütst* doo

Who's ...?　　*Wer ...?*　　　vair ...
　playing　　　*spielt*　　　　speelt
　winning　　　*gewinnt*　　　ge·*vint*

sports talk		
What a ...!	*Was für ...!*	vas für ...
goal	*ein Tor*	ain tawr
hit	*ein Treffer*	ain *tre*·fer
kick	*ein Schuss*	ain shus
pass	*ein Pass*	ain pas
performance	*eine Leistung*	*ai*·ne *lais*·tung

What was the final score?
Was war das Endergebnis?   vas vahr das *ent*·er·gayp·nis

It was a draw.
Es ging unentschieden aus.   es ging *un*·ent·shee·den ows

That was a	*Das war ein*	das vahr ain
... game!	*... Spiel!*	... shpeel
bad	*schlechtes*	*shlekh*·tes
boring	*langweiliges*	*lang*·vai·li·ges
great	*tolles*	*to*·les

scoring

What's the score?	*Wie steht es?*	vee shtayt es
draw/even	*unentschieden*	*un*·ent·shee·den
love (zero)	*null*	nul
match-point	*Matchball*	*mech*·bal
nil (zero)	*null*	nul
3–1	*3:1 (drei zu eins)*	drai tsoo ains

playing sport

sport treiben

Do you want to play?
Möchten Sie mitspielen? pol   *merkh*·ten zee *mit*·shpee·len
Möchtest du mitspielen? inf   *merkh*·test doo *mit*·shpee·len

Can I join in?
Kann ich mitspielen?   kan ikh *mit*·shpee·len

Yes, that'd be great.
Ja, das wäre toll.   yah das *vair*·re tol

I'm sorry, I can't.
Es tut mir Leid,   es toot meer lait
ich kann nicht.   ikh kan nikht

I have an injury.
Ich habe eine Verletzung.   ikh *hah*·be *ai*·ne fer·*le*·tsung

Your point.
Ihr/Dein Punkt. pol/inf — eer/dain pungkt

My point.
Mein Punkt. — main pungkt

Kick/Pass it to me!
Hierher! — heer·hair

You're a good player.
Sie sind — zee zint
ein guter Spieler/ — ain goo·ter shpee·ler/
eine gute Spielerin. m/f pol — ai·ne goo·te shpee·le·rin

You're a good player.
Du bist — doo bist ...
ein guter Spieler/ — ain goo·ter shpee·ler/
eine gute Spielerin. m/f inf — ai·ne goo·te shpee·le·rin

Thanks for the game.
Vielen Dank für das Spiel. — fee·len dangk für das shpeel

Where's the best place to jog/run around here?
Wo kann man hier am — vaw kan man heer am
besten joggen/laufen? — bes·ten dzho·gen/low·fen

Where's the nearest ...?
Wo ist ...? — vaw ist ...

gym
das nächste — das naykhs·te
Fitness-Studio — fit·nes·shtoo·di·o

swimming pool
das nächste — das naykhs·te
Schwimmbad — shvim·baht

tennis court
der nächste — dair naykhs·te
Tennisplatz — te·nis·plats

Do I have to be a member to attend?
Muss ich Mitglied sein, — mus ikh mit·gleet zain
um mitzumachen? — um mit·tsu·ma·khen

Is there a women-only session?
Gibt es eine Session   gipt es *ai*·ne ses·yawn
nur für Frauen?   noor für *frow*·en

Is there a women-only pool?
Gibt es ein Schwimmbecken   gipt es ain *shvim*·be·ken
nur für Frauen?   noor für *frow*·en

Where are the change rooms?
Wo sind die   vaw zint dee
Umkleideräume?   um·klai·de·roy·me

What's the	*Wie viel kostet*	vee feel *kos*·tet
charge per ...?	*es pro ...?*	es praw ...
day	*Tag*	tahk
game	*Spiel*	shpeel
hour	*Stunde*	*shtun*·de
visit	*Besuch*	be·*zookh*

Can I hire a ...?	*Kann ich ...?*	kan ikh ...
ball	*einen Ball leihen*	*ai*·nen bal *lai*·en
bicycle	*ein Fahrrad leihen*	ain *fahr*·raht *lai*·en
court	*einen Platz*	*ai*·nen plats
	mieten	*mee*·ten
racquet	*einen Schläger*	*ai*·nen *shlay*·ger
	leihen	*lai*·en

cycling

radsport

Where does the race finish?
Wo endet das Rennen?   vaw *en*·det das *re*·nen

Where does the race pass through?
Wo führt das Rennen lang?   vaw fürt das *re*·nen lang

Who's winning?
Wer gewinnt?   vair ge·*vint*

Is today's leg very hard?
Ist die Etappe heute   ist dee e·*ta*·pe *hoy*·te
sehr schwer?   zair shvair

How many kilometres is today's (leg)?
Wie viel Kilometer ist   vee feel ki·lo·*may*·ter ist
(die Etappe) heute?   (dee e·*ta*·pe) *hoy*·te

My favourite cyclist is ...
Mein Lieblings-   main *leep*·lingks·
radfahrer ist ...   *raht*·fah·rer ist ...

climbing stage	*Bergetappe* f	berk·e·ta·pe
cyclist	*Radfahrer(in)* m/f	*raht*·fah·rer/ *raht*·fah·re·rin
the (yellow) jersey	*das (gelbe) Trikot* n	das (*gel*·be) tri·*kaw*
leg (in race)	*Etappe* f *(des Rennens)*	e·*ta*·pe (des *re*·nens)
racing cyclist	*Radrenn-fahrer(in)* m/f	*raht*·ren·fah·rer/ *raht*·ren·fah·re·rin
time trial	*Zeitfahren* n	*tsait*·fah·ren
winner	*Sieger(in)* m/f	zee·ger/zee·ge·rin
winner of a leg	*Etappen-sieger(in)* m/f	e·*ta*·pen·zee·ger/ e·*ta*·pen·zee·ge·rin

For words and phrases on getting around by bicycle, see **transport**, page 45.

extreme sports

extremsportarten

Are you sure this is safe?
Sind Sie sicher, dass das   zint zee *zi*·kher das das
ungefährlich ist? pol   *un*·ge·fair·likh ist
Bist du sicher, dass das   bist doo *zi*·kher das das
ungefährlich ist? inf   *un*·ge·fair·likh ist

Is the equipment secure?
Ist die Ausrüstung sicher?   ist dee *ows*·rüs·tung *zi*·kher

This is insane.
Das ist verrückt!   das ist fer·*rükt*

abseiling	*Abseilen* n	*ap*·zai·len
bungy-jumping	*Bungyjumping* n	*ban*·dzhi·dzham·ping
caving	*Höhlenerforschung* f	*her*·len·er·for·shung
hanggliding	*Drachenfliegen* n	*dra*·khen·flee·gen
mountain biking	*Mountainbiken* n	*mown*·ten·bai·ken
parachuting	*Fallschirmspringen* n	*fal*·shirm·shpring·en
parasailing	*Parasailing* n	*pah*·ra·say·ling
rock-climbing	*Klettern* n	*kle*·tern
skydiving	*Skydiving* n	*skai*·dai·ving
snowboarding	*Snowboarden* n	*snoh*·bor·den
white-water rafting	*Wildwasser-fahrten* f pl	*vilt*·va·ser·fahr·ten

soccer

Who plays for (Bayern München)?
Wer spielt für (Bayern München)?   vair shpeelt für (*bai*·ern *mün*·khen)

What a terrible team!
Was für eine furchtbare Mannschaft!   vas für *ai*·ne *furkht*·bah·re *man*·shaft

Which team is at the top of the league?
Welcher Verein steht an der Tabellenspitze?   *vel*·kher fer·*ain* shtayt an dair ta·*be*·len·shpi·tse

She's a great player.
Sie ist eine tolle Spielerin.   zee ist ain·e *to*·le shpee·ler·in

He played brilliantly in the match against (Italy).
Im Spiel gegen (Italien) hat er fantastisch gespielt.   im shpeel gay·gen (i·*tah*·li·en) hat air fan·*tas*·tish ge·*shpeelt*

She scored (three) goals.
Sie hat (drei) Tore geschossen.   zee hat (drai) *taw*·re ge·*sho*·sen

corner	*Ecke* f	*e·ke*
free kick	*Freistoß* m	*frai·shtaws*
goalkeeper	*Torhüter(in)* m/f	*tawr·hü·ter/*
		tawr·hü·te·rin
offside	*Abseits* n	*ap·zaits*
penalty	*Strafstoß* m	*shtrahf·shtaws*

skiing

skifahren

How much is a pass?
Was kostet ein Skipass?   vas *kos*·tet ain *shee*·pas

Can I take lessons?
Kann ich Unterricht nehmen?   kan ikh *un*·ter·rikht *nay*·men

I'd like to hire ...	*Ich möchte ...*	ikh *merkh*·te ...
	leihen.	*lai*·en
boots	*Skistiefel*	*shee*·shtee·fel
goggles	*eine Skibrille*	*ai*·ne *shee*·bri·le
poles	*Skistöcke*	*shee*·shter·ke
skis	*Skier*	*shee*·er
a ski suit	*einen*	*ai*·nen
	Skianzug	*shee*·an·tsook
Is it possible to	*Kann man*	kan man
go ... here/there?	*hier/da ...?*	heer/dah ...
Alpine skiing	*Abfahrtsski*	*ap*·fahrts·shee
	fahren	*fah*·ren
cross-country	*Skilanglauf*	shee·*lang*·lowf
skiing	*machen*	*ma*·khen
snowboarding	*snowboarden*	*snoh*·bor·den
tobogganing	*Schlitten fahren*	*shli*·ten *fah*·ren

What are the skiing conditions like ...?	Wie sind die Schneebedingungen ...?	vee zint dee shnay·be·ding·ung·en ...
at (Lauberhorn)	am (Lauberhorn)	am (low·ber·horn)
on that run	an dieser Abfahrt	an dee·zer ap·fahrt
higher up	weiter oben	vai·ter aw·ben

What level is that slope?

| Wie schwierig ist dieser Hang? | vee shvee·rikh ist dee·zer hang |

Which are the ... slopes?	Welches sind die ...?	vel·khes zint dee ...
beginner	Anfängerhänge	an·feng·er·heng·e
intermediate	mittelschweren Hänge	mi·tel·shvair·ren heng·e
advanced	Fortgeschrittenen- hänge	fort·ge·shri·te·nen- heng·e

cable car	Seilbahn f	zail·bahn
chairlift	Sessellift m	ze·sel·lift
instructor	Skilehrer m	shee·lair·rer
resort	Ort m	ort
ski-lift	Skilift m	shee·lift
sled	Schlitten m	shli·ten

tennis

Would you like to play tennis?

| Möchten Sie Tennis spielen? pol | merkh·ten zee te·nis shpee·len |
| Möchtest du Tennis spielen? inf | merkh·test doo te·nis shpee·len |

Can we play at night?

| Können wir abends spielen? | ker·nen veer ah·bents shpee·len |

ace	*Ass* n	as
advantage	*Vorteil* m	*fawr*·tail
clay court	*Sandplatz* m	*zant*·plats
fault	*Fehler* m	*fay*·ler
game, set, match	*Spiel, Satz und Sieg*	shpeel *zats* unt zeek
grass court	*Rasenplatz* m	*rah*·zen·plats
hard court	*Hartplatz* m	*hart*·plats
play doubles	*ein Doppel spielen*	ain *do*·pel *shpee*·len
serve	*Aufschlag* m	*owf*·shlahk
set	*Satz* m	zats

könig fußball

The king of German amateur and professional sports is 'König Fußball' (king football). Football (or soccer as it's known in the US and Australia) is played at thousands of amateur clubs known as *Fußballvereine*. Germans are passionate about the game and professional games draw an average 25,000 fans. One of the longest words in the German language belongs to the football sphere. Try getting your tongue around *Fußballweltmeisterschafts-qualifikationsspiel* (World Cup Soccer qualifying game).

hiking

wandern

Where can I ...?	Wo kann ich ...?	vaw kan ikh ...
buy supplies	*Vorräte einkaufen*	*fawr·ray·te ain·kow·fen*
find out about hiking trails	*Informationen über Wanderwege bekommen*	*in·for·ma·tsyaw·nen ü·ber van·der·vay·ge be·ko·men*
find someone who knows this area	*jemanden finden, der die Gegend kennt*	*yay·man·den fin·den dair dee gay·gent kent*
get a map	*eine Karte bekommen*	*ai·ne kar·te be·ko·men*
hire hiking gear	*Wanderausrüstung leihen*	*van·der·ows·rüs·tung lai·en*
Do we need to take ...?	*Müssen wir ... mitnehmen?*	*mü·sen veer ... mit·nay·men*
bedding	*Bettzeug*	*bet·tsoyk*
food	*Essen*	*e·sen*
water	*Wasser*	*va·ser*

How long is the trail?
Wie lang ist der Weg?　　　vee lang ist dair vayk

How high is the climb?
Wie hoch führt die　　　vee hawkh fürt dee
Klettertour hinauf?　　　kle·ter·toor hi·nowf

Do we need a guide?
Brauchen wir einen Führer?　brow·khen veer ai·nen fü·rer

Are there guided treks?
Gibt es geführte　　　gipt es ge·für·te
Wanderungen?　　　van·de·rung·en

Is it safe?
Ist es ungefährlich?　　　ist es un·ge·fair·likh

Is there a hut there?
Gibt es dort eine Hütte?　gipt es dort ai·ne hü·te

When does it get dark?
Wann wird es dunkel?　　van virt es dung·kel

Is the track ...?	*Ist der Weg ...?*	ist dair vayk ...
(well-)marked	*(gut) markiert*	(goot) mar·keert
open	*offen*	o·fen
scenic	*schön*	shern

Which is the ...?	*Welches ist die ...?*	vel·khes ist dee ...
shortest route	*kürzeste Route*	kür·tses·te roo·te
easiest route	*einfachste Route*	ain·fakhs·te roo·te

Where's a/the ...?	*Wo ...?*	vaw ...
camp site	*ist ein Zeltplatz*	ist ain tselt·plats
nearest village	*ist das*	ist das
	nächste Dorf	naykhs·te dorf
showers	*sind (die) Duschen*	zint (dee) doo·shen
toilets	*sind (die)*	zint (dee)
	Toiletten	to·a·le·ten

Where have you come from?
Wo kommen Sie
gerade her? pol
vaw ko·men zee
ge·rah·de hair

How long did it take?
Wie lange hat
das gedauert?
vee lang·e hat
das ge·dow·ert

Does this path go to ...?
Führt dieser Weg nach ...?
fürt dee·zer vayk nahkh ...

Can we go through here?
Können wir hier
durchgehen?
ker·nen veer heer
durkh·gay·en

Is the water OK to drink?
Kann man das
Wasser trinken?
kan man das
va·ser tring·ken

I'm lost.
Ich habe mich verlaufen.
ikh hah·be mikh fer·low·fen

at the beach

am strand

Where's the ...	*Wo ist der ...*	vaw ist dair ...
beach?	*Strand?*	shtrant
best	*beste*	bes·te
nearest	*nächste*	naykhs·te
nudist	*FKK-*	ef·kah·kah·
public	*öffentliche*	er·fent·li·khe

---

signs

Schwimmen	shvi·men	**No Swimming!**
Verboten!	fer·baw·ten	
Sturmwarnung!	shturm var·nunk	**Storm Warning!**

outdoors

135

Is it safe to dive/swim here?
*Kann man hier gefahrlos
tauchen/schwimmen?*
kan man heer ge·*fahr*·laws
tow·khen/*shvi*·men

What time is high/low tide?
Wann ist Flut/Ebbe?
van ist floot/*e*·be

Do we have to pay?
Müssen wir bezahlen?
mü·sen veer be·*tsah*·len

listen for ...

akh·ten zee owf dayn zawk
Achten Sie auf den Sog. **Be careful of the undertow.**

es ist ge·*fair*·likh
Es ist gefährlich! **It's dangerous!**

zee *mü*·sen *ai*·ne *koor*·tak·se be·*tsah*·len
*Sie müssen eine
Kurtaxe bezahlen.* **You have to pay a health
resort visitor's tax.**

How much for a/an ...?	*Was kostet ein ...?*	vas *kos*·tet ain ...
canopied wicker beach-chair	*Strandkorb*	*shtrant*·korp
chair	*Stuhl*	shtool
hut	*Hut*	hoot
umbrella	*Schirm*	shirm

weather

What's the weather like?
Wie ist das Wetter?   vee ist das *ve*·ter

It's ...	*Es ist ...*	es ist ...
Will it be ...	*Wird es morgen*	virt es *mor*·gen
tomorrow?	*... sein?*	... zain
cloudy	*wolkig*	*vol*·kikh
cold	*kalt*	kalt
freezing	*eiskalt*	*ais*·kalt
hot	*heiß*	hais
raining	*regnerisch*	*rayg*·ne·rish
sunny	*sonnig*	*zo*·nikh
warm	*warm*	varm
windy	*windig*	*vin*·dikh

Where can I	*Wo kann ich*	vaw kan ikh
buy a/an ...?	*... kaufen?*	... *kow*·fen
rain jacket	*eine*	*ai*·ne
	Regenjacke	*ray*·gen·ya·ke
umbrella	*einen*	*ai*·nen
	Regenschirm	*ray*·gen·shirm

flora & fauna

What ... is that?	*Wie heißt ...?*	vee haist ...
animal	*dieses Tier*	*dee*·zes teer
flower	*diese Blume*	*dee*·ze *bloo*·me
plant	*diese Pflanze*	*dee*·ze *pflan*·tse
tree	*dieser Baum*	*dee*·zer bowm

Is it ...?	*Ist es ...?*	ist es ...
common	*weit verbreitet*	vait fer·*brai*·tet
dangerous	*gefährlich*	ge·*fair*·likh
endangered	*vom Aussterben*	fom *ows*·shter·ben
	bedroht	be·*drawt*
protected	*geschützt*	ge·*shütst*

What's it used for?
Wofür wird es benutzt?   vaw·*für* virt aes be·*nutst*

Can you eat it?
Kann man es essen?   kan man es e·sen

For geographical and agricultural terms and names of animals and plants, see the **dictionary**.

anyone for a dip?

Aquatic pursuits are popular in Germany and it's hard to find a town that doesn't have a public *Schwimmbad* (swimming pool). Often there's a *Hallenbad* (indoor pool) alongside the *Freibad* (outdoor pool). Spas are popular too, with people seeking to cure a variety of conditions. The most famous spa town in Germany is called *Baden Baden*. This double-barrelled name represents both the name of the surrounding region and the German word for bathing.

key language

wichtige wörter

breakfast	*Frühstück* n	*frü*·shtük
lunch	*Mittagessen* n	*mi*·tahk·e·sen
dinner	*Abendessen* n	*ah*·bent·e·sen
snack	*Snack* m	snek
eat	*essen*	e·sen
drink	*trinken*	*tring*·ken
Please.	*Bitte.*	*bi*·te
Thank you.	*Danke.*	*dang*·ke
I'd like ...	*Ich möchte ...*	ikh *merkh*·te ...
I'm starving!	*Ich bin am Verhungern!*	ikh bin am fer·*hung*·ern

finding a place to eat

ein restaurant suchen

Can you recommend a ...	*Können Sie ... empfehlen?* pol	*ker*·nen zee ... emp·*fay*·len
	Kannst du ... empfehlen? inf	kanst doo ... emp·*fay*·len
bar/pub	*eine Kneipe*	*ai*·ne *knai*·pe
cafe	*ein Café*	ain ka·*fay*
coffee bar	*eine Espressobar*	*ai*·ne es·*pre*·so·bahr
restaurant	*ein Restaurant*	ain res·to·*rang*
Where would you go for (a) ...?	*Wo kann man hingehen, um ...?*	vaw kan man *hin*·gay·en um ...
celebration	*etwas zu feiern*	*et*·vas tsoo *fai*·ern
cheap meal	*etwas Billiges zu essen*	*et*·vas *bi*·li·ges tsoo e·sen
local specialities	*örtliche Spezialitäten zu essen*	*ert*·li·khe shpe·tsya·li·*tay*·ten tsoo e·sen

I'd like to reserve a table for ...	Ich möchte einen Tisch für ... reservieren.	ikh *merkh*·te *ai*·nen tish für ... re·zer·*vee*·ren
(two) people	*(zwei) Personen*	(tsvai) per·*zaw*·nen
(eight) o'clock	*(acht) Uhr*	(akht) oor
I'd like ..., please.	*Ich hätte gern ..., bitte.*	ikh *he*·te gern ... *bi*·te
a table for (five)	*einen Tisch für (fünf) Personen*	*ai*·nen tish für (fünf) per·*zaw*·nen
the smoking section	*einen Raucher-tisch*	*ai*·nen *row*·kher· tish
the non-smoking section	*einen Nicht-rauchertisch*	*ai*·nen *nikht*· row·kher·tish
Do you have ...?	*Haben Sie ...?*	*hah*·ben zee ...
children's meals	*Kinderteller*	*kin*·der·te·ler
a menu in English	*eine englische Speisekarte*	*ai*·ne *eng*·li·she *shpai*·ze·kar·te

listen for ...

es toot meer lait veer *hah*·ben ge·*shlo*·sen
Es tut mir Leid, wir haben geschlossen. **Sorry, we're closed.**

veer zint fol *ows*·ge·bookht
Wir sind voll ausgebucht. **We're fully booked.**

veer *hah*·ben *kai*·nen tish frai
Wir haben keinen Tisch frei. **We have no free tables.**

vaw *merkh*·ten zee *zi*·tsen
Wo möchten Sie sitzen? **Where would you like to sit?**

merkh·ten zee *et*·vas *tring*·ken *vair*·rent zee *var*·ten
Möchten Sie etwas trinken, während Sie warten? **Would you like a drink while you wait?**

vas darf ikh *ee*·nen *bring*·en
Was darf ich Ihnen bringen? **What can I get for you?**

bi·te
Bitte! **Here you go!**

Are you still serving food?
Gibt es noch etwas zu essen? gipt es nokh *et*·vas tsoo *e*·sen

How long is the wait?
Wie lange muss man warten? vee *lang*·e mus man *var*·ten

at the restaurant

I'd like ...,	*Ich hätte gern ...,*	ikh *he*·te gern ...
please.	*bitte.*	*bi*·te
the drink list	*die Getränke-*	dee ge·*treng*·ke·
	karte	kar·te
the menu	*die Speisekarte*	dee *shpai*·ze·kar·te

What would you recommend?
Was empfehlen Sie? vas emp·*fay*·len zee

> ### listen for ...
>
> ikh emp·*fay*·le ee·nen ...
> *Ich empfehle Ihnen ...* **I suggest the ...**
>
> *mer*·gen zee ...
> *Mögen Sie ...?* **Do you like ...?**
>
> vee *merkh*·ten zee das *tsoo*·be·rai·tet *hah*·ben
> *Wie möchten Sie das* **How would you**
> *zubereitet haben?* **like that cooked?**

I'll have what they're having.
Ich nehme das ikh *nay*·me das
gleiche wie sie. *glai*·khe vee zee

I'd like a local speciality.
Ich möchte etwas ikh *merkh*·te et·vas
Typisches aus der Region. *tü*·pi·shes ows dair re·*gyawn*

What's in that dish?
Was ist in diesem Gericht? vas ist in *dee*·zem ge·*rikht*

Does it take long to prepare?
Dauert das lange?   *dow*·ert das *lang*·e

Is it self-serve?
Ist das Selbstbedienung?   ist das *zelpst*·be·dee·nung

Is service included in the bill?
Ist die Bedienung   ist dee be·*dee*·nung
inbegriffen?   *in*·be·gri·fen

Are these complimentary?
Sind die gratis?   zint dee *grah*·tis

We're just having drinks.
Wir möchten nur   veer *merkh*·ten noor
etwas trinken.   *et*·vas *tring*·ken

For more on special diets, see **vegetarian & special meals**, page 159.

---

look for ...

Vorspeisen	*fawr*·shpai·zen	appetisers/entrees
Suppen	*zu*·pen	soups
Salate	za·*lah*·te	salads
Hauptgerichte	*howpt*·ge·rikh·te	main courses
Beilagen	*bai*·lah·gen	side dishes
Nachspeisen	*nahkh*·shpai·zen	desserts
Aperitifs	a·pe·ri·*teefs*	aperitifs
Alkoholfreie	al·ko·*hawl*·frai·e	soft drinks
Getränke	ge·*treng*·ke	
Spirituosen	shpi·ri·tu·*aw*·zen	spirits
Bier	beer	beers
Schaumweine	*showm*·vai·ne	sparkling wines
Weißweine	*vais*·vai·ne	white wines
Rotweine	*rawt*·vai·ne	red wines
Dessertweine	de·*sair*·vai·ne	dessert wines
Digestifs	di·zhes·*teefs*	digestifs

For more words you might see on a menu, see the **culinary reader**, page 163.

at the table

Please bring ...	Bitte bringen Sie ...	bi·te bring·en zee ...
the bill	die Rechnung	dee rekh·nung
a cloth	eine Tischdecke	ai·ne tish·de·ke
a glass	ein Glas	ain (vain·)glahs

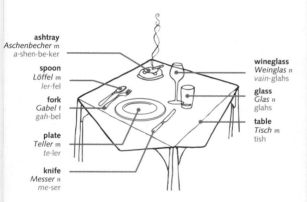

ashtray
Aschenbecher m
a·shen·be·ker

spoon
Löffel m
ler·fel

fork
Gabel f
gah·bel

plate
Teller m
te·ler

knife
Messer n
me·ser

wineglass
Weinglas n
vain·glahs

glass
Glas n
glahs

table
Tisch m
tish

talking food

I love this dish.
Ich mag dieses Gericht.
ikh mahk dee·zes ge·rikht

I love the local cuisine.
Ich mag die regionale Küche.
ikh mahk dee re·gyo·nah·le kü·khe

That was delicious!
Das hat hervorragend geschmeckt!
das hat her·fawr·rah·gent ge·shmekt

know your wurst

One of Germany's favourite and most famous foods is the not-so-humble *Wurst* (sausage). There are over 1500 types, some of the more common of which are listed below:

Blutwurst f	*bloot*·vurst	blood sausage
Bockwurst f	*bok*·vurst	pork sausage
Bratwurst f	*braht*·vurst	fried pork sausage
Bregenwurst f	*bray*·gen·vurst	brain sausage
Cervelatwurst f	ser·ve·*laht*·vurst	sausage made of a spicy pork and beef mixture
Katenwurst f	*kah*·ten·vurst	country-style smoked sausage
Knackwurst f	*knak*·vurst	mildly garlic-flavoured sausage
Krakauer f	*krah*·kow·er	thick, paprika-spiced sausage of Polish origin
Landjäger m	*lant*·yay·ger	thin, long, hard spicy sausage
Leberwurst f	*lay*·ber·vurst	liver sausage
Regensburger m	*ray*·gens·bur·ger	highly spiced smoked sausage
Rotwurst f	*rawt*·vurst	black pudding
Thüringer f	*tü*·ring·er	long, thin spicy sausage
Wiener	*vee*·ner	frankfurter
Würstchen n	*vürst*·khen	(small smoked sausage)
Weißwurst f	*vais*·vurst	veal sausage
Würstchen n	*vürst*·khen	small sausage
Zwiebelwurst f	*tsvee*·bel·vurst	liver and onion sausage

This is ...	*Das ist ...*	das ist ...
(too) cold	*(zu) kalt*	(tsoo) kalt
spicy	*scharf*	sharf
superb	*exzellent*	ek·se·*lent*

My compliments to the chef.
Mein Kompliment   main kom·pli·*ment*
an den Koch.   an dayn kokh

I'm full.
Ich bin satt.   ikh bin zat

meals

> breakfast

What's a typical breakfast in (Bavaria)?
Was ißt man in (Bayern)   vas ist man in (*bai*·ern)
normalerweise zum   nor·*mah*·ler·vai·ze tsum
Frühstück?   *frü*·shtük

---

when is a roll not a roll?

Bread rolls can be called many different things, depending on which area you're in. Below are five of the most common terms and where you'll hear them used:

Brötchen n	*brert*·khen	in Germany
Schrippe f	*shri*·pe	in Berlin
Semmel f	ze·mel	in Bavaria
Wecken m&f	ve·ken	in southern Germany and Austria
Weggli n	*veg*·li	in Switzerland

bread	*Brot* n	brawt
butter	*Butter* f	*bu*·ter
cereal	*Frühstücksflocken* f pl	*frü*·shtüks·flo·ken
cheese	*Käse* m	kay·ze
coffee	*Kaffee* m	ka·fay
cold cuts of meat/sausage	*Wurst/ Aufschnitt* f/m	vurst/ *owf*·shnit
croissant	*Hörnchen* n	*hern*·khen
egg/eggs	*Ei/Eier* n sg/pl	ai/ai·er
boiled egg	*gekochtes Ei* n	ge·*kokh*·tes ai
scrambled eggs	*Rührei* n	*rür*·ai
fried egg	*Spiegelei* n	*shpee*·gel·ai
poached egg	*pochiertes Ei*	po·*sheer*·tes ai
honey	*Honig* m	*haw*·nikh
jam	*Marmelade* f	mar·me·*lah*·de
omelette	*Omelette* n	om·*let*
orange juice	*Orangensaft* m	o·*rang*·zhen·zaft
milk	*Milch* f	milkh
muesli	*Müsli* n	*müs*·li
spreads	*Brotaufstrich* m	*brawt*·owf·shtrikh
tea	*Tee* m	tay
toast	*Toast* m	tawst

For other breakfast items see the **culinary reader**, page 163, and the **dictionary**.

> light meals

What's that called?	*Wie heißt das?*	vee haist das
I'd like	*Ich hätte gern*	ikh *he*·te gern
..., please	*..., bitte.*	... *bi*·te
one slice	*eine Scheibe*	*ai*·ne *shai*·be
a piece	*ein Stück*	ain shtük
a sandwich	*ein Sandwich*	ain *sent*·vich
that one	*dieses da*	*dee*·zes dah
two	*zwei*	tsvai

> condiments

Is there any ...?	Gibt es ...?	gipt es ...
chilli sauce	Chilisauce f	chi·li·zaw·se
ketchup	Ketchup m	ket·chap
pepper	Pfeffer m	pfe·fer
salt	Salz n	zalts
tomato sauce	Tomaten-ketchup n	to·mah·ten·ket·chap
vinegar	Essig m	e·sikh

For additional items, see the **culinary reader**, page 163, and the **dictionary**.

methods of preparation

zubereitungsarten

I'd like it ...	Ich hätte es gern ...	ikh he·te es gern ...
I don't want it ...	Ich möchte es nicht ...	ikh merkh·te es nikht ...
boiled	gekocht	ge·kokht
broiled	gegrillt	ge·grilt
deep-fried	frittiert	fri·teert
fried	gebraten	ge·brah·ten
grilled	gegrillt	ge·grilt
mashed	püriert	pü·reert
medium	halb durch	halp durkh
rare	englisch	eng·lish
re-heated	aufgewärmt	owf·ge·vermt
steamed	gedämpft	ge·dempft
well-done	gut durch-gebraten	goot durkh·ge·brah·ten
with the dressing on the side	mit dem Dressing daneben	mit daym dre·sing da·nay·ben
without ...	ohne ...	aw·ne ...

in the bar

Excuse me!	Entschuldigung!	ent·shul·di·gung
I'm next.	Ich bin dran.	ikh bin dran
I'll have ...	Ich hätte gern ...	ikh he·te gern ...

Same again, please.
  Dasselbe nochmal, bitte.   das·zel·be nokh·mahl bi·te

No ice, thanks.
  Kein Eis, bitte.   kain ais bi·te

I'll buy you a drink.
  Ich gebe Ihnen/dir   ikh gay·be ee·nen/deer
  einen aus. pol/inf   ai·nen ows

What would you like?
  Was möchten Sie? pol   vas merkh·ten zee
  Was möchtest du? inf   vas merkh·test doo

It's my round.
  Diese Runde geht auf mich.   dee·ze run·de gayt owf mikh

---

listen for ...

vas merkh·ten zee (tring·ken)
  Was möchten Sie   **What are you having**
  (trinken)? pol   **(to drink)?**

ikh glow·be zee ha·ten ge·nook
  Ich glaube, Sie hatten   **I think you've**
  genug. pol   **had enough.**

loy·te vee zee be·dee·nen veer heer nikht
  Leute wie Sie bedienen   **We don't serve**
  wir hier nicht. pol   **your type in here.**

You can get the next one.
  Sie können die nächste   zee ker·nen dee naykhs·te
  Runde bestellen. pol   run·de be·shte·len
  Du kannst die nächste   doo kanst dee naykhs·te
  Runde bestellen. inf   run·de be·shte·len

Do you serve meals here?
Gibt es hier auch   gipt es heer owkh
etwas zu essen?   *et·*vas tsoo *e·*sen

nonalcoholic drinks

alkoholfreie getränke

soft drink	*Softdrink* m	*soft·*dringk
coffee	*Kaffee* m	*ka·*fay
tea	*Tee* m	tay
... with (milk)	*... mit (Milch)*	... mit (milkh)
... without (sugar)	*... ohne (Zucker)*	... *aw·*ne (*tsu·*ker)
water	*Wasser* n	*va·*ser
boiled water	*heißes Wasser* n	*hai·*ses *va·*ser
mineral water	*Mineralwasser* n	mi·ne·*rahl·*va·ser

what's in a name?

In Germany, *Softdrink* (soft drink) only designates sweet fizzy drinks, such as lemonade or cola. Mineral water is not known as *ein Softdrink*, but as *ein alkoholfreies Getränk* (a nonalcoholic drink).

alcoholic drinks

alkoholische getränke

beer	*Bier* n	beer
light beer	*Leichtbier* n	*laikht*·beer
nonalcoholic beer	*alkoholfreies Bier* n	al·ko·*hawl*·frai·es beer
pilsner/lager	*Pils* n	pils
wheat beer	*Weißbier* n	*vais*·beer
brandy	*Weinbrand* m	*vain*·brant
(French) champagne	*Champagner* m	sham·*pan*·yer
cocktail	*Cocktail* m	*kok*·tayl
sparkling wine	*Sekt* m	zekt
a shot of ...	*einen ...*	*ai*·nen ...
gin	*Gin*	dzhin
rum	*Rum*	rum
tequila	*Tequila*	te·*kee*·la
vodka	*Wodka*	*vot*·ka
whisky	*Whisky*	*vis*·ki
a bottle of ... wine	*eine Flasche ...*	*ai*·ne *fla*·she ...
a glass of ... wine	*ein Glas ...*	ain glahs ...
dessert	*Dessertwein*	de·*sair*·vain
mulled	*Glühwein*	*glü*·vain
red	*Rotwein*	*rawt*·vain
rose	*Rosé*	ro·*zay*
sparkling	*Sekt*	zekt
white	*Weißwein*	*vais*·vain
a ... (of) beer	*ein ... Bier*	ain ... beer
glass	*Glas*	glahs
large	*großes*	*graw*·ses
pint	*halbes*	*halb*·es
small	*kleines*	*klai*·nes
a beer on tap	*ein Bier vom Fass*	ain beer fom fas

Germany is famous for its wines. There are three basic wine categories – *trocken* (dry), *halbtrocken* (medium-dry), and *lieblich* (sweet). Some of the more well-known grape varieties are listed below:

> white

Gewürztraminer m   ge·*vürts*·tra·mee·ner
very spicy with an intense bouquet

Müller-Thurgau m   mü·ler·*toor*·gow
early-ripening grape with a slight muscat flavour. Also called *Rivaner*, this wine is less acidic than *Riesling* and is best when young.

Riesling m   *rees*·ling
late-ripening grape with a fragrant, fruity bouquet, this wine can be drunk young or old

Ruländer/   *roo*·len·der/
Grauburgunder m   *grow*·bur·gun·der
robust, soft and full-bodied. Also known as *pinot gris* or *pinot grigio*.

Silvaner m   zil·*vah*·ner
full-bodied, mildly acidic wine with a neutral nose. Should be drunk young.

> red

Portugieser m   por·tu·*gee*·zer
light, mild red wine originally from Austria (not Portugal)

Spätburgunder m   *shpayt*·bur·gun·der
also known as Pinot Noir. A velvety and full-bodied wine – the best have an almond taste.

Trollinger m   *tro*·ling·er
hearty, full-bodied wine with a fragrant nose. *Trollinger* grapes ripen late and are only grown in Württemberg.

Alkoholfreies Bier n   al·ko·*hawl*·frai·es beer
nonalcoholic beer

Alster(wasser) n   *als*·ter(·*va*·ser)
mixture of pilsner and orange lemonade

Alt(bier) n   *alt*(·beer)
amber-coloured speciality beer from Düsseldorf, with
a strong taste of hops

Altbierbowle f   *alt*·beer·baw·le
Altbier with strawberries or other fruit

Alt-Schuss n   alt·*shus*
Altbier with a shot of syrup or *Malzbier*

Berliner Weiße f   ber·*lee*·ner *vai*·se
slightly fizzy and cloudy, often served with a shot of
raspberry (*rot*) or woodruff (*grün*) syrup

Bockbier n   *bok*·beer
light or dark beer with a high alcohol content

Eisbock m   *ais*·bok
Bockbier from which water has been extracted by
freezing thus increasing its alcoholic potency

Export n   eks·*port*
lager

Gose f   *gaw*·ze
wheat beer from Leipzig

Hefeweizen n   *hay*·fe·vai·tsen
cloudy wheat beer (with some yeast still in the
bottle) – comes in light (*hell*) or dark (*dunkel*) varieties

Helles n   *he*·les
lager (Bavaria)

Kölsch n   *kerlsh*
yellow-golden coloured beer from Cologne

Kräusen n   *kroy*·zen
unfiltered beer, gold-coloured or dark

Krefelder n   *kray*·fel·der
Altbier mixed with cola

Kristallweizen n   kris·*tal*·vai·tsen
clear light (*hell*) or dark (*dunkel*) wheat beer

Leichtbier n		*laikht*·beer
beer with half the alcohol content of normal beer		
Maibock m		*mai*·bok
special *Bockbier* brewed in May		
Malzbier n		*malts*·beer
nonalcoholic malt beer		
Märzen n		*mer*·tsen
special Bavarian beer brewed at the end of winter		
Pils/Pils(e)ner n		pils/*pil*·z(e·)ner
pilsner, similar to lager		
Radler n		*raht*·ler
mixture of pilsner or lager and sweet lemonade		
Rauchbier n		*rowkh*·beer
smoky-flavoured beer from Bamberg		
Schwarzbier n		*shvarts*·beer
stout (lit: black beer)		
Weizenbier/Weißbier n		*vai*·tsen·beer/*vais*·beer
wheat beer		

one too many?

einen über den durst?

Cheers!
Prost! — prawst

Thanks, but I don't feel like it.
Nein danke, ich möchte jetzt nichts. — nain *dang*·ke ikh *merkh*·te yetst nikhts

I don't drink alcohol.
Ich trinke keinen Alkohol. — ikh *tring*·ke *kai*·nen *al*·ko·hawl

This is hitting the spot.
Das kommt jetzt echt gut. — das komt yetst ekht goot

I'm tired, I'd better go home.
Ich bin müde, ich sollte besser nach Hause gehen. — ikh bin *mü*·de ikh *zol*·te *be*·ser nahkh *how*·ze *gay*·en

I'm feeling drunk.
Ich glaube, ich bin betrunken.   ikh *glow*·be ikh bin be·*trung*·ken

I feel fantastic!
Ich fühle mich fantastisch!   ikh *fü*·le mikh fan·*tas*·tish

I really, really love you.
Ich liebe dich echt total.   ikh *lee*·be dikh ekht to·*tahl*

I think I've had one too many.
Ich glaube, ich habe ein   ikh *glow*·be ikh *hah*·be ain
bisschen zu viel getrunken.   *bis*·khen tsoo feel ge·*trung*·ken

Can you call a taxi for me?
Können Sie mir ein   *ker*·nen zee meer ain
Taxi rufen? pol   *tak*·si *roo*·fen
Kannst du mir ein   kanst doo meer ain
Taxi rufen? inf   *tak*·si *roo*·fen

I don't think you should drive.
Ich glaube, Sie sollten   ikh *glow*·be zee *zol*·ten
nicht mehr fahren. pol   nikht mair *fah*·ren
Ich glaube, du solltest   ikh *glow*·be doo *zol*·test
nicht mehr fahren. inf   nikht mair *fah*·ren

There's still room for another!
Zwischen Leber und Milz   *tsvi*·shen *lay*·ber unt milts
ist noch Platz für ein Pils.   ist nokh plats für ain pils
(lit: between liver and spleen
   is still room for a beer)

Let's have a second drink.
Auf einem Bein steht   owf *ai*·nem bain shtayt
man schlecht.   man shlekht
(lit: on one leg
   stands one badly)

Where's the toilet?
Wo ist die Toilette?   vaw ist dee to·a·*le*·te

I'm pissed.	*Ich bin blau.*	ikh bin blow
	(lit: I am blue)	
I feel ill.	*Mir ist schlecht.*	meer ist shlekht
I've got a hangover.	*Ich habe einen Kater.*	ikh *hah*·be *ai*·nen *kah*·ter
	(lit: I have a tomcat)	

key language

wichtige wörter

cooked	*gekocht*	ge·*kokht*
dried	*getrocknet*	ge·*trok*·net
fresh	*frisch*	frish
frozen	*eingefroren*	*ain*·ge·fraw·ren
raw	*roh*	raw
A piece.	*Ein Stück.*	ain shtük
A slice.	*Eine Scheibe.*	*ai*·ne *shai*·be
That one.	*Dieses da.*	*dee*·zes dah
This.	*Dieses.*	*dee*·zes
A bit more.	*Ein bisschen mehr.*	ain *bis*·khen mair
Less.	*Weniger.*	*vay*·ni·ger
Enough.	*Genug.*	ge·*nook*

dining tips

The main meal of the day in the German-speaking countries is *das Mittagsessen* or lunch.

It's good manners to say *Guten Apetit* or *Mahlzeit* (Enjoy your meal) to your fellow diners. Observing German table etiquette is easy – it's enough to eat in a basically civilized manner. It's customary, however, to keep your hands on the table at all times.

To say you've really enjoyed your meal say *Das hat geschmeckt*.

To get the attention of a waiter call out *Herr Ober* (to a man) or *Fräulein* (to a woman). To indicate that you want to pay your bill say *Zahlen bitte!*

Germans are fond of toasts. If they break out the drink, wait until everyone is served. Then raise your glasses in unison, look your fellow toasters in the eye and give a hearty *Prost!* or *Zum Wohl!*

buying food

How much?
Wie viel? — vee feel

How much is (a kilo of cheese)?
Was kostet (ein Kilo Käse)? — vas *kos*·tet (ain *kee*·lo *kay*·ze)

What's the local speciality?
Was ist eine örtliche Spezialität? — vas ist *ai*·ne *ert*·li·khe shpe·tsya·li·*tayt*

What's that?
Was ist das? — vas ist das

Can I taste it?
Kann ich das probieren? — kan ikh das pro·*bee*·ren

Can I have a bag, please?
Könnte ich bitte eine Tüte haben? — *kern*·te ikh *bi*·te *ai*·ne *tü*·te *hah*·ben

I'd like ...	*Ich möchte ...*	ikh *merkh*·te ...
(three) pieces	*(drei) Stück*	(drai) shtük
(six) slices	*(sechs) Scheiben*	(zeks) *shai*·ben
some ...	*etwas ...*	*et*·vas ...
(two) kilos	*(zwei) Kilo*	(tsvai) *kee*·lo
(200) grams	*(200) Gramm*	(*tsvai*·hun·dert) gram

Do you have ...?	*Haben Sie ...?*	*hah*·ben zee ...
anything cheaper	*etwas Billigeres*	*et*·vas *bi*·li·ge·res
other kinds	*andere Sorten*	*an*·de·re *zor*·ten

Where can I find the ... section?	Wo kann ich die ... finden?	vaw kan ikh dee ... *fin*·den
dairy	*Abteilung für Milchprodukte*	ap·*tai*·lung für *milkh*·pro·duk·te
frozen goods	*Abteilung für Tiefkühlprodukte*	ap·*tai*·lung für *teef*·kül·pro·duk·te
fruit and vegetable	*Obst- und Gemüse-abteilung*	awpst· unt ge·*mü*·ze· ap·tai·lung
meat	*Fleischabteilung*	*flaish*·ap·tai·lung
poultry	*Geflügel-abteilung*	ge·*flü*·gel· ap·tai·lung

For food items see the **culinary reader** page 163 and the **dictionary**.

For food items see the culinary reader page 163

---

listen for ...

kan ikh *ee*·nen *hel*·fen
  Kann ich Ihnen helfen? — **Can I help you?**

vas *merkh*·ten zee?
  Was möchten Sie? — **What would you like?**

das ist (*ai*·ne *brat*·vurst)
  Das ist (eine Bratwurst). — **That's (a bratwurst).**

das ist ows
  Das ist aus. — **There's none left.**

das *hah*·ben veer nikht
  Das haben wir nicht. — **I don't have any.**

merkh·ten zee nokh *et*·vas
  Möchten Sie noch etwas? — **Would you like anything else?**

das *kos*·tet (fünf *oy*·ro)
  Das kostet (fünf Euro). — **That's (five euros).**

cooking utensils

Could I please borrow a ...?	Könnte ich bitte ... ausleihen?	kern·te ikh bi·te ... ows·lai·en
bottle opener	einen Flaschenöffner	ai·nen fla·shen·erf·ner
bowl	eine Schüssel	ai·ne shü·sel
can opener	einen Dosenöffner	ai·nen daw·zen·erf·ner
chopping board	ein Schneidebrett	ain shnai·de·bret
corkscrew	einen Korkenzieher	ai·nen kor·ken·tsee·er
cup	eine Tasse	ai·ne ta·se
fork	eine Gabel	ai·ne gah·bel
frying pan	eine Bratpfanne	ai·ne braht·pfa·ne
glass	ein Glas	ain glahs
knife	ein Messer	ain me·ser
plate	einen Teller	ai·nen te·ler
saucepan	einen Kochtopf	ai·nen kokh·topf
spoon	einen Löffel	ai·nen ler·fel
toaster	einen Toaster	ai·nen taws·ter
fridge	Kühlschrank m	kül·shrank
microwave	Mikrowelle f	mi·kro·ve·le
oven	Ofen m	aw·fen
stove	Kochplatte f	kokh·pla·te

vegetarian & special meals
vegetarische und besondere gerichte

ordering

Is there a (vegetarian) restaurant near here?
Gibt es ein (vegetarisches)   gipt es ain vege·*tar*·ish·shes
Restaurant hier in der Nähe?   res·to·*rang* heer in dair *nay*·e

Do you have   *Haben Sie*   *hah*·ben zee
... food?   *... Essen?*   ... e·sen
   halal   *Halal-*   ha·*lal*·
   kosher   *koscheres*   *kaw*·she·res
   vegetarian   *vegetarisches*   ve·ge·*tah*·ri·shes

Is it cooked   *Ist es in/mit*   ist es in/mit
in/with ...?   *... zubereitet?*   ... *tsoo*·be·rai·tet
   butter   *Butter*   *bu*·ter
   eggs   *Eiern*   *ai*·ern
   meat stock   *Fleischbrühe*   *flaish*·brü·e

I don't eat ...
Ich esse kein ...   ikh *e*·se kain ...

Does this dish have ... in it?
Enthält dieses Gericht ...?   ent·*helt* dee·zes ge·*rikht* ...

Can I get this without ... in it?
Kann ich das ohne ...   kan ikh das *aw*·ne ...
bekommen?   be·*ko*·men

Could you prepare a meal without ...?
Können Sie ein Gericht   *ker*·nen zee ain ge·*rikht*
ohne ... zubereiten?   *aw*·ne ... *tsoo*·be·rai·ten

Is this ...?	Ist das ...?	ist das ...
free of animal produce	*ohne tierische Produkte*	aw·ne *tee·ri·she* pro·*duk*·te
free-range	*von freilaufenden Tieren*	fon *frai*·low·fen·den *tee*·ren
genetically modified	*genmanipuliert*	*gayn*·ma·ni·pu·leert
gluten-free	*glutenfrei*	*gloo*·ten·frai
halal	*nach den Vorschriften des Koran zubereitet*	nahkh dayn *fawr*·shrif·ten des ko·*rahn* tsoo·be·rai·tet
kosher	*koscher*	*kaw*·sher
low in sugar	*zuckerarm*	*tsu*·ker·arm
low-fat	*fettarm*	*fet*·arm
organic	*organisch*	or·*gah*·nish
salt-free	*ohne Salz*	aw·ne zalts

special diets & allergies

spezielle diäten und allergien

I'm (a) ...	Ich bin ...	ikh bin ...
Buddhist	Buddhist(in) m/f	bu·dist/bu·dis·tin
Hindu	Hindu	hin·du
Jewish	Jude/Jüdin m/f	yoo·de/yü·din
Muslim	Moslem/	mos·lem/
	Moslime m/f	mos·lee·me
vegan	Veganer(in) m/f	ve·gah·ner/
		ve·gah·ne·rin
vegetarian	Vegetarier(in) m/f	ve·ge·tah·ri·er/
		ve·ge·tah·ri·e·rin

I'm allergic to ...	Ich bin allergisch gegen ...	ikh bin a·lair·gish gay·gen ...
animal products	Tierprodukte	teer·pro·duk·te
caffeine	Koffein	ko·fe·een
dairy produce	Milchprodukte	milkh·pro·duk·te
eggs	Eier	ai·er
fish	Fisch	fish
gelatin	Gelatine	zhe·la·tee·ne
genetically modified food	genmanipulierte Speisen	gayn·ma·ni·pu·leer·te shpai·zen
gluten	Gluten	gloo·ten
honey	Honig	haw·nikh
MSG	Natrium-glutamat	nah·tri·um·glu·ta·maht
nuts	Nüsse	nü·se
pork	Schweinefleisch	shvai·ne·flaish
poultry	Geflügelfleisch	ge·flü·gel·flaish
red meat	Rind- und Lammfleisch	rint· unt lam·flaish
seafood	Meeresfrüchte	mair·res·frükh·te
shellfish	Schaltiere	shahl·tee·re

I'm on a special diet.
Ich bin auf einer   ikh bin owf *ai*·ner
Spezialdiät.   shpe·*tsyahl*·di·et

I can't eat it because I'm allergic.
Ich kann es nicht essen   ikh kan es nikht *ess*·en
wiel ich allergisch bin.   vail ikh a·*lair*·gish bin

I can't eat it for ...	*Ich kann es nicht essen aus ...*	ikh kan es nikht ess·en ows ...
health reasons	*Gesundheits- gründen*	ge·*zunt*·haits· grün·den
religious reasons	*religiösen Gründen*	re·li·*gyer*·zen *grün*·den
philosophical reasons	*philosophischen Gründen*	fi·lo·*zaw*·fi·shen *grün*·den

A

Aachener Printen pl *ah·khe·ner prin·ten* cakes with chocolate, nuts, fruit peel, honey & spices

Aal ⓜ *ahl* eel
  —suppe ⓕ *ahl·zu·pe* eel soup
geräucherter Aal ⓜ *ge·roy·kher·ter ahl* smoked eel

Alpzirler ⓜ *alp·tsir·ler* cow's milk cheese from Austria

Apfel ⓜ *ap·fel* apple
  —strudel ⓜ *ap·fel·shtroo·del* apple strudel

Apfelsine ⓕ *ap·fel·zee·ne* orange

Aprikose ⓕ *a·pri·kaw·ze* apricot
  —nmarmelade ⓕ *a·pri·kaw·zen·mar·me·lah·de* apricot jam

Artischocke ⓕ *ar·ti·sho·ke* artichoke

Auflauf ⓜ *owf·lowf* souffle • casserole

Auster ⓕ *ows·ter* oyster

B

Bäckerofen ⓜ *be·ker·aw·fen* 'baker's oven' – pork & lamb bake from Saarland

Backhähnchen ⓝ *bak·hayn·khen* fried chicken

Backobst ⓝ *bak·awpst* dried fruit

Backpflaume ⓕ *bak·pflow·me* prune

Banane ⓕ *ba·nah·ne* banana

Barsch ⓜ *barsh* perch

Bauern
  —brot ⓝ *bow·ern·brawt* 'farmer's bread' – rye or wholemeal bread
  —frühstück ⓝ *bow·ern·frü·shtük* 'farmer's breakfast' – scrambled eggs, bacon, cooked diced potatoes, onions & tomatoes
  —schmaus ⓜ *bow·ern·shmows* 'farmer's feast' – sauerkraut garnished with bacon, smoked pork, sausages & dumpling or potatoes
  —suppe ⓕ *bow·ern·zu·pe* 'farmer's soup' – made from cabbage & sausage

Bayrisch Kraut ⓝ *bai·rish krowt* shredded cabbage cooked with sliced apples, wine & sugar

Beefsteak ⓝ *beef·stayk* hamburger patty

Berliner ⓜ *ber·lee·ner* jam doughnut

Beuschel ⓝ *boy·shel* heart, liver & kidney of a calf or lamb in a slightly sour sauce

Bienenstich ⓜ *bee·nen·shtikh* cake, baked on a tray with a coating of almonds & sugar

Birne ⓕ *bir·ne* pear

Bischofsbrot ⓝ *bi·shofs·brawt* fruit & nut cake

Blaubeere ⓕ *blow·bair·re* bilberry • blueberry

Blaukraut ⓝ *blow·krowt* red cabbage

Blumenkohl ⓜ *bloo·men·kawl* cauliflower

Blutwurst ⓕ *bloot·vurst* blood sausage

Bockwurst ⓕ *bok·vurst* pork sausage

Bohnen ⓕ pl *baw·nen* beans

Brat
  —huhn ⓝ *braht·hoon* roast chicken
  —kartoffeln ⓕ pl *braht·kar·to·feln* fried potatoes
  —wurst ⓕ *braht·vurst* fried pork sausage

Bregenwurst ⓕ *bray·gen·vurst* brain sausage, found mainly in Lower Saxony & Western Saxony-Anhalt

Brezel ⓕ *bray·tsel* pretzel

Brokkoli ⓜ pl *bro·ko·li broccoli*
Brombeere ⓕ *brom·bair·re blackberry*
Brot ⓝ *brawt bread*
  belegtes Brot ⓝ *be·layk·tes brawt open sandwich*
Brötchen ⓝ *brert·khen roll*
Brühwürfel ⓜ *brü·vür·fel stock cube*
Bulette ⓕ *bu·le·te meatball (Berlin)*
Butter ⓕ *bu·ter butter*

C

Cervelatwurst ⓕ *ser·ve·laht·vurst spicy pork & beef sausage*
Christstollen ⓜ *krist·shto·len spiced loaf with candied peel, traditionally eaten at Christmas*
Cremespeise ⓕ *kraym·shpai·ze mousse*

D

Damenkäse ⓜ *dah·men·kay·ze soft, buttery cheese*
Dampfnudeln ⓕ pl *dampf·noo·deln hot yeast dumplings with vanilla sauce*
Dattel ⓕ *da·tel date*
Dorsch ⓜ *dorsh cod*
Dotterkäse ⓜ *do·ter·kay·ze cheese made from skimmed milk & egg yolk*

E

Ei ⓝ ai *egg*
  gekochte Eier ⓝ pl *ge·kokh·te ai·er boiled eggs*
Eierkuchen ⓜ *ai·er·koo·khen pancake*
Eierschwammerln ⓜ pl *ai·er·shva·merln chanterelle mushrooms (Austria)*
Eierspeispfandl ⓝ *ai·er·shpais·pfandl special Viennese omelette (Austria)*
Eintopf ⓜ *ain·topf stew*
Eis ⓝ *ais ice cream*
Eisbein ⓝ *ais·bain pickled pork knuckles*
Emmentaler ⓜ *e·men·tah·ler Swiss Emmental, whole-milk hard cheese*
Ennstaler ⓜ *ens·tah·ler blue cheese produced from mixed milk*

Ente ⓕ *en·te duck*
Erbse ⓕ *erp·se pea*
Erbsensuppe ⓕ *erp·sen·zu·pe pea soup*
Erdäpfel ⓜ pl *ert·ep·fel potatoes*
  —gulasch ⓝ *ert·ep·fel·goo·lash spicy sausage & potato stew*
  —knödel ⓜ pl *ert·ep·fel·kner·del potato & semolina dumplings*
  —nudeln ⓕ pl *ert·ep·fel·noo·deln boiled potato balls fried & tossed in fried breadcrumbs*
Erdbeere ⓕ *ert·bair·re strawberry*
Erdbeermarmelade ⓕ *ert·bair·mar·me·lah·de strawberry jam*
Erdnuss ⓕ *ert·nus peanut*
Essig ⓜ *e·sikh vinegar*

F

Falscher Hase ⓜ *fal·sher hah·ze 'false hare' – baked mince meatloaf*
Fasan ⓜ *fa·zahn pheasant*
Feige ⓕ *fai·ge fig*
Filet ⓝ *fi·lay fillet*
Fisch ⓜ *fish fish*
Fladen ⓜ *flah·den round, flat dough cake*
Flädle ⓝ pl *flayt·le thin strips of pancake, added to soup*
Fledermaus ⓕ *flay·der·mows 'bat' – boiled beef in horseradish cream browned in the oven*
Fleisch ⓝ *flaish meat*
  —brühe ⓕ *flaish·brü·e bouillon*
  —pflanzerl ⓝ *flaish·pflan·tserl meatballs, a Bavarian speciality*
  —sülze ⓕ *flaish·zül·tse aspic*
Fondue ⓝ *fon·dü melted cheese with wine served with bread for dipping*
Forelle ⓕ *fo·re·le trout*
  — blau *fo·re·le blow steamed trout with potatoes & vegetables*
  — Müllerin *fo·re·le mü·le·rin trout fried in batter with almonds*
  geräucherte Forelle ⓕ *ge·roy·kher·te fo·re·le smoked trout*

Frankfurter Kranz ⓜ *frank·fur·ter krants sponge cake with rum, butter, cream & cherries (from Frankfurt)*

Frikadelle ⓕ *fri·ka·de·le meatball*

Frischling ⓜ *frish·ling young wild boar*

Frucht ⓕ *frukht fruit*

Frühlingssuppe ⓕ *frü·lingks·zu·pe vegetable soup*

Frühstücksspeck ⓜ *frü·shtüks·shpek bacon*

G

Gans ⓕ *gans goose*

Garnele ⓕ *gar·nay·le shrimp • prawn*

Gebäck ⓝ *ge·bek pastries*

Geflügel ⓝ *ge·flü·gel poultry*

gekocht *ge·kokht boiled • cooked*

Gemüse ⓝ *ge·mü·ze vegetables*
 —suppe ⓕ *ge·mü·ze·zu·pe vegetable soup*

geräuchert *ge·roy·khert smoked*

Geschnetzeltes ⓝ *ge·shne·tsel·tes small slices of meat*
 Züricher Geschnetzeltes ⓝ *tsü·ri·kher ge·shne·tsel·tes sliced veal with mushrooms & onions cooked in a white wine & cream sauce*

Gitziprägel ⓝ *gi·tsi·pray·gel baked rabbit in batter (Switzerland)*

Graf Görz ⓜ *grahf gerts Austrian soft cheese*

Granat ⓜ *gra·naht shrimp*

Granatapfel ⓜ *gra·naht·ap·fel pomegranate*

Gratin ⓜ *gra·teng a dish topped with cheese & baked in the oven*

Graupensuppe ⓕ *grow·pen·zu·pe barley soup*

Greyerzer ⓜ *grai·er·tser Gruyère, a smooth, rich cheese*

Grießklößchensuppe ⓕ *grees·klers·khen·zu·pe soup with semolina dumplings*

Gröstl ⓝ *grerstl grated fried potatoes with meat (Tyrol)*

grüner Salat ⓜ *grü·ner za·laht green salad*

Grünkohl mit Pinkel *grün·kawl mit ping·kel cabbage with sausages (Bremen)*

Güggeli ⓝ *gü·ge·lee spring chicken (Switzerland)*

Gurke ⓕ *gur·ke cucumber • gherkin*

H

Hack
 —braten ⓜ *hak·brah·ten meatloaf*
 —fleisch ⓝ *hak·flaish minced meat*

Haferbrei ⓜ *hah·fer·brai porridge*

Hähnchen ⓝ *hayn·khen chicken*

Hämchen ⓝ *hem·khen pork or hock shank, served with sauerkraut & potatoes (Cologne)*

Handkäs mit Musik ⓜ *hant·kays mit mu·zeek spicy cheese, marinated in vinegar & white wine*

Hartkäse ⓜ *hart·kay·ze hard cheese*

Hase ⓜ *hah·ze hare*
 —nläufe pl **in Jägerrahmsauce** *hah·zen·loy·fe in yay·ger·rahm·zaw·se hare thigh in dark cream sauce of mushroom, shallots, white wine & parsley*
 —npfeffer ⓜ *hah·zen·pfe·fer hare stew with mushrooms & onions*

Haselnuß ⓕ *hah·zel·nus hazelnut*

Haxe ⓕ *hak·se knuckle*

Hecht ⓜ *hekht pike*

Heidelbeere ⓕ *hai·del·bair·re bilberry • blueberry*

Heidelbeermarmelade ⓕ *hai·del·bair·mar·me·lah·de blueberry/bilberry jam*

Heilbutt ⓜ *hail·but halibut*

Hering ⓜ *hay·ring herring*
 —sschmaus ⓜ *hay·ringks·shmows herring in creamy sauce*
 —ssalat ⓜ *hay·ringks·za·laht salad with herring & beetroot*

Himbeere ⓕ *him·bair·re raspberry*

Himmel und Erde *hi·mel unt er·de 'Heaven & Earth' – mashed potatoes & apple sauce, sometimes served with slices of black pudding*

Hirsch ⓜ *hirsh male deer*

Holsteiner Schnitzel ⓜ *hol·*shtai·ner
*shni·tsel veal schnitzel with fried egg,
accompanied by seafood*
Honig ⓜ *haw·*nikh *honey*
Hörnchen ⓝ *hern·*khen *croissant*
Hühnerbrust ⓕ *hü·*ner·brust *chicken
breast*
Hühnersuppe ⓕ *hü·*ner·zu·pe *chicken
soup*
Hummer ⓜ *hu·*mer *lobster*
Husarenfleisch ⓝ *hu·zah·*ren·flaish
*braised beef, veal & pork fillets with
sweet peppers, onions & sour cream*
Hutzelbrot ⓝ *hu·*tsel·brawt *bread
made of prunes & other dried fruit*

I

Ingwer ⓜ *ing·*ver *ginger*
italienischer Salat ⓜ *i·tal·yay·*ni·sher
*za·laht finely sliced veal, salami,
anchovies, tomatoes, cucumber &
celery in mayonnaise*

J

Joghurt ⓜ *yaw·*gurt *yogurt*

K

Kabeljau ⓜ *kah·*bel·yow *cod*
Kaiserschmarren ⓜ *kai·zer·*shmar·ren
*'emperor's pancakes' – fluffy
pancakes with raisins, served with
fruit compote or chocolate sauce*
Kaisersemmeln ⓕ pl *kai·zer·*ze·meln
'emperor's rolls' – Austrian bread rolls
Kalbfleisch ⓝ *kalp·*flaish *veal*
Kalbsnierenbraten ⓜ
*kalps·nee·ren·*brah·ten *roast veal
stuffed with kidneys*
Kaninchen ⓝ *ka·neen·*khen *rabbit*
Kapern ⓕ pl *kah·*pern *capers*
Karotte ⓕ *ka·ro·*te *carrot*
Karpfen ⓜ *karp·*fen *carp*
Kartoffel ⓕ *kar·to·*fel *potato*
　—**auflauf** ⓜ *kar·to·fel·*owf·lowf
potato casserole

—**brei** ⓜ *kar·to·fel·*brai
mashed potatoes
—**püree** ⓝ *kar·to·fel·*pü·ray
mashed potatoes
—**salat** ⓜ *kar·to·fel·*za·laht
potato salad
Käse ⓜ *kay·*ze *cheese*
—**fondue** ⓝ *kay·ze·fon·*dü *melted
cheese flavoured with wine & kirsch,
into which bread is dipped*
Kasseler ⓜ *kas·*ler *smoked pork*
　— **Rippe** ⓕ **mit Sauerkraut**
*kas·ler ri·*pe mit zow·er·krowt
smoked pork rib with sauerkraut
Katenwurst ⓕ *kah·*ten·vurst
country-style smoked sausage
Katzenjammer ⓜ *ka·tsen·ya·*mer
*cold slices of beef in mayonnaise
with cucumbers or gherkin*
Keule ⓕ *koy·*le *leg • haunch*
Kieler Sprotten ⓕ pl *kee·*ler *shpro·*ten
small smoked herring
Kirsche ⓕ *kir·*she *cherry*
Kirtagssuppe ⓕ *kir·*tahks·zu·pe
*soup with caraway seed, thickened
with potato*
Klöße ⓜ pl *kler·*se *dumplings*
Knackwurst ⓕ *knak·*vurst
sausage lightly flavoured with garlic
Knoblauch ⓜ *knawp·*lowkh *garlic*
Knödel ⓜ *kner·*del *dumpling*
—**beignets** ⓜ pl *kner·del·ben·*yays
fruit dumplings
Kohl ⓜ *kawl *cabbage*
—**rabi** ⓜ *kawl·rah·*bi *kohlrabi*
—**roulade** ⓕ *kawl·ru·lah·*de *cabbage
leaves stuffed with minced meat*
Kompott ⓝ *kom·*pot *stewed fruit*
Königinsuppe ⓕ *ker·ni·gin·*zu·pe
*creamy chicken soup with pieces of
chicken breast*
Königsberger Klopse ⓜ pl
*ker·niks·ber·ger klop·*se *meatballs in a
sour cream & caper sauce*
Königstorte ⓕ *ker·niks·*tor·te
rum-flavoured fruit cake

Kopfsalat ⓜ *kopf·za·laht lettuce*
Kotelett ⓝ *kot·let chop*
Krabbe ⓕ *kra·be crab*
Krakauer ⓕ *krah·kow·er thick, paprika-spiced sausage of Polish origin*
Kraut ⓝ *krowt cabbage*
 —salat ⓜ *krowt·za·laht coleslaw*
Kräuter ⓝ pl *kroy·ter herbs*
Krebs ⓜ *krayps crab • crayfish*
Kren ⓜ *krayn horseradish (Bavaria & Austria)*
Krokette ⓕ *kro·ke·te croquette*
Kuchen ⓜ *koo·khen cake*
Kümmel ⓜ *kü·mel caraway (seeds)*
Kürbis ⓜ *kür·bis pumpkin*
Kutteln ⓕ pl *ku·teln tripe*

L

Labskaus ⓝ *laps·kows thick meat & potato stew*
Lachs ⓜ *laks salmon*
 geräucherter Lachs ⓜ *ge·roy·kher·ter laks smoked salmon*
Lamm
 —fleisch ⓝ *lam·flaish lamb*
 —keule ⓕ *lam·koy·le leg of lamb*
Landjäger ⓜ *lant·yay·ger thin, long, hard, spicy sausage*
Languste ⓕ *lan·gus·te crayfish*
Lappenpickert ⓜ *la·pen·pi·kert pan-sized potato pancake usually served with jam or salted fish (Westphalia)*
Lauch ⓜ *lowkh leek*
Leber ⓕ *lay·ber liver*
 —käse ⓜ *lay·ber·kay·ze seasoned meatloaf made of minced liver, pork & bacon*
 —knödel ⓜ *lay·ber·kner·del liver dumpling*
 —knödelsuppe ⓕ *lay·ber·kner·del·zu·pe hot broth with liver dumplings*
 —wurst ⓕ *lay·ber·vurst liver sausage*
Lebkuchen ⓜ *layp·koo·khen gingerbread*
Leckerli ⓝ *le·ker·lee honey-flavoured ginger biscuit*

Leipziger Allerlei ⓝ *laip·tsi·ger a·ler·lai mixed vegetable stew (Leipzig)*
Lende ⓕ *len·de loin*
Limburger ⓜ *lim·bur·ger strong cheese flavoured with herbs*
Linsen ⓕ pl *lin·zen lentils*
 — mit Spätzle *mit shpets·le lentil stew with noodles & sausages*
 —suppe ⓕ *lin·zen·zu·pe lentil soup*
Linzer Torte ⓕ *lin·tser tor·te latticed tart with jam topping*
Lorbeerblätter ⓝ pl *lor·bair·ble·ter bay leaves*
Lübecker Marzipan ⓝ *lü·be·ker mar·tsi·pahn marzipan (Lübeck)*
Lucullus-Eier ⓝ pl *lu·ku·lus·ai·er poached, boiled or scrambled eggs with goose liver, truffle & other garnishes, served with a sauce*

M

Mais ⓜ *mais sweet corn*
Majonnaise ⓕ *ma·yo·nay·ze mayonnaise*
Makrele ⓕ *ma·kray·le mackerel*
Mandarine ⓕ *man·da·ree·ne mandarine • tangerine*
Mandel ⓕ *man·del almond*
Marmelade ⓕ *mar·me·lah·de jam*
Matjes ⓜ *mat·yes young herring*
Maultasche ⓕ *mowl·ta·she filled pasta (Swabia)*
Meeresfrüchte ⓕ pl *mair·res·frükh·te seafood*
Meerrettich ⓜ *mair·re·tikh horseradish*
Mehl ⓝ *mayl flour*
Mett ⓝ *met lean minced pork*
Mettentchen ⓝ *met·ent·khen beer stick*
Milch ⓕ *milkh milk*
 —rahmstrudel ⓜ *milkh·rahm·shtroo·del strudel filled with egg custard & soft cheese*
Mohnbrötchen ⓝ *mawn·brert·khen bread roll with poppy seeds*
Möhre ⓕ *mer·re carrot*

Muschel ① mu·shel *clam • mussel*
Muskat ⓜ mus·kaht *nutmeg*
Müesli ⓝ mü·es·li *muesli*
Müsli ⓝ müs·li *muesli*

N

Nelken ① pl nel·ken *cloves*
Niere ① nee·re *kidney*
Nockerl ⓝ no·kerl *small dumpling (Austria)*
Nudeln ① pl noo·deln *noodles*
Nudelauflauf ⓜ noo·del·owf·lowf *pasta casserole*
Nürnberger Lebkuchen ⓜ nürn·ber·ger layp·koo·khen *cakes with chocolate, nuts, fruit peel, honey & spices*

O

Obatzter ⓜ aw·bats·ter *Bavarian soft cheese mousse*
Obst ⓝ awpst *fruit*
 —salat ⓜ awpst·za·laht *fruit salad*
Ochsenschwanz ⓜ ok·sen·shvants *oxtail*
 —suppe ① ok·sen·shvants·zu·pe *oxtail soup*
Öl ⓝ erl *oil*
Orangenmarmelade ① o·rahng·zhen·mar·me·lah·de *marmelade*

P

Palatschinken ⓜ pa·lat·shing·ken *pancake, usually filled with jam or cheese, sometimes served with a hot chocolate & nut topping*
Pampelmuse ① pam·pel·moo·ze *grapefruit*
Paprika ① pap·ri·kah *sweet pepper*
Pastetchen ⓝ pas·tayt·khen *filled puff-pastry case*
Pastete ① pas·tay·te *pastry • pie*
Pellkartoffeln ① pl pel·kar·to·feln *small jacket potatoes served in their skins, often served with quark*
Petersilie ① pa·ter·zee·li·e *parsley*
Pfälzer Saumagen ⓜ pfel·tser zow·mah·gen *stuffed stomach of pork*

Pfannkuchen ⓜ pfan·koo·khen *pancake*
Pfeffer ⓜ pfe·fer *pepper*
Pfifferling ⓜ pfi·fer·ling *chanterelle mushroom*
Pfirsich ⓜ pfir·zikh *peach*
Pflaume ① pflow·me *plum*
Pilz ⓜ pilts *mushroom*
Pichelsteiner ⓝ pi·khel·shtai·ner *meat & vegetable stew*
Pökelfleisch ⓝ per·kel·flaish *marinated meat*
Pomeranzensoße ① po·me·ran·tsen·zaw·se *sauce made of bitter oranges, wine & brandy, usually served with duck*
Pommes Frites pl pom frit *French fries*
Porree ⓜ por·ray *leek*
Preiselbeere ① prai·zel·bair·re *cranberry*
Printe ① prin·te *honey-flavoured biscuit*
Pumpernickel ⓜ pum·per·ni·kel *very dark bread made with coarse wholemeal rye flour*
Putenbrust ① poo·ten·brust *turkey breast*
Puter ⓜ poo·ter *turkey*

Q

Quargel ⓜ kvar·gel *small, round, salty & slightly acidic cheese*
Quark ⓜ kvark *quark (curd cheese)*
Quitte ① kvi·te *quince*

R

Radieschen ⓝ ra·dees·khen *radish*
Ragout ⓝ ra·goo *stew*
Rahm ⓜ rahm *cream*
Rebhuhn ⓝ rayp·hoon *partridge*
Regensburger ⓜ ray·gens·bur·ger *highly spiced smoked sausage*
Reh ⓝ ray *venison*
 —pfeffer ⓜ ray·pfe·fer *jugged venison, fried & braised in its marinade, served with sour cream*
 —rücken ⓜ ray·rü·ken *saddle of venison*

Reibekuchen ⓜ *rai*·be·koo·khen potato cake

Reis ⓜ rais rice

Remouladensauce ⓕ re·mu·*lah*·den·zaw·se mayonnaise sauce with mustard, anchovies, capers, gherkins, tarragon & chervil

Rettich ⓜ *re*·tikh radish

Rhabarber ⓜ ra·*bar*·ber rhubarb

Rheinischer Sauerbraten ⓜ **mit Kartoffelklößen** *rai*·ni·sher zow·er·*brah*·ten mit kar·*to*·fel·kler·sen roasted marinated meat, slightly sour, often served with potato dumpling

Rindfleisch ⓝ *rint*·flaish beef

Rippenspeer ⓜ *ri*·pen·shpair spare ribs

Rogen ⓜ *raw*·gen roe

Roggenbrot ⓝ *ro*·gen·brawt rye bread

Rohkost ⓕ *raw*·kost uncooked vegetables • vegetarian food

Rollmops ⓜ *rol*·mops pickled herring fillet rolled around chopped onions or gherkins

Rosenkohl ⓜ *raw*·zen·kawl Brussels sprouts

Rosinen ⓕ pl ro·*zee*·nen raisins

Rosmarin ⓜ *raws*·ma·reen rosemary

Rost
  —braten ⓜ *rost*·brah·ten roast
  —brätl ⓝ *rost*·braytl grilled meat
  —hähnchen ⓝ *rost*·hayn·khen roast chicken

Rösti pl *rers*·tee grated, fried potatoes (Switzerland)

rot rawt red
  —e Beete ⓕ *raw*·te bay·te beetroot
  —e Grütze ⓕ *raw*·te grü·tse fruit pudding of cooked & sweetened berries, thickened & put in moulds
  —e Johannisbeere ⓕ *raw*·te yo·ha·nis·bair·re redcurrant
  —kohl ⓜ *rawt*·kawl red cabbage
  —e Rüben ⓕ pl *raw*·te rü·ben beetroot
  —wurst ⓕ *rawt*·vurst black pudding

Roulade ⓕ ru·*lah*·de collared beef – thin slices of beef stuffed with onion, bacon and dill pickles then rolled & braised

Rührei ⓝ pl *rür*·ai·er scrambled eggs

Russische Eier ⓝ pl *ru*·si·she ai·er 'Russian eggs' – eggs with mayonnaise

S

Sahne ⓕ *zah*·ne cream

Salat ⓜ za·*laht* salad
  grüner Salat ⓜ *grü*·ner za·*laht* green salad
  italienischer Salat ⓜ i·tal·*yay*·ni·sher za·*laht* finely sliced veal, salami, anchovies, tomatoes, cucumber & celery in mayonnaise

Salbei ⓜ *zal*·bai sage

Salz ⓝ zalts salt

Salzburger Nockerln ⓝ pl *zalts*·bur·ger no·kerln Austrian dessert of sweet dumplings poached in milk & served with warm vanilla sauce

Salzkartoffeln ⓕ pl *zalts*·kar·to·feln boiled potatoes

Sauerbraten ⓜ zow·er·*brah*·ten marinated roasted beef served with a sour cream sauce

Sauerkraut ⓝ *zow*·er·krowt pickled cabbage

Schafskäse ⓜ *shahfs*·kay·ze sheep's milk feta

Schellfisch ⓜ *shel*·fish haddock

Schinken ⓜ *shing*·ken ham
  gekochter Schinken ⓜ ge·*kokh*·ter *shing*·ken cooked ham
  geräucherter Schinken ⓜ ge·*roy*·kher·ter *shing*·ken gammon

Schlachtplatte ⓕ *shlakht*·pla·te selection of pork & sausage

Schmalzbrot ⓝ *shmalts*·brawt slice of bread with dripping

Schmorbraten ⓜ *shmawr*·brah·ten beef pot roast

Schnitte ⓕ *shni*·te slice of bread • small square piece of cake

Schnittlauch ⑩ *shnit-lowkh* chives
Schnitzel ⑪ *shni-tsel* pork, veal or chicken breast pounded flat, covered in breadcrumbs & pan-fried
Holsteiner Schnitzel ⑩ *hol-shtai-ner shni-tsel* veal schnitzel with fried egg, accompanied by seafood
Wiener Schnitzel ⑪ *vee-ner shni-tsel* crumbed veal
Scholle ① *sho-le* plaice
schwarze Johannisbeere ① *shvar-tse yo-ha-nis-bair-re* blackcurrant
Schwarzwälder Kirschtorte ① *shvarts-vel-der kirsh-tor-te* Black Forest cake (chocolate layer cake filled with cream & cherries)
Schwein ⑩ *shvain* pork
—ebraten ⑩ *shvai-ne-brah-ten* roast pork
—efleisch ⑪ *shvai-ne-flaish* pork
—shaxe ① *shvains-hak-se* crispy leg of pork served with dumplings
Seezunge ① *zay-tsung-e* sole
Seidfleisch ⑪ *zait-flaish* boiled meat
Sekt ⑩ *zekt* German champagne
Selchfleisch ⑪ *zelkh-flaish* smoked pork
Sellerie ① *ze-le-ree* celery
Semmel ① *ze-mel* bread roll (Austria & Bavaria)
—knödel ⑩ pl *ze-mel-kner-del* dumplings made of dry rolls dunked in milk (Bavaria)
Senf ⑩ *zenf* mustard
Sonnenblumenkerne ⑩ pl *zo-nen-bloo-men-ker-ne* sunflower seeds
Soße ① *zaw-se* sauce • gravy
spanische Soße ① *shpah-ni-she zaw-se* brown sauce with herbs
Spanferkel ⑩ *shpahn-fer-kel* suckling pig
Spargel ⑩ *shpar-gel* asparagus
Spätzle pl *shpets-le* thick noodles
Speck ⑩ *shpek* bacon
Spekulatius ⑩ *shpe-ku-lah-tsi-us* almond biscuits

Spiegelei ⑪ *shpee-gel-ai* fried egg
Spinat ⑩ *shpi-naht* spinach
Sprossenkohl ⑩ *shpro-sen-kawl* Brussels sprouts
Sprotten ① pl *shpro-ten* sprats (small herring-like fish)
Steckrübe ① *shtek-rü-be* turnip
Steinbuscher ⑩ *shtain-bu-sher* semi-hard, creamy cheese with a strong, slightly bitter flavour
Steinbutt ⑩ *shtain-but* turbot (flatfish)
Stelze ① *shtel-tse* knuckle of pork
Sterz ⑩ *shterts* Austrian polenta
Stollen ⑩ *shto-len* spiced loaf with candied peel, traditionally eaten at Christmas
Strammer Max ⑩ *shtra-mer maks* sandwich with ham (or sausage or spiced minced pork), served with fried eggs & sometimes onions
Streichkäse ⑩ *shtraikh-kay-ze* any kind of soft cheese spread
Streuselkuchen ⑩ *shtroy-zel-koo-khen* coffee cake topped with a mixture of butter, sugar, flour & cinnamon
Strudel ⑩ *shtroo-del* loaf-shaped pastry filled with something sweet or savoury
Suppe ① *zu-pe* soup

T

Tascherl ⑪ *ta-sherl* pastry turnover with meat, cheese or jam filling
Tatarenbrot ⑪ *ta-tah-ren-brawt* open sandwich topped with raw spiced minced beef
Teigwaren pl *taik-vah-ren* pasta
Thunfisch ⑩ *toon-fish* tuna
Thüringer ① *tü-ring-er* long, thin, spiced sausage
Thymian ⑩ *tü-mi-ahn* thyme
Toast ⑩ *tawst* toast
Tomate ① *to-mah-te* tomato
—nketchup ⑩ *to-mah-ten-ket-chap* tomato sauce
—nsuppe ① *to-mah-ten-zu-pe* tomato soup

Topfen ⓜ *top·fen* curd cheese (Austria)
Törtchen ⓝ *tert·khen* small tart or cake
Torte ⓕ *tor·te* layer cake
Truthahn ⓜ *troot·hahn* turkey
Tunke ⓕ *tung·ke* sauce • gravy

V

Vollkornbrot ⓝ *fol·korn·brawt* wholemeal bread
Voressen ⓝ *fawr·e·sen* meat stew

W

Wachtel ⓕ *vakh·tel* quail
Walnuss ⓕ *val·nus* walnut
Wecke ⓕ *ve·ke* bread roll (Austria & southern Germany)
Weichkäse ⓜ *vaikh·kay·ze* soft cheese
Weinbergschnecken ⓕ pl *vain·berk·shne·ken* snails
Weinkraut ⓝ *vain·krowt* white cabbage, braised with apples & simmered in wine
Weintraube ⓕ *vain·trow·be* grape
Weißbrot ⓝ *vais·brawt* white bread
Weißwurst ⓕ *vais·vurst* veal sausage, found mainly in southern Germany
Westfälischer Schinken ⓜ *vest·fay·li·sher shing·ken* variety of cured & smoked ham
Wiener *vee·ner* in the Viennese style
— **Würstchen** ⓝ *vee·ner vürst·khen* frankfurter (sausage)
— **Schnitzel** ⓝ *vee·ner shni·tsel* crumbed veal

Wiezenbrot ⓝ *vai·tsen·brawt* wheat bread
Wild ⓝ *vilt* game
—**braten** ⓜ *vilt·brah·ten* roast venison
—**ente** ⓕ *vilt·en·te* wild duck
—**schwein** ⓝ *vilt·shvain* wild boar
Wilstermarschkäse ⓜ *vils·ter·marsh·kay·ze* semi-hard cheese
Wurst ⓕ *vurst* sausage
Würstchen ⓝ *vürst·khen* small sausage
Wurstplatte ⓕ *vurst·pla·te* cold cuts

Z

Ziege ⓕ *tsee·ge* goat
Zimt ⓜ *tsimt* cinnamon
Zitrone ⓕ *tsi·traw·ne* lemon
Zucker ⓜ *tsu·ker* sugar
Zunge ⓕ *tsung·e* tongue
Zwetschge ⓕ *tsvetsh·ge* plum
—**ndatschi** ⓜ *tsvetsh·gen·dat·shi* damson plum tart
Zwieback ⓜ *tsvee·bak* rusk
Zwiebel ⓕ *tsvee·bel* onion
—**fleisch** ⓝ *tsvee·bel·flaish* beef sauteed with onion
—**kuchen** ⓝ *tsvee·bel·koo·khen* onion quiche, often served with Federweißer (new wine)
—**suppe** ⓕ *tsvee·bel·zu·pe* onion soup
—**wurst** ⓕ *tsvee·bel·vurst* liver & onion sausage
Zwischenrippenstück ⓝ *tsvi·shen·ri·pen·shtük* rib eye steak

emergencies

notfälle

Help!	*Hilfe!*	hil·fe
Stop!	*Halt!*	halt
Go away!	*Gehen Sie weg!*	gay·en zee vek
Thief!	*Dieb!*	deeb
Fire!	*Feuer!*	foy·er
Watch out!	*Vorsicht!*	for·zikht

signs

Unfallstation	un·fal·sta·tsyawn	**Casualty**
Polizei	po·li·tsai	**Police**
Polizeirevier	po·li·tsai·re·veer	**Police Station**

It's an emergency!
Es ist ein Notfall! — es ist ain *nawt*·fal

Call the police!
Rufen Sie die Polizei! — *roo*·fen zee dee po·li·*tsai*

Call a doctor!
Rufen Sie einen Arzt! — *roo*·fen zee *ai*·nen artst

Call an ambulance!
Rufen Sie einen Krankenwagen! — *roo*·fen zee *ai*·nen *krang*·ken·vah·gen

I'm ill.
Ich bin krank. — ikh bin krank

My friend is ill.
Mein Freund/Meine Freundin ist krank. m/f — main froynd/*mai*·ne *froyn*·din ist krank

Could you please help me/us?
Könnten Sie mir/ uns bitte helfen? — *kern*·ten zee meer/ uns *bi*·te *hel*·fen

I have to use the telephone.
*Ich muss das Telefon
benutzen.*
ikh mus das te·le·*fawn*
be·*nu*·tsen

I'm lost.
Ich habe mich verirrt.
ikh *hah*·be mikh fer·*irt*

police

Where's the police station?
Wo ist das Polizeirevier?
vaw ist das po·li·*tsai*·re·veer

I want to report an offence.
*Ich möchte eine
Straftat melden.*
ikh *merkh*·te *ai*·ne
shtrahf·taht *mel*·den

My ... was/	*Man hat mir ...*	man hat meer ...
were stolen.	*gestohlen.*	ge·*shtaw*·len
I've lost my...	*Ich habe ... verloren.*	ikh *hah*·be ... fer·*law*·ren
backpack	*meinen Rucksack*	*mai*·nen *ruk*·zak
bags	*meine Reisetaschen*	*mai*·ne rai·ze·ta·shen
credit card	*meine Kreditkarte*	*mai*·ne kre·*deet*·karte
handbag	*meine Handtasche*	*mai*·ne *hant*·ta·she
jewellery	*meinen Schmuck*	*mai*·nen shmuk
money	*mein Geld*	main gelt
papers	*meine Papiere*	*mai*·ne pa·*pee*·re
travellers cheques	*meine Reiseschecks*	*mai*·ne rai·ze·sheks
passport	*meinen Pass*	*mai*·nen pas
purse	*mein Portemonnaie*	main port·mo·*nay*
wallet	*meine Brieftasche*	*mai*·ne *breef*·ta·she
She/He tried	*Sie/Er hat versucht,*	zee/air hat fer·*zookht*
to ... me.	*mich zu ...*	mikh tsoo ...
assault	*überfallen*	an·ge·*gri*·fen
rape	*vergewaltigen*	fer·ge·*val*·ti·gen
rob	*bestehlen*	be·*shtay*·len

I've been ...	*Ich bin ... worden.*	ikh bin ... *vor·*den
He/She	*Er/Sie ist ...*	air·zee ist ...
has been ...	*worden.*	*vor·*den
assaulted	*angegriffen*	*an·*ge·gri·fen
raped	*vergewaltigt*	fer·ge·*val·*tikht
robbed	*bestohlen*	be·*shtaw·*len

I have insurance.
Ich bin versichert.   ikh bin fer·*zi·*khert

I apologise.
Entschuldigen Sie bitte.   ent·*shul·*di·gen zee *bi·*te

I didn't realise I was doing anything wrong.
Ich war mir nicht bewusst,   ikh vahr meer nikht be·*vust*
etwas Unrechtes getan   et·vas *un·*rekh·tes ge·*tahn*
zu haben.   tsoo *hah·*ben

I didn't do it.
Das habe ich nicht getan.   das *hah·*be ikh nikht ge·*tahn*

I'm innocent.
Ich bin unschuldig.   ikh bin *un·*shul·dikh

Can I call someone?
Kann ich jemanden   kan ikh *yay·*man·den
anrufen?   *an·*roo·fen

Can I call a lawyer?
Kann ich einen   kan ikh *ai·*nen
Rechtsanwalt anrufen?   *rekhts·*an·valt *an·*roo·fen

Can I have a lawyer who speaks English?
Kann ich einen Rechtsanwalt   kan ikh *ai·*nen *rekhts·*an·valt
haben, der Englisch spricht?   *hah·*ben dair *eng·*lish shprikht

Is there a fine we can pay to clear this?
Können wir eine Geldbuße   *ker·*nen veer *ai·*ne *gelt·*boo·se
dafür bezahlen?   da·*für* be·*tsah·*len

I want to	*Ich möchte*	ikh *merkh·*te
contact my ...	*mich mit ... in*	mikh mit ... in
	Verbindung setzen.	fer·*bin·*dung ze·tsen
consulate	*meinem Konsulat*	*mai·*nem kon·zu·*laht*
embassy	*meiner Botschaft*	*mai·*ner *bawt·*shaft

This drug is for personal use.
Diese Droge ist für meinen   *dee·ze draw·ge ist für mai·nen*
persönlichen Gebrauch.   *per·zern·li·khen ge·browkh*

I have a prescription for this drug.
Ich habe ein Rezept für   *ikh hah·be ain re·tsept für*
dieses Medikament.   *dee·zes me·di·ka·ment*

I (don't) understand.
Ich verstehe (nicht).   *ikh fer·shtay·e (nikht)*

I know my rights.
Ich kenne meine Rechte.   *ikh ke·ne mai·ne rekh·te*

What am I accused of?
Wessen werde ich   *ve·sen ver·de ikh*
beschuldigt?   *be·shul·dikht*

the police may say ...

You'll be	*Sie werden ...*	zee ver·den ...
charged with ...	*beschuldigt.*	be·shul·dikht
She/He will be	*Sie/Er wird ...*	zee/air virt ...
charged with ...	*beschuldigt.*	be·shul·dikht
assault	*des Überfalls*	des ü·ber·fals
possession (of	*des Besitzes*	des be·zi·tses
illegal	*(illegaler*	*(i·le·gah·ler*
substances)	*Substanzen)*	zup·stan·tsen)
not having	*der Einreise*	dair ain·rai·ze
a visa	*ohne Visum*	aw·ne vee·zum
overstaying	*der Über-*	dair ü·ber·
your visa	*schreitung*	shrai·tung
	der Gültigkeits-	dair gül·tikh·kaits·
	dauer Ihres	dow·er ee·res
	Visums	vee·zums
shoplifting	*des Laden-*	des lah·den·
	diebstahls	deep·shtahls
speeding	*der Geschwin-*	dair ge·shvin·
	digkeitsüber-	dikh·kaits·ü·ber·
	schreitung	shrai·tung

Where's the nearest ...?	*Wo ist der/die/das nächste ...?* m/f/n	vaw ist dair/dee/das naykhs·te ...
chemist	*Apotheke* f	a·po·*tay*·ke
dentist	*Zahnarzt* m	*tsahn*·artst
doctor	*Arzt* m	artst
hospital	*Krankenhaus* n	*krang*·ken·hows
optometrist	*Augenoptiker* m	*ow*·gen·op·ti·ker

I need a doctor (who speaks English).
Ich brauche einen Arzt   ikh *brow*·khe *ai*·nen artst
(der Englisch spricht).   (dair *eng*·lish shprikht)

Could I see a female doctor?
Könnte ich von einer   *kern*·te ikh fon *ai*·ner
Ärztin behandelt werden?   *erts*·tin be·*han*·delt *ver*·den

Could the doctor come here?
Könnte der Arzt hierher   *kern*·te dair artst heer·*hair*
kommen?   *ko*·men

Is there a (night) chemist nearby?
Gibt es in der Nähe eine   gipt es in dair *nay*·e *ai*·ne
(Nacht)Apotheke?   (nakht·)a·po·*tay*·ke

I don't want a blood transfusion.
Ich möchte keine   ikh *merkh*·te *kai*·ne
Bluttransfusion.   *bloot*·trans·fu·zyawn

Please use a new syringe.
Bitte benutzen   *bi*·te be·*nu*·tsen
Sie eine neue Spritze.   zee *ai*·ne *noy*·e *shpri*·tse

I have my own syringe.
Ich habe meine   ikh *hah*·be *mai*·ne
eigene Spritze.   *ai*·ge·ne *shpri*·tse

I've been	Ich bin gegen ...	ikh bin *gay*·gen ...
vaccinated for ...	*geimpft worden.*	ge·*impft vor*·den
He's/She's been	*Er/Sie ist gegen*	air/zee ist *gay*·gen
vaccinated for ...	*... geimpft worden.*	... ge·*impft vor*·den
... fever	*...Fieber*	...*fee*·ber
hepatitis A/B/C	*Hepatitis*	he·pa·*tee*·tis
	A/B/C	ah/bay/tsay
tetanus	*Tätanus*	*tay*·ta·nus
typhoid	*Typhus*	*tü*·fus
I need new ...	*Ich brauche ...*	ikh *brow*·khe ...
contact lenses	*neue*	*noy*·e
	Kontaktlinsen	kon·*takt*·lin·zen
glasses	*eine neue Brille*	*ai*·ne *noy*·e *bri*·le

I've run out of my medication.
Ich habe keine   ikh *hah*·be *kai*·ne
Medikamente mehr.   me·di·ka·*men*·te mair

My prescription is ...
Mein Rezept ist ...   main re·*tsept* ist ...

Can I have a receipt for my insurance?
Kann ich eine Quittung für   kan ikh *ai*·ne *kvi*·tung für
meine Versicherung   *mai*·ne fer·*zi*·khe·rung
bekommen?   be·*ko*·men

the doctor may say ...

What's the problem?
vas faylt *ee*·nen   *Was fehlt Ihnen?*

Where does it hurt?
vaw toot es vay   *Wo tut es weh?*

Do you have a temperature?
hah·ben zee *fee*·ber   *Haben Sie Fieber?*

How long have you been like this?
zait van *hah*·ben zee   *Seit wann haben Sie*
dee·ze be·*shver*·den   *diese Beschwerden?*

Have you had this before?
ha·ten zee das　　　　　*Hatten Sie das*
shawn ain·mahl　　　　　*schon einmal?*

How long are you travelling for?
vee lang·e dow·ert　　　　*Wie lange dauert*
ee·re rai·ze　　　　　　　*Ihre Reise?*

Are you on medication?
nay·men zee ir·gent·vel·khe　*Nehmen Sie irgendwelche*
me·di·ka·men·te　　　　　*Medikamente?*

Are you allergic to anything?
zint zee gay·gen be·shtim·te　*Sind Sie gegen bestimmte*
shto·fe a·lair·gish　　　　*Stoffe allergisch?*

Do you ...?
drink	*tring·ken zee*	*Trinken Sie?*
smoke	*row·khen zee*	*Rauchen Sie?*
take drugs	*nay·men*	*Nehmen*
	zee draw·gen	*Sie Drogen?*

Are you sexually active?
zint zee zek·su·el ak·teef　　*Sind Sie sexuell aktiv?*

Have you had unprotected sex?
ha·ten zee un·ge·shüts·ten　*Hatten Sie ungeschützten*
ge·shlekhts·fer·kair　　　　*Geschlechtsverkehr?*

You need to be admitted to hospital.
zee mü·sen in ain　　　　*Sie müssen in ein*
krang·ken·hows　　　　　*Krankenhaus*
ain·ge·vee·zen ver·den　　*eingewiesen werden.*

You should have it checked when you go home.
zee zol·ten es tsoo how·ze　*Sie sollten es zu Hause*
un·ter·zoo·khen la·sen　　*untersuchen lassen.*

You should return home for treatment.
zee zol·ten nahkh how·ze　*Sie sollten nach Hause*
fah·ren um zikh　　　　　*fahren, um sich*
be·han·deln tsoo la·sen　　*behandeln zu lassen.*

symptoms & conditions

I'm sick.
Ich bin krank. ikh bin krangk

My friend is sick.
Mein Freund/Meine main froynt/*mai*·ne
Freundin ist krank. m/f *froyn*·din ist krangk

It hurts here.
Es tut hier weh. es toot heer *vay*

I've been vomiting.
Ich habe mich übergeben. ikh *hah*·be mikh *ü*·ber·*gay*·ben

I can't sleep.
Ich kann nicht schlafen. ikh kan nikht *shlah*·fen

I feel ...

anxious	*Ich habe Ängste.*	ikh *hah*·be *engs*·te
better	*Ich fühle*	ikh *fü*·le
	mich besser.	mikh *be*·ser
depressed	*Ich bin deprimiert.*	ikh bin de·pri·*meert*
dizzy	*Mir ist*	meer ist
	schwindelig.	*shvin*·de·likh
hot and cold	*Mir ist*	meer ist
	abwechselnd	*ap*·vek·selnt
	heiß und kalt.	hais unt kalt
nauseous	*Mir ist übel.*	meer ist *ü*·bel
shivery	*Mich fröstelt.*	mikh *frers*·telt
strange	*Mir ist komisch.*	meer ist *kaw*·mish
weak	*Ich fühle mich*	ikh *fü*·le mikh
	schwach.	shvakh
worse	*Ich fühle mich*	ikh *fü*·le mikh
	schlechter.	*shlekh*·ter

I have (a) ... *Ich habe ...* ikh *hah*·be ...

diarrhoea	*Durchfall*	*durkh*·fal
fever	*Fieber*	*fee*·ber
headache	*Kopfschmerzen*	*kopf*·shmer·tsen
pain	*Schmerzen*	*shmer*·tsen

I've noticed a lump here.
Ich habe hier einen   ikh *hah*·be heer *ai*·nen
Knoten bemerkt.   *knaw*·ten be·*merkt*

I've recently had ...
Ich hatte vor kurzem ...   ikh *ha*·te fawr *kur*·tsem ...

He's/She's recently had ...
Er/Sie hatte vor kurzem ...   air/zee *ha*·te fawr *kur*·tsem ...

There's a history of ...
Es gibt eine   es gipt *ai*·ne
Vorgeschichte mit ...   *fawr*·ge·shikh·te mit ...

I'm on medication for ...
Ich nehme   ikh *nay*·me
Medikamente gegen ...   me·di·ka·*men*·te gay·gen ...

He's/She's on medication for ...
Er/Sie nimmt   air/zee nimt
Medikamente gegen ...   me·di·ka·*men*·te gay·gen ...

asthma	*Asthma* n	*ast*·ma
heart condition	*Herzbeschwerden* f	*herts*·be·shver·den
venereal disease	*Geschlechts-*	ge·*shlekhts*·
	krankheit f	krangk·hait

For more symptoms and conditions, see the **dictionary**.

women's health

gesundheit bei frauen

(I think) I'm pregnant.
(Ich glaube,) Ich bin   (ikh *glow*·be) ikh bin
schwanger.   *shvang*·er

I'm on the Pill.
Ich nehme die Pille.   ikh *nay*·me dee *pi*·le

I haven't had my period for ... weeks.
Ich habe seit ...   ikh *hah*·be zait ...
Wochen meine   *vo*·khen *mai*·ne
Periode nicht   pe·ri·*aw*·de nikht
gehabt.   ge·*hahpt*

Are you using contraception?
be·*nu*·tsen zee
fer·*hü*·tungks·mi·tel

*Benutzen Sie
Verhütungsmittel?*

Are you menstruating?
hah·ben zee *ee*·re
pe·ri·*aw*·de

*Haben Sie Ihre
Periode?*

Are you pregnant?
zint zee *shvang*·er

Sind Sie schwanger?

When did you last have your period?
van *ha*·ten zee
ee·re *lets*·te pe·ri·*aw*·de

*Wann hatten Sie
Ihre letzte Periode?*

You're pregnant.
zee zint *shvang*·er

Sie sind schwanger.

allergies

allergien

I have a skin allergy.
Ich habe eine Hautallergie.   ikh *hah*·be *ai*·ne howt·a·ler·gee

I'm allergic to ...	*Ich bin allergisch gegen ...*	ikh bin a·*lair*·gish *gay*·gen ...
He/She's allergic to ...	*Er/Sie ist allergisch gegen ...*	air/zee ist a·*lair*·gish *gay*·gen ...
antibiotics	*Antibiotika*	an·ti·bi·*aw*·ti·ka
anti-inflammatories	*entzündungs-hemmende Mittel*	en·*tsün*·dungks·he·men·de *mi*·tel
aspirin	*Aspirin*	as·pi·*reen*
bees	*Bienen*	*bee*·nen
codeine	*Kodein*	ko·de·*een*
penicillin	*Penizillin*	pe·ni·tsi·*leen*
pollen	*Pollen*	*po*·len
inhaler	*Inhalator* m	in·ha·*lah*·tor
injection	*Injektion* f	in·yek·*tsyawn*
antihistamines	*Antihistamine* n pl	an·ti·his·ta·*mee*·ne

For food-related allergies, see **special diets & allergies**, page 161.

parts of the body

My ... hurts.
*Mir tut der/die/
das ... weh.* m/f/n

meer toot dair/dee/
das ... vay

I can't move my ...
*Ich kann meinen/meine/
mein ... nicht bewegen.* m/f/n

ikh kan *mai*·nen/*mai*·ne/
main ... nikht be·*vay*·gen

I have a cramp in my ...
*Ich habe einen Krampf in
meinem/meiner/
meinem ...* m/f/n

ikh *hah*·be *ai*·nen krampf in
mai·nem/*mai*·ner/
mai·nem ...

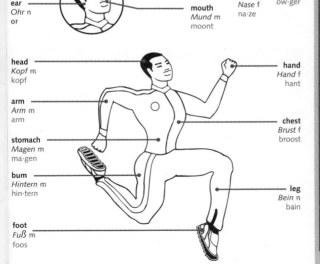

ear
Ohr n
or

eye
Auge n
ow·ger

nose
Nase f
na·ze

mouth
Mund m
moont

head
Kopf m
kopf

hand
Hand f
hant

arm
Arm m
arm

chest
Brust f
broost

stomach
Magen m
ma·gen

bum
Hintern m
hin·tern

leg
Bein n
bain

foot
Fuß m
foos

My ... is swollen.
> *Mein/Meine/Mein ... ist*   main/*mai*·ne/main ... ist
> *geschwollen.* m/f/n   ge·*shvo*·len

For other body parts, see the **dictionary**.

chemist

die apotheke

I need something for ...
> *Ich brauche etwas gegen ...*   ikh *brow*·khe *et*·vas *gay*·gen ...

Do I need a prescription for ...?
> *Brauche ich für ... ein Rezept?*   *brow*·khe ikh für ... ain re·*tsept*

How many times a day?
> *Wie oft am Tag?*   vee oft am tahk

Will it make me drowsy?
> *Macht es müde?*   makht es *mü*·de

For chemist items, see the **dictionary**.

---

listen for ...

hah·ben zee das shawn ain·mahl ain·ge·no·men
> *Haben Sie das schon*   **Have you taken**
> *einmal eingenommen?*   **this before?**

tsvai·mahl am tahk (tsum e·sen)
> *Zweimal am Tag*   **Twice a day**
> *(zum Essen).*   **(with food).**

zee ker·nen es in (tsvan·tsikh mi·noo·ten) ap·haw·len
> *Sie können es in (zwanzig*   **It'll be ready to pick up**
> *Minuten) abholen.*   **in (20 minutes).**

zee mü·sen dee me·di·ka·men·te bis tsum en·de ain·nay·men
> *Sie müssen die*   **You must complete**
> *Medikamente bis zum*   **the course.**
> *Ende einnehmen.*

dentist

der zahnartz

I have a ...	*Ich habe...*	ikh *hah·*be ...
broken tooth	*einen abgebro-chenen Zahn*	*ai·*nen *ap·*ge·bro·khe·nen tsahn
cavity	*ein Loch*	ain lokh
toothache	*Zahnschmerzen*	*tsahn·*shmer·tsen

I need ...	*Ich brauche ...*	ikh *brow·*khe ...
an anaesthetic	*eine Betäubung*	*ai·*ne be·*toy·*bung
a filling	*eine Füllung*	*ai·*ne *fü·*lung

listen for ...

*bai·*sen zee heer drowf
Beißen Sie hier drauf.   **Bite down on this.**

be·*vay·*gen zee zikh nikht
Bewegen Sie sich nicht.   **Don't move.**

*bi·*te dayn munt vait *erf·*nen
Bitte den Mund weit öffnen.   **Open wide.**

das toot fi·*laikht* ain *bis·*khen *vay*
Das tut vielleicht ein bisschen weh.   **This might hurt a little.**

das toot gar nikht vay
Das tut gar nicht weh.   **This won't hurt a bit.**

*ko·*men zee tsu·*rük* ikh bin nokh nikht *fer·*tikh
Kommen Sie zurück, ich bin noch nicht fertig!   **Come back, I haven't finished!**

*shpü·*len
Spülen.   **Rinse.**

health

185

I've lost a filling.
Ich habe eine
Füllung verloren.

ikh *hah*·be ai·ne
fü·lung fer·*law*·ren

My dentures are broken.
Mein Gebiss ist zerbrochen.

main ge·*bis* ist tser·*bro*·khen

My gums hurt.
Das Zahnfleisch
tut mir weh.

das *tsahn*·flaish
toot meer vay

I don't want it extracted.
Ich will ihn nicht
ziehen lassen.

ikh vil een nikht
tsee·en *la*·sen

Ouch!
Au!

ow

DICTIONARY > english–german
englisch–deutsch

Nouns in the dictionary, and adjectives affected by gender, have their gender indicated by ⓜ, ⓕ or ⓝ. If it's a plural noun, you'll also see pl. Where a word that could be either a noun or a verb has no gender indicated, it's a verb.

A

(to be) able können *ker*·nen
aboard *an Bord* an bort
abortion *Abtreibung* ⓕ *ap*·trai·bung
about *über* ü·ber
above *über* ü·ber
abroad *im Ausland* im ows·lant
accident *Unfall* ⓜ *un*·fal
accommodation *Unterkunft* ⓕ
un·ter·kunft
accountant *Buchhalter(in)* ⓜ/ⓕ
bookh·hal·ter/*bookh*·hal·te·rin
across (from) *gegenüber* gay·gen·ü·ber
across (to) *hinüber* hi·nü·ber
activist *Aktivist(in)* ⓜ/ⓕ
ak·ti·*vist*/ak·ti·*vis*·tin
actor *Schauspieler(in)* ⓜ/ⓕ
show·shpee·ler/*show*·shpee·le·rin
acupuncture *Akupunktur* ⓕ
a·ku·pungk·*toor*
adaptor *Adapter* ⓜ a·*dap*·ter
addicted *abhängig* ap·heng·ikh
address *Adresse* ⓕ a·*dre*·se
administration *Verwaltung* ⓕ
fer·*val*·tung
admire *bewundern* be·*vun*·dern
admission price *Eintrittspreis* ⓜ
ain·trits·prais
admit (allow to enter) *einlassen*
ain·la·sen
admit (accept as true) *zugeben*
tsoo·gay·ben
adult *Erwachsene* ⓜ&ⓕ er·*vak*·se·ne
advertisement *Anzeige* ⓕ *an*·tsai·ge
advice *Rat* ⓜ raht
advise *raten* *rah*·ten
aerobics *Aerobics* pl e·*ro*·biks
aerogram *Aerogramm* ⓝ *air*·ro·gram
aeroplane *Flugzeug* ⓝ *flook*·tsoyk
(to be) afraid *Angst (haben)*
angst (*hah*·ben)
Africa *Afrika* ⓝ a·*fri*·kah

after *nach* nahkh
(this) afternoon *(heute) Nachmittag* ⓜ
(*hoy*·te) *nahkh*·mi·tahk
aftershave *Aftershave* ⓝ *ahf*·ter·shayf
again *wieder* vee·der
against *gegen* gay·gen
age *Alter* ⓝ *al*·ter
(three days) ago *vor (drei Tagen)* fawr
(drai *tah*·gen)
agree *zustimmen* *tsoo*·shti·men
agriculture *Landwirtschaft* ⓕ
lant·virt·shaft
ahead *vor uns* fawr uns
AIDS *AIDS* ⓝ aydz
air *Luft* ⓕ luft
airmail *Luftpost* ⓕ *luft*·post
air pollution *Luftverschmutzung* ⓕ
luft·fer·shmu·tsung
air-conditioned *mit Klimaanlage* ⓕ
mit *klee*·ma·an·lah·ge
airline *Fluglinie* ⓕ *flook*·lee·ni·e
airplane *Flugzeug* ⓝ *flook*·tsoyk
airport *Flughafen* ⓜ *flook*·hah·fen
airport tax *Flughafengebühr* ⓕ
flook·hah·fen·ge·bür
airsickness *Luftkrankheit* ⓕ
luft·krangk·hait
aisle *Gang* ⓜ gang
aisle seat *Platz* ⓜ *am Gang*
plats am gang
alarm clock *Wecker* ⓜ *ve*·ker
alcohol *Alkohol* ⓜ al·ko·hawl
alcoholic *Alkoholiker(in)* ⓜ/ⓕ
al·ko·*haw*·li·ker/al·ko·*haw*·li·ke·rin
alcoholic *alkoholisch* al·ko·*haw*·lish
all *alle* a·le
allergy *Allergie* ⓕ a·*lair*·gee
allow *erlauben* er·*low*·ben
almond *Mandel* ⓕ *man*·del
almost *fast* fast
alone *allein* a·*lain*
already *schon* shawn
also *auch* owkh

altar *Altar* ⓜ al·tahr
altitude *Höhe* ① her·e
always *immer* i·mer
amateur(in) ⓜ/①
a·ma·ter/a·ma·te·rin
amazing *erstaunlich* er·shtown·likh
ambassador *Botschafter(in)* ⓜ/①
bawt·shaf·ter/bawt·shaf·te·rin
ambulance *Krankenwagen* ⓜ
krang·ken·vah·gen
among *unter* un·ter
amount *Betrag* ⓜ be·trahk
anaesthetic *Betäubung* ① be·toy·bung
anarchist *Anarchist(in)* ⓜ/①
a·nar·khist/a·nar·khis·tin
ancient *alt* alt
and *und* unt
angry *wütend* vü·tent
animal *Tier* ⓝ teer
ankle *Knöchel* ⓜ kner·khel
answer *Antwort* ① ant·vort
answer *antworten* ant·vor·ten
ant *Ameise* ① ah·mai·ze
antibiotics *Antibiotika* ⓝ pl
an·ti·bi·aw·ti·ka
antinuclear *Anti-Atom-* an·ti·a·tawm
antique *Antiquität* ① an·ti·kvi·tayt
antiseptic *Antiseptikum* ⓝ
an·ti·zep·ti·kum
any *irgendein* ir·gent·ain
anything *(irgend)etwas* (ir·gent·)et·vas
anywhere *irgendwo* ir·gent·vaw
apart from (besides) *außer* ow·ser
apartment *Wohnung* ① vaw·nung
appendix *Blinddarm* ⓜ blint·darm
apple *Apfel* ⓜ ap·fel
appointment *Termin* ⓜ ter·meen
apprentice *Auszubildende* ⓜ&①
ows·tsu·bil·den·de
approximately *ungefähr* un·ge·fair
apricot *Aprikose* ① a·pri·kaw·ze
archaeological *archäologisch*
ar·khe·o·law·gish
architecture *Architektur* ①
ar·khi·tek·toor
area code *Vorwahl* ① fawr·vahl
argue *streiten* shtrai·ten
arm *Arm* ⓜ arm
arrest *Verhaftung* ① fer·haf·tung

arrivals *Ankunft* ① an·kunft
arrive *ankommen* an·ko·men
art *Kunst* ① kunst
art collection *Kunstsammlung* ①
kunst·zam·lung
art gallery *Kunstgalerie* ①
kunst·ga·le·ree
artist *Künstler(in)* ⓜ/①
künst·ler/künst·le·rin
arts & crafts *Kunstgewerbe* ⓝ
kunst·ge·ver·be
as far as *bis zu* bis tsoo
ashtray *Aschenbecher* ⓜ
a·shen·be·kher
Asia *Asien* ⓝ ah·zi·en
ask a question *eine Frage stellen*
ai·ne frah·ge shte·len
ask (for something) *um etwas bitten*
um et·vas bi·ten
asleep *schlafen* shlah·fen
asparagus *Spargel* ⓜ shpar·gel
aspirin *Kopfschmerztablette* ①
kopf·shmerts·ta·ble·te
asthma *Asthma* ⓝ ast·ma
asylum seeker *Asylant(in)* ⓜ/①
a·zü·lant/a·zü·lan·tin
at *in* • *an* • *auf* • *bei* • *zu*
in • an • owf • bai • tsoo
athletics *Leichtathletik* ①
laikht·at·lay·tik
atmosphere *Atmosphäre* ①
at·mos·fair·re
attic *Dachboden* ⓜ dakh·baw·den
aubergine *Aubergine* ①
aw·ber·zhee·ne
aunt *Tante* ① tan·te
Australia *Australien* ⓝ ows·trah·li·en
Austria *Österreich* ⓝ ers·ter·raikh
author *Autor(in)* ⓜ/①
ow·tor/ow·taw·rin
automatic *automatisch* ow·to·mah·tish
automatic teller machine (ATM)
Geldautomat ⓜ gelt·ow·to·maht
autumn *Herbst* ⓜ herpst
avalanche *Lawine* ① la·vee·ne
avenue *Allee* ① a·lay
avocado *Avokado* ⓝ a·vo·kah·do
axe *Axt* ① akst

B

baby *Baby* ⓝ bay·bi
baby food *Babynahrung* ⓕ
　bay·bi·nah·rung
baby powder *Babypuder* ⓝ
　bay·bi·poo·der
babysitter *Babysitter* ⓜ bay·bi·si·ter
back (body) *Rücken* ⓜ rü·ken
back (return) *zurück* tsu·rük
backpack *Rucksack* ⓜ ruk·zak
bacon *Frühstücksspeck* ⓜ
　frü·shtüks·shpek
bad *schlecht* shlekht
badger *Dachs* ⓜ daks
bag *Tasche* ⓕ ta·she
baggage *Gepäck* ⓝ ge·pek
baggage allowance *Freigepäck* ⓝ
　frai·ge·pek
baggage claim *Gepäckausgabe* ⓕ
　ge·pek·ows·gah·be
bait *Köder* ⓜ ker·der
bakery *Bäckerei* ⓕ be·ke·rai
balance (account) *Kontostand* ⓜ
　kon·to·shtant
balcony *Balkon* ⓜ bal·kawn
ball *Ball* ⓜ bal
ballet *Ballett* ⓝ ba·let
banana *Banane* ⓕ ba·nah·ne
band (music) *Band* ⓕ bent
bandage *Verband* ⓜ fer·bant
Band-aids *Pflaster* ⓝ pflas·ter
bank *Bank* ⓕ bangk
bank account *Bankkonto* ⓝ
　bangk·kon·to
bankdraft *Bankauszug* ⓜ
　bangk·ows·tsook
banknote *Geldschein* ⓜ gelt·shain
baptism *Taufe* ⓕ tow·fe
bar *Lokal* ⓝ lo·kahl
baseball *Baseball* ⓜ bays·bawl
basket *Korb* ⓜ korp
bath *Bad* ⓝ baht
bath towel *Badetuch* ⓝ bah·de·tookh
bathing suit *Badeanzug* ⓜ
　bah·de·an·tsook
bathroom *Badezimmer* ⓝ
　bah·de·tsi·mer

battery *Batterie* ⓕ ba·te·ree
bay *Bucht* ⓕ bukht
be *sein* zain
beach *Strand* ⓜ shtrant
bean *Bohne* ⓕ baw·ne
bear *Bär* ⓜ bair
beautiful *schön* shern
beauty salon *Schönheitssalon* ⓜ
　shern·haits·za·long
because *weil* vail
because of *wegen* vay·gen
bed *Bett* ⓝ bet
bed & breakfast *Pension* ⓕ
　pahng·zyawn
bedding *Bettzeug* ⓝ bet·tsoyk
bedroom *Schlafzimmer* ⓝ
　shlahf·tsi·mer
bee *Biene* ⓕ bee·ne
beef *Rindfleisch* ⓝ rint·flaish
beer *Bier* ⓝ beer
beetroot *rote Beete* ⓕ raw·te bay·te
before *vor* fawr
beggar *Bettler(in)* ⓜ/ⓕ bet·ler/bet·le·rin
begin *beginnen* be·gi·nen
behind *hinter* hin·ter
below *unter* un·ter
belt *Gürtel* ⓜ gür·tel
beside *neben* nay·ben
best *beste* bes·te
bet *Wette* ⓕ ve·te
better *besser* be·ser
between *zwischen* tsvi·shen
bible *Bibel* ⓕ bee·bel
bicycle *Fahrrad* ⓝ fahr·raht
big *groß* graws
bike *Fahrrad* ⓝ fahr·raht
bike chain *Fahrradkette* ⓕ
　fahr·raht·ke·te
bike path *Radweg* ⓜ raht·vayk
bill (account) *Rechnung* ⓕ rekh·nung
bin (rubbish) *Mülleimer* ⓜ mül·ai·mer
binoculars *Fernglas* ⓝ fern·glahs
bird *Vogel* ⓜ faw·gel
birth certificate *Geburtsurkunde* ⓕ
　ge·burts·oor·kun·de
birthday *Geburtstag* ⓜ ge·burts·tahk
biscuit *Keks* ⓜ kayks
bite (dog) *Biss* ⓜ bis
bite (insect) *Stich* ⓜ shtikh

bitter *bitter* bi·ter
black *schwarz* shvarts
B&W (film) *schwarzweiß* shvarts·vais
blanket *Decke* ① de·ke
bless *segnen* zayg·nen
blind *blind* blint
blister *Blase* ① blah·ze
blocked *blockiert* blo·keert
blood *Blut* ① bloot
blood group *Blutgruppe* ①
  bloot·gru·pe
blood pressure *Blutdruck* ⓜ *bloot*·druk
blood test *Bluttest* ⓜ *bloot*·test
blue *blau* blow
boar *Wildschwein* ① *vilt*·shvain
board *Brett* ⓝ bret
board (plane, ship) *besteigen*
  be·*shtai*·gen
boarding house *Pension* ①
  pahng·zyawn
boarding pass *Bordkarte* ① *bort*·kar·te
boat *Boot* ⓝ bawt
body *Körper* ⓜ *ker*·per
bone *Knochen* ⓜ *kno*·khen
book *Buch* ⓝ bookh
book (reserve) *buchen* *boo*·khen
booked out *ausgebucht* ows·ge·bookht
bookshop *Buchhandlung* ①
  bookh·hand·lung
boot (trunk) *Kofferraum* ⓜ ko·fer·rowm
boot (footwear) *Stiefel* ⓜ *shtee*·fel
border *Grenze* ① *gren*·tse
bored *gelangweilt* ge·*lang*·vailt
boring *langweilig* *lang*·vai·likh
borrow *(aus)leihen* (ows·)*lai*·en
boss *Chef(in)* ⓜ/① shef/*she*·fin
botanic garden *Botanischer Garten* ⓜ
  bo·*tah*·ni·sher gar·ten
both *beide* *bai*·de
bottle *Flasche* ① *fla*·she
bottle opener *Flaschenöffner* ⓜ
  fla·shen·erf·ner
at the bottom *unten* *un*·ten
bouncer (doorman) *Türsteher* ⓜ
  tür·shtay·er
bowl *Schüssel* ① *shü*·sel
box *Karton* ⓜ kar·tong
boxer shorts *Shorts* pl shorts
boxing *Boxen* ⓝ *bok*·sen

boy *Junge* ⓜ *yung*·e
boyfriend *Freund* ⓜ froynt
bra *BH* ⓜ bay·hah
Braille *Blindenschrift* ① *blin*·den·shrift
brake fluid *Bremsflüssigkeit* ①
  brems·flü·sikh·kait
brakes *Bremsen* ⓜ pl *brem*·zen
brandy *Weinbrand* ⓜ *vain*·brant
brave *mutig* *moo*·tikh
bread *Brot* ⓝ brawt
bread roll *Brötchen* ⓝ *brert*·khen
break *(zer)brechen* (tser·)*bre*·khen
break down *eine Panne haben* ai·ne
  pa·ne *hah*·ben
breakdown service *Abschleppdienst* ⓜ
  ap·shlep·deenst
breakfast *Frühstück* ⓝ *frü*·shtük
breast *Brust* ① brust
breathe *atmen* *aht*·men
bribe *bestechen* be·*shte*·khen
bricklayer *Maurer(in)* ⓜ/①
  mow·rer/*mow*·re·rin
bridge *Brücke* ① *brü*·ke
bridle path *Reitweg* ⓜ *rait*·vayk
briefcase *Aktentasche* ① *ak*·ten·ta·she
brilliant *brillant* bril·*yant*
bring *bringen* *bring*·en
broccoli *Brokkoli* ⓜ pl bro·ko·li
brochure *Broschüre* ① bro·*shü*·re
broken *kaputt* ka·*put*
bronchitis *Bronchitis* ① bron·*khee*·tis
brother *Bruder* ⓜ *broo*·der
brown *braun* brown
bruise *Schramme* ① *shra*·me
Brussels sprouts *Rosenkohl* ⓜ
  raw·zen·kawl
bucket *Eimer* ⓜ *ai*·mer
Buddhist *Buddhist(in)* ⓜ/①
  bu·*dist*/bu·*dis*·tin
buffet *Buffet* ⓝ bü·*fay*
bug (animal) *Insekt* ⓝ in·*zekt*
build *bauen* *bow*·en
building *Gebäude* ⓝ ge·*boy*·de
bumbag *Hüfttasche* ① *hüft*·ta·she
burn *(ver)brennen* (fer·)*bre*·nen
bus (city) *Bus* ⓜ bus
bus (intercity) *Fernbus* ⓜ *fern*·bus
bus station *Busbahnhof* ⓜ
  bus·bahn·hawf
bus stop *Bushaltestelle* ①
  bus·hal·te·shte·le

business *Geschäft* ⑩ ge·*sheft*
business class *Business Class* ①
bi·zi·nes klahs
business person *Geschäftsmann/*
Geschäftsfrau ⑩/①
ge·*shefts*·man/ge·*shefts*·frow
business trip *Geschäftsreise* ①
ge·*shefts*·rai·ze
busker *Straßenmusiker(in)* ⑩/①
shtrah·sen·moo·zi·ker/
shtrah·sen·moo·zi·ke·rin
busy (person) *beschäftigt* be·*shef*·tikht
busy (phone) *besetzt* be·*zetst*
but *aber* ah·ber
butcher's shop *Metzgerei* ①
mets·ge·*rai*
butter *Butter* ⑩ bu·ter
butterfly *Schmetterling* ⑩ shme·ter·ling
button *Knopf* ⑩ knopf
buy *kaufen* kow·fen

C

cabbage *Kohl* ⑩ kawl
cable *Kabel* ⑩ kah·bel
cable car *Seilbahn* ① zail·bahn
cafe *Café* ⑩ ka·fay
cake *Kuchen* ⑩ koo·khen
cake shop *Konditorei* ① kon·dee·to·*rai*
calculator *Taschenrechner* ⑩
ta·shen·rekh·ner
calendar *Kalender* ⑩ ka·*len*·der
camera *Kamera* ① ka·me·ra
camp *zelten* tsel·ten
camping ground *Campingplatz* ⑩
kem·ping·plats
camping stove *Kocher* ⑩ ko·kher
camp site *Zeltplatz* ⑩ tselt·plats
can (be able) *können* ker·nen
can (have permission) *können* ker·nen
can (tin) *Dose* ① daw·ze
can opener *Dosenöffner* ⑩
daw·zen·erf·ner
Canada *Kanada* ⑩ ka·na·dah
canary *Kanarienvogel* ⑩
ka·*nah*·ri·en·faw·gel
cancel *stornieren* shtor·*nee*·ren
cancer *Krebs* ⑩ krayps
candle *Kerze* ① ker·tse

candy *Bonbon* ⑩ bong·bong
cantaloupe *Beutelmelone* ①
boy·tel·me·law·ne
canteen *Kantine* ① kan·tee·ne
cape (offshore) *Kap* ⑩ kap
capitalism *Kapitalismus* ⑩
ka·pi·ta·*lis*·mus
capsicum *Paprika* ① pap·ri·kah
car *Auto* ⑩ ow·to
car hire *Autoverleih* ⑩ ow·to·fer·lai
car owner's title (document)
Fahrzeugpapiere ⑰ pl
fahr·tsoyk·pa·pee·re
car registration (PKW-)Zulassung ①
(pay·kah·vay·)tsoo·la·sung
caravan *Wohnwagen* ⑩ vawn·vah·gen
carburettor *Vergaser* ⑩ fer·*gah*·zer
cards *Karten* ⑰ pl kar·ten
care (for someone) *sich kümmern um*
zikh *kü*·mern um
careful *vorsichtig* fawr·zikh·tikh
caring *liebevoll* lee·be·fol
carpark *Parkplatz* ⑩ park·plats
carpenter *Schreiner(in)* ⑩/①
shrai·ner/shrai·ne·rin
carriage (train) *Wagen* ⑩ vah·*gen*
carrot *Mohrrübe* ① mawr·rü·be
carry *tragen* trah·gen
carton *Karton* ⑩ kar·*tong*
carton (milk) *Tüte* ① tü·te
cash *Bargeld* ⑩ bahr·gelt
cash (a cheque) (einen Scheck)
einlösen (ai·nen shek) ain·ler·zen
cash register *Kasse* ① ka·se
cashew *Cashewnuss* ① kesh·yoo·nus
cashier *Kassierer(in)* ⑩/① ka·see·rer/
ka·see·re·rin
casino *Kasino* ⑩ ka·zee·no
cassette *Kassette* ① ka·se·te
castle *Burg* ① burk
casual work *Gelegenheitsarbeit* ①
ge·*lay*·gen·haits·ar·bait
cat *Katze* ① ka·tse
cathedral *Dom* ⑩ dawm
Catholic *Katholik(in)* ⑩/①
ka·to·*leek*/ka·to·lee·kin
cauliflower *Blumenkohl* ⑩
bloo·men·kawl
cave *Höhle* ① her·le

caviar *Kaviar* ⓜ *kah·vi·ahr*
CD *CD* ⓝ *tsay·day*
celebration *Feier* ⓕ *fai·er*
cellar *Keller* ⓜ *ke·ler*
cemetery *Friedhof* ⓜ *freet·hawf*
centigrade *Celsius* ⓜ *tsel·zi·us*
centimetre *Zentimeter* ⓜ
  tsen·ti·may·ter
central heating *Zentralheizung* ⓕ
  tsen·trahl·hai·tsung
centre *Zentrum* ⓝ *tsen·trum*
ceramic *Keramik* ⓕ *ke·rah·mik*
cereal *Frühstücksflocke* ⓕ
  frü·shtüks·flo·ke
certificate *Zertifikat* ⓝ *tser·ti·fi·kaht*
chain *Kette* ⓕ *ke·te*
chair *Stuhl* ⓜ *shtool*
chairlift (skiing) *Sessellift* ⓜ *ze·se·lift*
championships *Meisterschaften* ⓕ pl
  mais·ter·shaf·ten
chance *Zufall* ⓜ *tsoo·fal*
change (coins) *Wechselgeld* ⓝ
  vek·sel·gelt
change (money) *wechseln* *vek·seln*
change (trains) *umsteigen* *um·shtai·gen*
changing room *Umkleideraum* ⓜ
  um·klai·de·rowm
chapel *Kapelle* ⓕ *ka·pe·le*
charming *charmant* *shar·mant*
chat up *anbaggern* *an·ba·gern*
cheap *billig* *bi·likh*
cheat *Betrüger(in)* ⓜ/ⓕ
  be·trü·ger/be·trü·ge·rin
check (banking) *Scheck* ⓜ *shek*
check (bill) *Rechnung* ⓕ *rekh·nung*
check *prüfen* *prü·fen*
check-in (desk) *Abfertigungsschalter* ⓜ
  ap·fer·ti·gungks·shal·ter
checkpoint *Kontrollstelle* ⓕ
  kon·trol·shte·le
cheese *Käse* ⓜ *kay·ze*
chef *Koch/Köchin* ⓜ/ⓕ *kokh/ker·khin*
chemist *Apotheke* ⓕ *a·po·tay·ke*
cheque (banking) *Scheck* ⓜ *shek*
chess *Schach* ⓝ *shakh*
chest *Brustkorb* ⓜ *brust·korp*
chewing gum *Kaugummi* ⓝ *kow·gu·mi*
chicken *Huhn* ⓝ *hoon*
chicken breast *Hühnerbrust* ⓕ
  hü·ner·brust

chicken drumstick *Hähnchenschenkel* ⓜ
  hayn·khen·sheng·kel
chickpea *Kichererbse* ⓕ *ki·kher·erp·se*
child *Kind* ⓝ *kint*
child seat *Kindersitz* ⓜ *kin·der·zits*
childminding *Kinderbetreuung* ⓕ
  kin·der·be·troy·ung
children *Kinder* ⓝ pl *kin·der*
chilli *Chili* ⓝ *chi·li*
chocolate *Schokolade* ⓕ *sho·ko·lah·de*
choose *(aus)wählen* *(ows)vay·len*
christening *Taufe* ⓕ *tow·fe*
Christian *Christ(in)* ⓜ/ⓕ *krist/kris·tin*
Christian name *Vorname* ⓜ
  fawr·nah·me
Christmas *Weihnachten* ⓝ
  vai·nakh·ten
Christmas Day *(erster)
  Weihnachtsfeiertag* ⓜ *(ers·ter)*
  vai·nakhts·fai·er·tahk
Christmas Eve *Heiligabend* ⓜ
  hai·likh·ah·bent
Christmas tree *Weihnachtsbaum* ⓜ
  vai·nakhts·bowm
church *Kirche* ⓕ *kir·khe*
cider *Apfelmost* ⓜ *ap·fel·most*
cigar *Zigarre* ⓕ *tsi·ga·re*
cigarette *Zigarette* ⓕ *tsi·ga·re·te*
cigarette lighter *Feuerzeug* ⓝ
  foy·er·tsoyk
cinema *Kino* ⓝ *kee·no*
circus *Zirkus* ⓜ *tsir·kus*
citizenship *Staatsbürgerschaft* ⓕ
  shtahts·bür·ger·shaft
city *Stadt* ⓕ *shtat*
city centre *Innenstadt* ⓕ *i·nen·shtat*
civil rights *Bürgerrechte* ⓝ pl
  bür·ger·rekh·te
civil servant *Beamte/Beamtin* ⓜ/ⓕ
  be·am·te/be·am·tin
class *Klasse* ⓕ *kla·se*
classical *klassisch* *kla·sish*
clean *sauber* *zow·ber*
cleaning *Reinigung* ⓕ *rai·ni·gung*
client *Kunde/Kundin* ⓜ/ⓕ
  kun·de/kun·din
cliff *Klippe* ⓕ *kli·pe*
climate *Klima* ⓝ *klee·ma*
climb *klettern* *kle·tern*

cloak *Mantel* ⓜ man·tel
cloakroom *Garderobe* ⓕ gar·draw·be
clock *Uhr* ⓕ oor
close (shut) *schließen* shlee·sen
close (nearby) *nahe* nah·e
closed *geschlossen* ge·shlo·sen
clothesline *Wäscheleine* ⓕ
ve·she·lai·ne
clothing *Kleidung* ⓕ klai·dung
clothing store *Bekleidungsgeschäft* ⓝ
be·klai·dungks·ge·sheft
cloud *Wolke* ⓕ vol·ke
cloudy *wolkig* vol·kikh
clove (spice) *Gewürznelke* ⓕ
ge·vürts·nel·ke
clove (of garlic) *Zehe* ⓕ tsay·e
clutch (car) *Kupplung* ⓕ kup·lung
coach (bus) *Bus* ⓜ bus
coach (sport) *Trainer(in)* ⓜ/ⓕ
tray·ner/tray·ne·rin
coast *Küste* ⓕ küs·te
coat *Mantel* ⓜ man·tel
cocaine *Kokain* ⓝ ko·ka·een
cockroach *Kakerlake* ⓕ kah·ker·lah·ke
cocoa *Kakao* ⓝ ka·kow
coffee *Kaffee* ⓜ ka·fay
coins *Münzen* ⓕ pl mün·tsen
cold *kalt* kalt
have a cold *erkältet sein* er·kel·tet zain
colleague *Kollege/Kollegin* ⓜ/ⓕ
ko·lay·ge/ko·lay·gin
collect call *R-Gespräch* ⓝ
air·ge·shpraykh
college *College* ⓝ ko·lidzh
colour *Farbe* ⓕ far·be
comb *Kamm* ⓜ kam
come *kommen* ko·men
comedy *Komödie* ⓕ ko·mer·di·e
comfortable *bequem* be·kvaym
communion *Kommunion* ⓕ
ko·mun·yawn
companion *Begleiter(in)* ⓜ/ⓕ
be·glai·ter/be·glai·te·rin
company *Firma* ⓕ fir·ma
compass *Kompass* ⓜ kom·pas
complain *sich beschweren* zikh
be·shvair·ren
computer *Computer* ⓜ kom·pyoo·ter
computer game *Computerspiel* ⓝ
kom·pyoo·ter·shpeel

concert *Konzert* ⓝ kon·tsert
concert hall *Konzerthalle* ⓕ
kon·tsert·ha·le
conditioner *Spülung* ⓕ shpü·lung
condom *Kondom* ⓝ kon·dawm
conductor *Schaffner(in)* ⓜ/ⓕ
shaf·ner/shaf·ne·rin
confession (religious) *Beichte* ⓕ
baikh·te
confirm (a booking) *bestätigen*
be·shtay·ti·gen
connection *Verbindung* ⓕ fer·bin·dung
conservative *konservativ*
kon·zer·va·teef
constipation *Verstopfung* ⓕ
fer·shtop·fung
consulate *Konsulat* ⓝ kon·zu·laht
contact lenses *Kontaktlinsen* ⓕ pl
kon·takt·lin·zen
contraceptives *Verhütungsmittel* ⓝ
fer·hü·tungks·mi·tel
contract *Vertrag* ⓜ fer·trahk
convenience store *Kiosk* ⓜ kee·osk
convent *Kloster* ⓝ klaws·ter
cook *Koch/Köchin* ⓜ/ⓕ kokh/ker·khin
cook *kochen* ko·khen
cookie *Keks* ⓜ kayks
corner *Ecke* ⓕ e·ke
cornflakes *Cornflakes* pl korn·flayks
corrupt *korrupt* ko·rupt
cost *kosten* kos·ten
cottage cheese *Hüttenkäse* ⓜ
hü·ten·kay·ze
cotton *Baumwolle* ⓕ bowm·vo·le
cotton balls *Watte-Pads* pl va·te·pedz
cough *husten* hoos·ten
cough medicine *Hustensaft* ⓜ
hoos·ten·zaft
count *zählen* tsay·len
counter (at bar) *Theke* ⓕ tay·ke
country *Land* ⓝ lant
countryside *Land* ⓝ lant
coupon *Coupon* ⓜ ku·pong
courgette *Zucchini* ⓕ tsu·kee·ni
court (legal) *Gericht* ⓝ ge·rikht
court (tennis) *Platz* ⓜ plats
couscous *Couscous* ⓜ kus·kus
cousin *Cousin(e)* ⓜ/ⓕ ku·zen/ku·zee·ne

cover charge Eintrittsgeld ⓝ
ain·trits·gelt
cow Kuh ① koo
cracker Cracker ⓜ kre·ker
crafts Handwerk ⓝ hant·verk
cramp Krampf ⓜ krampf
crash Zusammenstoß ⓜ
tsu·za·men·staws
crazy verrückt fe·rükt
cream Sahne ① zah·ne
cream cheese Frischkäse ⓜ frish·kay·ze
creche Kinderkrippe ① kin·der·kri·pe
credit card Kreditkarte ①
kre·deet·kar·te
cricket Cricket ⓝ kri·ket
crop Feldfrucht ① felt·frukht
cross (religious) Kreuz ⓝ kroyts
cross (angry) wütend vü·tent
crowded überfüllt ü·ber·fült
cuckoo clock Kuckucksuhr ①
ku·kuks·oor
cucumber Gurke ① gur·ke
cup Tasse ① ta·se
cupboard Schrank ⓜ shrangk
currency Währung ① vair·rung
currency exchange Geldwechsel ⓜ
gelt·vek·sel
current (electricity) Strom ⓜ shtrawm
current affairs Aktuelles ⓝ ak·tu·e·les
curry (powder) Curry(pulver) ⓝ
ker·ri(·pul·ver)
customs Zoll ⓜ tsol
cut schneiden shnai·den
cutlery Besteck ⓝ be·shtek
CV Lebenslauf ⓜ lay·bens·lowf
cycle radfahren raht·fah·ren
cycling Radsport ⓜ raht·shport
cyclist Radfahrer(in) ⓜ/①
raht·fah·rer/raht·fah·re·rin
cystitis Blasenentzündung ①
blah·zen·en·tsün·dung

D

dad Papa ⓜ pa·pa
daily täglich tayk·likh
dairy products Milchprodukte ⓝ pl
milkh·pro·duk·te
damp feucht foykht

dance tanzen tan·tsen
dangerous gefährlich ge·fair·likh
dark dunkel dung·kel
date (a person)
mit jemandem ausgehen
mit yay·man·dem ows·gay·en
date (appointment) Verabredung ①
fer·ap·ray·dung
date (day) Datum ⓝ dah·tum
date of birth Geburtsdatum ⓝ
ge·burts·dah·tum
daughter Tochter ① tokh·ter
daughter-in-law Schwiegertochter ①
shvee·ger·tokh·ter
dawn Dämmerung ① de·me·rung
day Tag ⓜ tahk
day after tomorrow übermorgen
ü·ber·mor·gen
day before yesterday vorgestern
fawr·ges·tern
dead tot tawt
deaf taub towp
deal (cards) austeilen ows·tai·len
decide entscheiden ent·shai·den
deep tief teef
deforestation Abholzung ①
ap·hol·tsung
degree Grad ⓜ graht
delay Verspätung ① fer·shpay·tung
delicatessen Feinkostgeschäft ⓝ
fain·kost·ge·sheft
delicious köstlich kerst·likh
deliver (aus)liefern (ows·)lee·fern
demand Forderung ① for·de·rung
democracy Demokratie ①
de·mo·kra·tee
demonstration Demonstration ①
de·mons·tra·tsyawn
dental floss Zahnseide ① tsahn·zai·de
dentist Zahnarzt/Zahnärztin ⓜ/①
tsahn·artst/tsahn·erts·tin
deodorant Deo ⓝ day·o
depart (leave) abfahren ap·fah·ren
department store Warenhaus ⓝ
vah·ren·hows
departure Abfahrt ① ap·fahrt
deposit Anzahlung ① an·tsah·lung
descendant Nachkomme ⓜ
nahkh·ko·me

desert *Wüste* ① *vüs·*te
design *entwerfen* ent·*ver·*fen
destination *(Reise)Ziel* ⑩ *(rai·ze·)tseel*
detail *Detail* ⑩ de·*tai*
diabetes *Diabetis* ① di·a·*bay·*tis
dial tone *Wählton* ⑩ *vayl·*tawn
diaper *Windel* ① *vin·*del
diaphragm (body) *Zwerchfell* ⑩
 *tsverkh·*fel
diarrhoea *Durchfall* ⑩ *durkh·*fal
diary (for appointments)
 Terminkalender ⑩
 ter·*meen·*ka·len·der
diary (record of events) *Tagebuch* ⑩
 *tah·*ge·bookh
dice (die) *Würfel* ⑩ *vür·*fel
dictionary *Wörterbuch* ⑩ *ver·*ter·bookh
die *sterben* *shter·*ben
diet *Diät* ① di·*ayt*
different *andere* *an·*de·re
difficult *schwierig* *shvee·*rikh
dining car *Speisewagen* ⑩
 *shpai·*ze·vah·gen
dinner *Abendessen* ⑩ *ah·*bent·e·sen
direct *direkt* di·*rekt*
direct-dial *Durchwahl* ① *durkh·*vahl
director *Regisseur(in)* ⑩/① re·zhi·*ser/*
 re·zhi·*ser·*rin
directory enquiries *Telefonauskunft* ①
 te·le·*fawn·*ows·kunft
dirty *schmutzig* *shmu·*tsikh
disabled *behindert* be·*hin·*dert
disco *Disko(thek)* ① *dis·*ko(·*tayk*)
discount *Rabatt* ⑩ ra·*bat*
discrimination *Diskriminierung* ①
 dis·kri·mi·*nee·*rung
disease *Krankheit* ① *krangk·*hait
disk (computer) *Diskette* ① dis·*ke·*te
diving *Tauchen* ⑩ *tow·*khen
dizzy *schwindelig* *shvin·*de·likh
do *tun* toon
doctor (medical) *Arzt/Ärztin* ⑩/①
 artst/*erts·*tin
doctor (title) *Doktor(in)* ⑩/①
 *dok·*tor/dok·*taw·*rin
documentary *Dokumentation* ①
 do·ku·men·ta·*tsyawn*
dog *Hund* ⑩ hunt

dole (unemployment benefit)
 Arbeitslosengeld ⑩
 ar·*baits·*law·zen·gelt
doll *Puppe* ① *pu·*pe
dollar *Dollar* ⑩ *do·*lahr
door *Tür* ① tür
dope (drugs) *Dope* ⑩ dawp/dohp
double *doppelt* *do·*pelt
double bed *Doppelbett* ⑩ *do·*pel·bet
down (nach) unten (nahkh) *un·*ten
downhill *abwärts* *ap·*verts
dozen *Dutzend* ⑩ *du·*tsent
drama *Schauspiel* ⑩ *show·*shpeel
dream *träumen* *troy·*men
dress *Kleid* ⑩ klait
dried fruit *Trockenobst* ⑩
 *tro·*ken·awpst
drink *Getränk* ⑩ ge·*trengk*
drink *trinken* *tring·*ken
drive *fahren* *fah·*ren
driving licence *Führerschein* ⑩
 *fü·*rer·shain
drug *Droge* ① *draw·*ge
drug addiction *Drogenabhängigkeit* ①
 *draw·*gen·ap·heng·ikh·kait
drug dealer *Drogenhändler* ⑩
 *draw·*gen·hen·dler
drunk *betrunken* be·*trung·*ken
dry (clothes) *trocknen* *trok·*nen
dry (wine) *trocken* *tro·*ken
dry-cleaner *chemische Reinigung* ①
 *khay·*mi·she *rai·*ni·gung
duck *Ente* ① *en·*te
dummy (pacifier) *Schnuller* ⑩ *shnu·*ler
during *während* *vair·*rent
dusk *Dämmerung* ① *de·*me·rung

E

each *jeder/jede/jedes* ⑩/①/⑩
 *yay·*der/yay·*de/yay·*des
ear *Ohr* ⑩ awr
early *früh* frü
earn *verdienen* fer·*dee·*nen
earplugs *Ohrenstöpsel* ⑩
 aw·ren·*shterp·*sel
earrings *Ohrringe* ⑩ pl *awr·*ring·e
Earth *Erde* ① *er·*de

earthquake Erdbeben ⓝ ert·bay·ben
east Osten ⓜ os·ten
Easter Ostern ⓝ aws·tern
easy leicht laikht
eat essen e·sen
economy class Touristenklasse ⓕ
   tu·ris·ten·kla·se
eczema Ekzem ⓝ ek·tsaym
editor Herausgeber(in) ⓜ/ⓕ
   he·rows·gay·ber/he·rows·gay·be·rin
education Erziehung ⓕ er·tsee·ung
egg Ei ⓝ ai
eggplant Aubergine ⓕ aw·ber·zhee·ne
elections Wahlen ⓕ pl vah·len
electrical store Elektrogeschäft ⓝ
   e·lek·tro·ge·sheft
electrician Elektriker(in) ⓜ/ⓕ
   e·lek·tri·ker/e·lek·tri·ke·rin
electricity Elektrizität ⓕ e·lek·tri·tsi·tayt
elevator Lift ⓜ lift
embarrassed verlegen fer·lay·gen
embassy Botschaft ⓕ bawt·shaft
embroidery Stickerei ⓕ shti·ke·rai
emergency Notfall ⓜ nawt·fal
emotional emotional e·mo·tsyo·nahl
employee Angestellte ⓜ&ⓕ
   an·ge·shtel·te
employer Arbeitgeber ⓜ
   ar·bait·gay·ber
empty leer lair
end Ende ⓝ en·de
end beenden be·en·den
endangered (species) bedrohte (Art) ⓕ
   be·draw·te art
energy Energie ⓕ e·ner·gee
engagement (marriage) Verlobung ⓕ
   fer·law·bung
engine Motor ⓜ maw·tor/mo·tawr
engineer Ingenieur(in) ⓜ/ⓕ
   in·zhe·nyer/in·zhe·nye·rin
engineering Ingenieurwesen ⓝ
   in·zhe·nyer·vay·zen
England England ⓝ eng·lant
English Englisch ⓝ eng·lish
enjoy (oneself) sich amüsieren zikh
   a·mü·zee·ren
enough genug ge·nook
enter eintreten ain·tray·ten

entertainment guide
   Veranstaltungskalender ⓜ fer·an·shtal·
   tungks·ka·len·der
envelope Briefumschlag ⓜ
   breef·um·shlahk
environment Umwelt ⓕ um·velt
epilepsy Epilepsie ⓕ e·pi·lep·see
equal opportunity Chancengleichheit ⓕ
   shahng·sen·glaikh·hait
equality Gleichheit ⓕ glaikh·hait
equipment Ausrüstung ⓕ ows·rüs·tung
escalator Rolltreppe ⓕ rol·tre·pe
euro Euro ⓜ oy·ro
Europe Europa ⓝ oy·raw·pa
euthanasia Euthanasie ⓕ oy·ta·na·zee
evening Abend ⓜ ah·bent
every jeder/jede/jedes ⓜ/ⓕ/ⓝ
   yay·der/yay·de/yay·des
every day alltäglich al·tayk·likh
everyone jeder yay·der
everything alles a·les
example Beispiel ⓝ bai·shpeel
for example zum Beispiel tsum
   bai·shpeel
excellent ausgezeichnet
   ows·ge·tsaikh·net
excess baggage Übergepäck ⓝ
   ü·ber·ge·pek
exchange Umtausch ⓜ um·towsh
exchange wechseln vek·seln
exchange rate Wechselkurs ⓜ
   vek·sel·kurs
excluded ausgeschlossen
   ows·ge·shlo·sen
exhaust (car) Auspuff ⓜ ows·puf
exhibition Ausstellung ⓕ
   ows·shte·lung
exit Ausgang ⓜ ows·gang
expensive teuer toy·er
experience Erfahrung ⓕ er·fah·rung
exploitation Ausbeutung ⓕ
   ows·boy·tung
express Express- eks·pres·
express mail Expresspost ⓕ
   eks·pres·post
extension (visa) Verlängerung ⓕ
   fer·leng·e·rung
eye Auge ⓝ ow·ge
eye drops Augentropfen ⓜ pl
   ow·gen·trop·fen

F

fabric *Gewebe* ⁿ ge·vay·be
face *Gesicht* ⁿ ge·zikht
face cloth *Waschlappen* ⓜ vash·la·pen
factory *Fabrik* ① fa·breek
factory worker *Fabrik-
  arbeiter(in)* ⓜ/①
  fa·breek·ar·bai·ter/fa·breek·ar·bai·te·rin
fair (trade) *Messe* ① me·se
fall (autumn) *Herbst* ⓜ herpst
false *falsch* falsh
family *Familie* ① fa·mee·li·e
family name *Familienname* ⓜ
  fa·mee·li·en·nah·me
famous *berühmt* be·rümt
fan (sports) *Fan* ⓜ fen
fan (machine) *Ventilator* ⓜ
  ven·ti·lah·tor
fanbelt *Keilriemen* ⓜ kail·ree·men
far *weit* vait
farm *Bauernhof* ⓜ bow·ern·hawf
farmer *Bauer/Bäuerin* ⓜ/①
  bow·er/boy·e·rin
fast *schnell* shnel
fat *dick* dik
father *Vater* ⓜ fah·ter
father-in-law *Schwiegervater* ⓜ
  shvee·ger·fah·ter
faucet *Wasserhahn* ⓜ va·ser·hahn
fault (someone's) *Schuld* ① shult
faulty *fehlerhaft* fay·ler·haft
fax *Fax* ⓝ faks
feed *füttern* fü·tern
feel *fühlen* fü·len
feelings *Gefühle* ⓝ pl ge·fü·le
fence *Zaun* ⓜ tsown
fencing (sport) *Fechten* ⓝ fekh·ten
festival *Fest* ⓝ fest
fever *Fieber* ⓝ fee·ber
few *wenige* vay·ni·ge
a few *ein paar* ain pahr
fiance/fiancee *Verlobte* ⓜ&①
  fer·lawp·te
fiction *Prosa* ① praw·za
field *Feld* ⓝ felt
fig *Feige* ① fai·ge
fight *Kampf* ⓜ kampf
fill *füllen* fü·len

fillet *Filet* ⓝ fi·lay
film (cinema & camera) *Film* ⓜ film
film (for camera) *Film* ⓜ film
film speed *Empfindlichkeit* ①
  emp·fint·likh·kait
filtered *gefiltert* ge·fil·tert
find *finden* fin·den
fine (payment) *Geldbuße* ① gelt·boo·se
finger *Finger* ⓜ fing·er
finish *beenden* be·en·den
fire *Feuer* ⓝ foy·er
firewood *Brennholz* ⓝ bren·holts
first *erste* ers·te
first class *erste Klasse* ① ers·te kla·se
first-aid kit *Verbandskasten* ⓜ
  fer·bants·kas·ten
fish *Fisch* ⓜ fish
fish shop *Fischgeschäft* ⓝ fish·ge·sheft
fishing *Fischen* ⓝ fi·shen
fishing rod *Angel* ① ang·el
flag *Flagge* ① fla·ge
flash *Blitz* ⓜ blits
flashlight *Taschenlampe* ①
  ta·shen·lam·pe
flat *flach* flakh
flea *Floh* ⓜ flaw
flea-market *Flohmarkt* ⓜ flaw·markt
flight *Flug* ⓜ flook
flooding *Überschwemmung* ①
  ü·ber·shve·mung
floor *Boden* ⓜ baw·den
floor (storey) *Stock* ⓜ shtok
florist *Blumenhändler* ⓜ
  bloo·men·hen·dler
flour *Mehl* ⓝ mayl
flower *Blume* ① bloo·me
fly *Fliege* ① flee·ge
fly *fliegen* flee·gen
foggy *neblig* nay·blikh
follow *folgen* fol·gen
food *Essen* ⓝ e·sen
food poisoning *Lebensmittelvergiftung* ①
  lay·bens·mi·tel·fer·gif·tung
foot *Fuß* ⓜ foos
football (soccer) *Fußball* ⓜ foos·bal
American football *American Football*
  e·me·ri·ken fut·bawl
Australian Rules football *Australian
  Rules Football* ⓜ aws·tray·li·en roolz
  fut·bawl

footpath *Gehweg* ⓜ gay·vayk
for *für* für
foreign *ausländisch* ows·len·dish
forest *Wald* ⓜ valt
forever *immer* i·mer
forget *vergessen* fer·ge·sen
forgive *verzeihen* fer·tsai·en
fork *Gabel* ① gah·bel
formal *formell* for·mel
fortnight *vierzehn Tage* ⓝ pl
   feer·tsayn tah·ge
foul *Foul* ⓝ fowl
fountain *Brunnen* ⓜ bru·nen
foyer *Foyer* ⓝ fo·a·yay
fragile *zerbrechlich* tser·brekh·likh
frame *Rahmen* ⓜ rah·men
France *Frankreich* ⓝ frangk·raikh
free (gratis) *gratis* grah·tis
free (not bound) *frei* frai
freeze *gefrieren* ge·free·ren
fresh (not stale) *frisch* frish
Friday *Freitag* ⓜ frai·tahk
friend *Freund(in)* ⓜ/① froynt/froyn·din
friendly *freundlich* froynt·likh
frog *Frosch* ⓜ frosh
from *aus* • *von* ows • fon
in front of *vor* fawr
frost *Frost* ⓜ frost
fruit *Frucht* ① frukht
fruit picking *Obsternte* ① awpst·ern·te
fry *braten* brah·ten
frying pan *Bratpfanne* ① braht·pfa·ne
fuel *Brennstoff* ⓜ bren·shtof
full *voll* fol
full-time *Vollzeit* ① fol·tsait
fun *Spaß* ⓜ shpahs
funeral *Begräbnis* ⓝ be·grayp·nis
funny *lustig* lus·tikh
furniture *Möbel* ⓝ pl mer·bel
fuse *Sicherung* ① zi·khe·rung
future *Zukunft* ① tsoo·kunft

G

game (sport) *Spiel* ⓝ shpeel
garage (car repair) *Werkstatt* ①
   verk·shtat
garage (car shelter) *Garage* ①
   ga·rah·zhe

garbage *Abfall* ⓜ ap·fal
garden *Garten* ⓜ gar·ten
garlic *Knoblauch* ⓜ knawp·lowkh
gas (for cooking) *Gas* ⓝ gahs
gas (petrol) *Benzin* ⓝ ben·tseen
gas cartridge *Gaskartusche* ①
   gahs·kar·tu·she
gas cylinder *Gasflasche* ① gahs·fla·she
gastroenteritis *Magen-Darm-Katarrh* ⓜ
   mah·gen·darm·ka·tar
gate *Tor* ⓝ tawr
gay *schwul* shvool
gears *Gänge* ⓝ pl geng·e
general *allgemein* al·ge·main
German *Deutsch* ⓝ doytsh
Germany *Deutschland* ⓝ doytsh·lant
gift *Geschenk* ⓝ ge·shengk
gig *Auftritt* ⓜ owf·trit
gin *Gin* ⓜ dzhin
ginger *Ingwer* ⓜ ing·ver
girl *Mädchen* ⓝ mayt·khen
girlfriend *Freundin* ① froyn·din
give *geben* gay·ben
glacier *Gletscher* ⓜ glet·sher
glandular fever *Drüsenfieber* ⓝ
   drü·zen·fee·ber
glass *Glas* ⓝ glahs
glasses (spectacles) *Brille* ① bri·le
glove *Handschuh* ⓜ hant·shoo
go (on foot) *gehen* gay·en
go (by vehicle) *fahren* fah·ren
go out with *ausgehen mit*
   ows·gay·en mit
go shopping *einkaufen gehen*
   ain·kow·fen gay·en
goal *Tor* ⓝ tawr
goalkeeper *Torwart/Torhüterin* ⓜ/①
   tawr·vart/tawr·hü·te·rin
goat *Ziege* ① tsee·ge
god *Gott* ⓜ got
goggles (skiing) *Skibrille* ① shee·bri·le
gold *Gold* ⓝ golt
golf ball *Golfball* ⓜ golf·bal
golf course *Golfplatz* ⓜ golf·plats
good *gut* goot
gorge *Schlucht* ① shlukht
government *Regierung* ① re·gee·rung
gram *Gramm* ⓝ gram
grandchild *Enkelkind* ⓝ eng·kel·kint

grandfather *Großvater • Opa* ⓜ
graws·fah·ter • aw·pa
grandmother *Großmutter • Oma* ⓕ
graws·mu·ter • aw·ma
grandparents *Großeltern* ⓝ pl
graws·el·tern
grapefruit *Pampelmuse* ⓕ
pam·pel·moo·ze
grapes *Weintrauben* ⓕ pl *vain·trow·ben*
graphic art *grafische Kunst* ⓕ
grah·fi·she kunst
grass *Gras* ⓝ *grahs*
grave *Grab* ⓝ *grahp*
gray *grau* grow
great *groß* graws
green *grün* grün
greengrocer *Lebensmittelhändler* ⓜ
lay·bens·mi·tel·hen·dler
grey *grau* grow
grocery store *Lebensmittelladen* ⓜ
lay·bens·mi·tel·lah·den
groundnut *Erdnuss* ⓕ *ert·nus*
grow *wachsen* vak·sen
guess *raten* rah·ten
guide (audio) *Führer* ⓜ *fü·rer*
guide (person) *Führer* ⓜ *fü·rer*
guide dog *Blindenhund* ⓜ
blin·den·hunt
guidebook *Reiseführer* ⓜ *rai·ze·fü·rer*
guided tour *Führung* ⓕ *fü·rung*
guilty *schuldig* shul·dikh
guitar *Gitarre* ⓕ *gi·ta·re*
gum (mouth) *Zahnfleisch* ⓝ
tsahn·flaish
gym *Fitness-Studio* ⓝ *fit·nes·shtoo·di·o*
gymnastics *Gymnastik* ⓕ *güm·nas·tik*
gynaecologist
Gynäkologe/Gynäkologin ⓜ/ⓕ
gü·ne·ko·law·ge/gü·ne·ko·law·gin

H

hair *Haar* ⓝ *hahr*
hairbrush *Haarbürste* ⓕ *hahr·bürs·te*
hairdresser *Friseur(in)* ⓜ/ⓕ *fri·zer/
fri·zer·rin*
Halal *Halal-* ha·*lal·*
half *Hälfte* ⓕ *helf·te*
half a litre *ein halber Liter* ⓜ *ain
hal·ber lee·ter*

hallucinate *halluzinieren*
ha·lu·tsi·nee·ren
ham *Schinken* ⓜ *shing·ken*
hammer *Hammer* ⓜ *ha·mer*
hammock *Hängematte* ⓕ *heng·e·ma·te*
hamster *Hamster* ⓜ *hams·ter*
hand *Hand* ⓕ *hant*
handbag *Handtasche* ⓕ *hant·ta·she*
handicrafts *Kunsthandwerk* ⓝ
kunst·hant·verk
handlebar *Lenker* ⓜ *leng·ker*
handmade *handgemacht*
hant·ge·makht
handsome *gutaussehend*
goot·ows·zay·ent
hang-gliding *Drachenfliegen* ⓝ
dra·khen·flee·gen
happy *glücklich* glük·likh
harassment *Belästigung* ⓕ
be·les·ti·gung
harbour *Hafen* ⓜ *hah·fen*
hard (difficult) *schwer* shvair
hard (not soft) *hart* hart
hardware store *Eisenwarengeschäft* ⓝ
ai·zen·vah·ren·ge·sheft
hash *Haschee* ⓝ *ha·shay*
hat *Hut* ⓜ *hoot*
hate *hassen* ha·sen
have *haben* hah·ben
hay fever *Heuschnupfen* ⓜ
hoy·shnup·fen
he *er* air
head *Kopf* ⓜ kopf
headache *Kopfschmerzen* ⓜ pl
kopf·shmer·tsen
headlights *Scheinwerfer* ⓜ pl
shain·ver·fer
health *Gesundheit* ⓕ *ge·zunt·hait*
hear *hören* her·ren
hearing aid *Hörgerät* ⓝ *her·ge·rayt*
heart *Herz* ⓝ herts
heart condition *Herzleiden* ⓝ
herts·lai·den
heat *Hitze* ⓕ *hi·tse*
heater *Heizgerät* ⓝ *haits·ge·rayt*
heavy *schwer* shvair
hello *hallo* ha·lo
helmet *Helm* ⓜ helm

help *helfen* hel·fen
hepatitis *Hepatitis* ① he·pa·tee·tis
her *ihr* eer
herbalist *Naturheilkundige* ⓜ&① na·toor·hail·kun·di·ge
herbs *Kräuter* ⓝ pl kroy·ter
here *hier* heer
heroin *Heroin* ⓝ he·ro·een
herring *Hering* ⓜ hay·ring
high *hoch* hawkh
high school *Sekundarschule* ① ze·kun·dahr·shoo·le
hike *wandern* van·dern
hiking *Wandern* ⓝ van·dern
hiking boots *Wanderstiefel* ⓜ pl van·der·shtee·fel
hiking route *Wanderweg* ⓜ van·der·vayk
hill *Hügel* ⓜ hü·gel
Hindu *Hindu* ⓜ&① hin·du
hire *mieten* mee·ten
his *sein* zain
historical *historisch* his·taw·rish
hitchhike *trampen* trem·pen
HIV positive *HIV-positiv* hah·ee·fow·paw·zi·teef
hockey *Hockey* ⓝ ho·ki
holiday *Urlaub* ⓜ oor·lowp
holidays *Ferien* pl fair·ri·en
holy *heilig* hai·likh
Holy Week *Karwoche* ① kahr·vo·khe
home *Heim* ⓝ haim
(at) home *zu Hause* tsoo how·ze
(go) home *nach Hause* nahkh how·ze
homeless *obdachlos* op·dakh·laws
homemaker *Hausmann/Hausfrau* ⓜ/① hows·man/hows·frow
to be homesick *Heimweh haben* haim·vay hah·ben
homeopathic medicine *homöopathisches Mittel* ⓝ haw·mer·o·pah·ti·shes mi·tel
homosexual *homosexuell* haw·mo·zek·su·el
honest *ehrlich* air·likh
honey *Honig* ⓜ haw·nikh
honeymoon *Flitterwochen* ① pl fli·ter·vo·khen

horoscope *Horoskop* ⓝ ho·ros·kawp
horse *Pferd* ⓝ pfert
horse riding *Reiten* ⓝ rai·ten
horseradish *Meerrettich* ⓜ mair·re·tikh
hospital *Krankenhaus* ⓝ krang·ken·hows
hospitality *Gastfreundschaft* ① gast·froynt·shaft
hot *heiß* hais
hot water *warmes Wasser* ⓝ var·mes va·ser
hotel *Hotel* ⓝ ho·tel
house *Haus* ⓝ hows
housework *Hausarbeit* ① hows·ar·bait
how *wie* vee
hug *umarmen* um·ar·men
huge *riesig* ree·zikh
human *menschlich* mensh·likh
human rights *Menschenrechte* ⓝ pl men·shen·rekh·te
humanities *Geisteswissenschaften* ① pl gais·tes·vi·sen·shaf·ten
hundred *hundert* hun·dert
hungry *hungrig* hung·rikh
hunting *Jagd* ① yahkt
in a hurry *in Eile* in ai·le
hurt *verletzen* fer·le·tsen
hurt (yourself) *sich weh tun* zikh vay toon
husband *Ehemann* ⓜ ay·e·man
hut *Hütte* ① hü·te

I

I *ich* ikh
ice *Eis* ⓝ ais
ice axe *Eispickel* ⓜ ais·pi·kel
ice cream *Eiscreme* ① ais·kraym
ice cream parlour *Eisdiele* ① ais·dee·le
ice hockey *Eishockey* ⓝ ais·ho·ki
ice skating *Eislaufen* ⓝ ais·low·fen
idea *Idee* ① i·day
identification *Ausweis* ⓜ ows·vais
identification card *Personalausweis* ⓜ per·zo·nahl·ows·vais
idiot *Idiot* ⓜ i·di·awt
if *wenn* ven
ignition *Zündung* ① tsün·dung

ill *krank* krangk
illegal *illegal* i·le·gahl
imagination *Phantasie* ⓕ fan·ta·zee
immediately *sofort* zo·fort
immigration *Immigration* ⓕ
  i·mi·gra·tsyawn
important *wichtig* vikh·tikh
impossible *unmöglich* un·merk·likh
in *in* in
in front of *vor* fawr
included *inbegriffen* in·be·gri·fen
income tax *Einkommensteuer* ⓕ
  ain·ko·men·shtoy·er
India *Indien* ⓝ in·di·en
indicator *Blinker* ⓜ bling·ker
indigestion *Magenverstimmung* ⓕ
  mah·gen·fer·shti·mung
industry *Industrie* ⓕ in·dus·tree
inequality *Ungleichheit* ⓕ
  un·glaikh·hait
infection *Entzündung* ⓕ en·tsün·dung
inflammation *Entzündung* ⓕ
  en·tsün·dung
influenza *Grippe* ⓕ gri·pe
information *Auskunft* ⓕ ows·kunft
ingredient *Zutat* ⓕ tsoo·taht
inject *injizieren* in·yi·tsee·ren
injection (car) *Einspritzung* ⓕ
  ain·shpri·tsung
injection (medical) *Injektion* ⓕ
  in·yek·tsyawn
injury *Verletzung* ⓕ fer·le·tsung
in-line skating *Rollschuhfahren* ⓝ
  rol·shoo·fah·ren
innocent *unschuldig* un·shul·dikh
insect repellent *Insektenschutzmittel* ⓝ
  in·zek·ten·shuts·mi·tel
inside *innen* i·nen
instead of *(an)statt* (an·)shtat
instructor *Lehrer(in)* ⓜ/ⓕ
  lair·rer/lair·re·rin
insurance *Versicherung* ⓕ
  fer·zi·khe·rung
interesting *interessant* in·tre·sant
intermission *Pause* ⓕ pow·ze
international *international*
  in·ter·na·tsyo·nahl
Internet *Internet* ⓝ in·ter·net

Internet cafe *Internetcafé* ⓝ
  in·ter·net·ka·fay
interpreter *Dolmetscher(in)* ⓜ/ⓕ
  dol·met·sher/dol·met·she·rin
interview *Interview* ⓝ in·ter·vyoo
invite *einladen* ain·lah·den
Ireland *Irland* ⓝ ir·lant
iron (clothes) *bügeln* bü·geln
island *Insel* ⓕ in·zel
IT *Informationstechnologie* ⓕ
  in·for·ma·tsyawns·tekh·no·lo·gee
itch *Juckreiz* ⓜ yuk·raits
itemised *einzeln aufgeführt*
  ain·tseln owf·ge·fürt
itinerary *Reiseroute* ⓕ rai·ze·roo·te
IUD *Intrauterinpessar* ⓝ
  in·tra·u·te·reen·pe·sahr

J

jacket *Jacke* ⓕ ya·ke
jail *Gefängnis* ⓝ ge·feng·nis
jam *Marmelade* ⓕ mar·me·lah·de
Japan *Japan* ⓝ yah·pahn
jar *Glas* ⓝ glahs
jaw *Kiefer* ⓜ kee·fer
jealous *eifersüchtig* ai·fer·zükh·tikh
jeans *Jeans* ⓕ pl dzheens
jeep *Jeep* ⓜ dzheep
jet lag *Jetlag* ⓜ dzhet·leg
jewellery *Schmuck* ⓜ shmuk
Jewish *jüdisch* yü·dish
job *Arbeitsstelle* ⓕ ar·baits·shte·le
jockey *Jockey* ⓜ dzho·ki
jogging *Joggen* ⓝ dzho·gen
joke *Witz* ⓜ vits
journalist *Journalist(in)* ⓜ/ⓕ
  zhur·na·list/zhur·na·lis·tin
journey *Reise* ⓕ rai·ze
judge *Richter(in)* ⓜ/ⓕ rikh·ter/
  rikh·te·rin
juice *Saft* ⓜ zaft
jump *springen* shpring·en
jumper (sweater) *Pullover* ⓜ
  pu·law·ver
jumper leads *Überbrückungskabel* ⓝ
  ü·ber·brü·kungks·kah·bel
justice *Gerechtigkeit* ⓕ
  ge·rekh·tikh·kait

K

ketchup *Ketchup* ⓜ *ket*·chap
kettle *Kessel* ⓜ *ke*·sel
key *Schlüssel* ⓜ *shlü*·sel
keyboard *Tastatur* ⓕ tas·ta·*toor*
kick *treten* tray·ten
kill *töten* ter·ten
kilogram *Kilogramm* ⓝ *kee*·lo·gram
kilometre *Kilometer* ⓝ ki·lo·*may*·ter
kind *nett* net
kindergarten *Kindergarten* ⓜ
  kin·der·gar·ten
king *König* ⓜ *ker*·nikh
kiss *Kuss* ⓜ kus
kiss *küssen* kü·sen
kitchen *Küche* ⓕ *kü*·khe
kitten *Kätzchen* ⓝ *kets*·khen
kiwifruit *Kiwifrucht* ⓕ *kee*·vi·frukht
knapsack *Rucksack* ⓜ *ruk*·zak
knee *Knie* ⓝ knee
knife *Messer* ⓝ *me*·ser
know (a person) *kennen* ke·nen
know (something) *wissen* vi·sen
kosher *koscher* kaw·sher

L

labourer *Arbeiter(in)* ⓜ/ⓕ
  ar·bai·ter/ar·bai·te·rin
lace *Spitze* ⓕ *shpi*·tse
lager *Lager* ⓝ *lah*·ger
lake *See* ⓜ zay
lamb *Lamm* ⓝ lam
land *Land* ⓝ lant
landlady *Vermieterin* ⓕ fer·*mee*·te·rin
landlord *Vermieter* ⓜ fer·*mee*·ter
language *Sprache* ⓕ *shprah*·khe
laptop *Laptop* ⓜ *lep*·top
lard *Schmalz* ⓝ shmalts
large *groß* graws
last (week) *letzte (Woche)*
  lets·te (vo·khe)
late *spät* shpayt
laugh *lachen* la·khen
laundrette *Wäscherei* ⓕ ve·she·*rai*
laundry (room) *Waschküche* ⓕ
  vash·kü·khe

law (subject) *Jura* ⓝ *yoo*·ra
law (rules) *Gesetz* ⓝ ge·*zets*
lawyer *Rechtsanwalt/*
  Rechtsanwältin ⓜ/ⓕ
  rekhts·an·valt/*rekhts*·an·vel·tin
laxatives *Abführmittel* ⓝ *ap*·für·mi·tel
lazy *faul* fowl
leader *Anführer* ⓜ *an*·fü·rer
leaf *Blatt* ⓝ blat
learn *lernen* *ler*·nen
lease *Mietvertrag* ⓜ *meet*·fer·trahk
leather *Leder* ⓝ *lay*·der
leave (depart) *abfahren* *ap*·fah·ren
lecturer *Dozent(in)* ⓜ/ⓕ
  do·*tsent*/do·*tsen*·tin
leek *Lauch* ⓜ lowkh
left (direction) *links* lingks
left luggage *Gepäckaufbewahrung* ⓕ
  ge·*pek*·owf·be·vah·rung
left-wing *links(gerichtet)*
  lingks(·ge·rikh·tet)
leg (body) *Bein* ⓝ bain
legal *legal* le·*gahl*
legislation *Gesetzgebung* ⓕ
  ge·*zets*·gay·bung
legume *Hülsenfrucht* ⓕ *hül*·zen·frukht
lemon *Zitrone* ⓕ tsi·*traw*·ne
lemonade *Limonade* ⓕ li·mo·*nah*·de
lens (camera) *Objektiv* ⓝ op·yek·*teef*
Lent *Fastenzeit* ⓕ *fas*·ten·tsait
lentil *Linse* ⓕ *lin*·ze
lesbian *Lesbierin* ⓕ *les*·bi·e·rin
less *weniger* *vay*·ni·ger
letter *Brief* ⓜ breef
lettuce *Kopfsalat* ⓜ *kopf*·za·laht
liar *Lügner(in)* ⓜ/ⓕ *lüg*·ner/*lüg*·ne·rin
library *Bibliothek* ⓕ bi·bli·o·*tayk*
lice *Läuse* ⓕ pl *loy*·ze
license plate number *Auto-*
  kennzeichen ⓝ *ow*·to·ken·tsai·khen
lie (not stand) *liegen* lee·gen
life *Leben* ⓝ *lay*·ben
lifejacket *Schwimmweste* ⓕ
  shvim·ves·te
lift (elevator) *Lift* ⓜ lift
light *Licht* ⓝ likht
light *hell* hel
light bulb *Glühbirne* ⓕ *glü*·bir·ne
light meter *Belichtungsmesser* ⓜ
  be·*likh*·tungks·me·ser

lighter (cigarette) *Feuerzeug* ⓝ
  foy·er·tsoyk
lightning *Blitz* ⓜ blits
lights (on car) *Scheinwerfer* ⓜ pl
  shain·ver·fer
like *mögen* mer·gen
lime *Limone* ⓕ li·maw·ne
line *Linie* ⓕ lee·ni·e
linen (bed) *Bettwäsche* ⓕ bet·ve·she
linen (fabric) *Leinen* ⓝ lai·nen
lip balm *Lippenbalsam* ⓜ
  li·pen·bal·zahm
lips *Lippen* ⓕ pl li·pen
lipstick *Lippenstift* ⓜ li·pen·shtift
liquor store *Getränkehandel* ⓜ
  ge·treng·ke·han·del
listen *hören* her·ren
little *klein* klain
little (not much) *wenig* vay·nikh
a little *ein bisschen* ain bis·khen
live *leben* lay·ben
live (reside) *wohnen* vaw·nen
liver *Leber* ⓕ lay·ber
lizard *Echse* ⓕ ek·se
local *örtlich* ert·likh
lock *Schloss* ⓝ shlos
locked *abgeschlossen* ap·ge·shlo·sen
lollies *Süßigkeiten* ⓕ pl zü·sikh·kai·ten
lonely *einsam* ain·zahm
long *lang* lang
long-sleeved *langärmelig*
  lang·er·me·likh
look (an)sehen (an·)zay·en
look after *sich kümmern um* zikh
  kü·mern um
look for *suchen nach* zoo·khen nahkh
lookout *Aussichtspunkt* ⓜ
  ows·zikhts·pungkt
loose change *Kleingeld* ⓝ klain·gelt
lose *verlieren* fer·lee·ren
lost *verloren* fer·law·ren
lost property office *Fundbüro* ⓝ
  funt·bü·raw
a lot (of) *viel* feel
loud *laut* lowt
love *lieben* lee·ben
lover *Liebhaber(in)* ⓜ/ⓕ
  leep·hah·ber/leep·hah·be·rin
low *niedrig* nee·drikh
lubricant *Schmiermittel* ⓝ
  shmeer·mi·tel

luck *Glück* ⓝ glük
lucky *glücklich* glük·likh
luggage *Gepäck* ⓝ ge·pek
luggage lockers *Schließfächer* ⓝ pl
  shlees·fe·kher
luggage tag *Adressanhänger* ⓜ
  a·dres·an·heng·er
lump (health) *Knoten* ⓜ knaw·ten
lunch *Mittagessen* ⓝ mi·tahk·e·sen
lungs *Lungen* ⓕ pl lung·en
luxury *luxuriös* luk·su·ri·ers

M

machine *Maschine* ⓕ ma·shee·ne
made of (cotton) *aus (Baumwolle)*
  ows (bowm·vo·le)
magazine *Zeitschrift* ⓕ tsait·shrift
magician *Zauberer(in)* ⓜ/ⓕ
  tsow·be·rer/tsow·be·re·rin
mail *Post* ⓕ post
mailbox *Briefkasten* ⓜ breef·kas·ten
main *Haupt-* howpt·
main square *Hauptplatz* ⓜ howpt·plats
make *machen* ma·khen
make-up *Schminke* ⓕ shming·ke
mammogram *Mammogramm* ⓝ
  ma·mo·gram
man *Mann* ⓜ man
man (human being) *Mensch* ⓜ mensh
manager *Manager(in)* ⓜ/ⓕ
  me·ne·dzher/me·ne·dzhe·rin
mandarin *Mandarine* ⓕ man·da·ree·ne
mango *Mango* ⓜ mang·go
manual worker *Arbeiter(in)* ⓜ/ⓕ
  ar·bai·ter/ar·bai·te·rin
many *viele* fee·le
map *Karte* ⓕ kar·te
margarine *Margarine* ⓕ mar·ga·ree·ne
marijuana *Marihuana* ⓕ ma·ri·hu·ah·na
marital status *Familienstand* ⓜ
  fa·mee·li·en·shtant
market *Markt* ⓜ markt
market square *Marktplatz* ⓜ
  markt·plats
marmalade *Orangenmarmelade* ⓕ
  o·rahng·zhen·mar·me·lah·de
marriage *Ehe* ⓕ ay·e
marry *heiraten* hai·rah·ten

martial arts *Kampfsport* ⓜ
  kampf-shport
mass (Catholic) *Messe* ⓕ *me*-se
massage *Massage* ⓕ ma-*sah*-zhe
masseur *Masseur* ⓜ ma-*ser*
masseuse *Masseurin* ⓕ ma-*ser*-rin
mat *Matte* ⓕ *ma*-te
match (sport) *Spiel* ⓜ shpeel
matches *Streichhölzer* ⓝ pl
  shtraikh-herl-tser
material *Material* ⓝ ma-te-ri-*ahl*
mattress *Matratze* ⓕ ma-*tra*-tse
maybe *vielleicht* fi-*laikht*
mayonnaise *Majonnaise* ⓕ
  ma-yo-*nay*-ze
mayor *Bürgermeister(in)* ⓜ/ⓕ
  bür-ger-mais-ter/*bür*-ger-mais-te-rin
measles *Masern* pl *mah*-zern
meat *Fleisch* ⓝ flaish
mechanic *Mechaniker(in)* ⓜ/ⓕ
  me-*khah*-ni-ker/me-*khah*-ni-ke-rin
media *Medien* pl *may*-di-en
medicine *Medizin* ⓕ me-di-*tseen*
meditation *Meditation* ⓕ
  me-di-ta-*tsyawn*
meet *treffen* *tre*-fen
melon *Melone* ⓕ me-*law*-ne
member *Mitglied* ⓝ *mit*-gleet
member of parliament *Abgeordnete* ⓜ&ⓕ *ap*-ge-ord-ne-te
menstruation *Menstruation* ⓕ
  mens-tru-a-*tsyawn*
menu *Speisekarte* ⓕ *shpai*-ze-kar-te
message *Mitteilung* ⓕ *mi*-tai-lung
metal *Metall* ⓝ me-*tal*
metre *Meter* ⓜ *may*-ter
metro station *U-Bahnhof* ⓜ
  oo-bahn-hawf
microwave *Mikrowelle* ⓕ *mee*-kro-ve-le
Middle East *Nahe Osten* ⓜ *nah*-e os-ten
midnight *Mitternacht* ⓕ *mi*-ter-nakht
migraine *Migräne* ⓕ mi-*gray*-ne
military *Militär* ⓝ mi-li-*tair*
military service *Wehrdienst* ⓜ
  vair-deenst
milk *Milch* ⓕ milkh
millimetre *Millimeter* ⓜ mi-li-*may*-ter
million *Million* ⓕ mi-*lyawn*
mince *Gehacktes* ⓝ ge-*hak*-tes

mind (look after) *aufpassen* *owf*-pa-sen
mineral water *Mineralwasser* ⓝ
  mi-ne-*rahl*-va-ser
mints *Pfefferminzbonbons* ⓝ pl
  pfe-fer-*mints*-bong-bongs
minute *Minute* ⓕ mi-*noo*-te
mirror *Spiegel* ⓜ *shpee*-gel
miscarriage *Fehlgeburt* ⓕ *fayl*-ge-burt
miss (feel absence of) *vermissen*
  fer-*mi*-sen
miss (the bus) *verpassen* fer-*pa*-sen
mistake *Fehler* ⓜ *fay*-ler
mix *mischen* *mi*-shen
mobile phone *Handy* ⓝ *hen*-di
modem *Modem* ⓝ *maw*-dem
moisturiser *Feuchtigkeitscreme* ⓕ
  foykh-tikh-kaits-kraym
monastery *Kloster* ⓝ *klaws*-ter
Monday *Montag* ⓜ *mawn*-tahk
money *Geld* ⓝ gelt
month *Monat* ⓜ *maw*-nat
monument *Denkmal* ⓝ *dengk*-mahl
(full) moon *(Voll) Mond* ⓜ
  *(fol-)*mawnt
more *mehr* mair
morning (6am–10am) *Morgen* ⓜ
  mor-gen
morning (10am–12pm) *Vormittag* ⓜ
  fawr-mi-tahk
morning sickness
  (Schwangerschafts-)Erbrechen ⓝ
  (shvang-er-shafts-)er-bre-khen
mosque *Moschee* ⓕ mo-*shay*
mosquito *Stechmücke* ⓕ *shtekh*-mü-ke
mosquito coil *Moskitospirale* ⓕ
  mos-*kee*-to-shpi-rah-le
mother *Mutter* ⓕ *mu*-ter
mother-in-law *Schwiegermutter* ⓕ
  shvee-ger-mu-ter
motorboat *Motorboot* ⓝ
  maw-tor-bawt
motorcycle *Motorrad* ⓝ *maw*-tor-raht
motorway (tollway) *Autobahn* ⓕ
  ow-to-bahn
mountain *Berg* ⓜ berk
mountain bike *Mountainbike* ⓝ
  mown-ten-baik
mountain hut *Berghütte* ⓕ *berk*-hü-te

mountain path *Bergweg* ⓜ *berk·vayk*
mountain range *Gebirgszug* ⓜ
  ge·birks·tsook
mountaineering *Bergsteigen* ⓝ
  berk·shtai·gen
mouse *Maus* ⓕ mows
mouth *Mund* ⓜ munt
movie *Film* ⓜ film
mud *Schlamm* ⓜ shlam
muesli *Müsli* ⓝ *müs·li*
muggy *schwül* shvül
mum *Mama* ⓕ *ma·ma*
muscle *Muskel* ⓜ *mus·kel*
museum *Museum* ⓝ mu·zay·um
mushroom *Pilz* ⓜ pilts
music *Musik* ⓕ mu·zeek
musician *Musiker(in)* ⓜ/ⓕ
  moo·zi·ker/moo·zi·ke·rin
Muslim *Moslem/Moslime* ⓜ/ⓕ
  mos·lem/mos·lee·me
mussel *Muschel* ⓕ *mu·shel*
mustard *Senf* ⓜ zenf
mute *stumm* shtum
my *mein/meine/mein* ⓜ/ⓕ/ⓝ
  main/mai·ne/main

N

nail clippers *Nagelknipser* ⓜ pl
  nah·gel·knip·ser
name *Name* ⓜ *nah·me*
napkin *Serviette* ⓕ *zer·vye·te*
nappy *Windel* ⓕ *vin·del*
nappy rash *Windeldermatitis* ⓕ
  vin·del·der·ma·tee·tis
national park *Nationalpark* ⓜ
  na·tsyo·nahl·park
nationality *Staatsangehörigkeit* ⓕ
  shtahts·an·ge·her·rikh·kait
nature *Natur* ⓕ *na·toor*
nature reserve *Naturreservat* ⓝ
  na·toor·re·zer·vaht
naturopathy *Naturheilkunde* ⓕ
  na·toor·hail·kun·de
nausea *Übelkeit* ⓕ *ü·bel·kait*
near *nah* *nah·e*
nearby *in der Nähe* in dair *nay·e*
nearest *nächste* naykhs·te
necessary *notwendig* nawt·ven·dikh

necklace *Halskette* ⓕ *hals·ke·te*
need *brauchen* brow·khen
needle (sewing) *Nadel* ⓕ *nah·del*
needle (syringe) *Nadel* ⓕ *nah·del*
neither *auch nicht* owkh nikht
nephew *Neffe* ⓜ *ne·fe*
net *Netz* ⓝ nets
Netherlands *Niederlande* pl
  nee·der·lan·de
never *nie* nee
new *neu* noy
New Year's Day *Neujahrstag* ⓜ
  noy·yahrs·tahk
New Year's Eve *Silvester* ⓜ *zil·ves·ter*
New Zealand *Neuseeland* ⓝ
  noy·zay·lant
news *Nachrichten* ⓕ pl nahkh·rikh·ten
newsagency *Zeitungshändler* ⓜ
  tsai·tungks·hen·dler
newspaper *Zeitung* ⓕ *tsai·tung*
newsstand *Zeitungskiosk* ⓜ
  tsai·tungks·kee·osk
next *nächste* naykhs·te
next to *neben* nay·ben
nice *nett* net
nickname *Spitzname* ⓜ shpits·nah·me
niece *Nichte* ⓕ nikh·te
night *Nacht* ⓕ nakht
no *nein* nain
noisy *laut* lowt
none *keine* kai·ne
non-smoking *Nichtraucher-*
  nikht·row·kher·
noodles *Nudeln* ⓕ pl noo·deln
noon *Mittag* ⓜ *mi·tahk*
north *Norden* ⓜ *nor·den*
nose *Nase* ⓕ *nah·ze*
not *nicht* nikht
notebook *Notizbuch* ⓝ no·teets·bookh
nothing *nichts* nikhts
now *jetzt* yetst
nuclear energy *Atomenergie* ⓕ
  a·tawm·e·ner·gee
nuclear testing *Atomtest* ⓜ
  a·tawm·test
nuclear waste *Atommüll* ⓜ
  a·tawm·mül
number (numeral) *Zahl* ⓕ tsahl
number (telephone) *Nummer* ⓕ nu·mer

nun *Nonne* ⓕ *no·ne*
nurse *Krankenpfleger/*
Krankenschwester ⓜ/ⓕ
krang·ken·pflay·ger/
krang·ken·shves·ter
nut *Nuss* ⓕ *nus*

O

oats *Hafer(flocken)* ⓜ pl
hah·fer(·flo·ken)
obvious *offensichtlich* o·fen·zikht·likh
occupation *Beruf* ⓜ be·roof
ocean *Ozean* ⓜ aw·tse·ahn
off (food) *schlecht* shlekht
office *Büro* ⓝ bü·raw
office worker *Büroangestellte* ⓜ&ⓕ
bü·raw·an·ge·shtel·te
offside *abseits* ap·zaits
often *oft* oft
oil *Öl* ⓝ erl
OK *okay* o·kay
old *alt* alt
olive *Olive* ⓕ o·lee·ve
olive oil *Olivenöl* ⓝ o·lee·ven·erl
Olympic Games *Olympische*
Spiele pl o·lüm·pi·she shpee·le
on *auf* owf
once *einmal* ain·mahl
one *ein(s)* ain(s)
onion *Zwiebel* ⓕ tsvee·bel
only *nur* noor
open *offen* o·fen
open (unlock) *öffnen* erf·nen
opening hours *Öffnungszeiten* ⓕ pl
erf·nungks·tsai·ten
opera *Oper* ⓕ aw·per
opera house *Opernhaus* ⓝ
aw·pern·hows
operation *Operation* ⓕ o·pe·ra·tsyawn
operator *Vermittlung* ⓕ fer·mit·lung
opinion *Meinung* ⓕ mai·nung
opposite *gegenüber* gay·gen·ü·ber
optician *Optiker(in)* ⓜ/ⓕ
op·ti·ker/op·ti·ke·rin
or *oder* aw·der
orange (fruit) *Orange* ⓕ o·rahng·zhe
orange (colour) *orange* o·rahngzh
orange juice *Orangensaft* ⓜ
o·rahng·zhen·zaft

orchestra *Orchester* ⓝ or·kes·ter
order (restaurant) *Bestellung* ⓕ
be·shte·lung
order *bestellen* be·shte·len
ordinary *normal* nor·mahl
organ (church) *Orgel* ⓕ or·gel
organise *organisieren* or·ga·ni·zee·ren
orgasm *Orgasmus* ⓜ or·gas·mus
original (not copied) *Original-*
o·ri·gi·nahl-
other *andere* an·de·re
our *unser* un·zer
out *aus* ows
outside *draußen* drow·sen
ovarian cyst *Eierstockzyste* ⓕ
ai·er·shtok·tsüs·te
oven *Ofen* ⓜ aw·fen
over *über* ü·ber
overcoat *Mantel* ⓜ man·tel
overdose *Überdosis* ⓕ ü·ber·daw·zis
overnight *über Nacht* ü·ber nakht
owe *schulden* shul·den
owner *Besitzer(in)* ⓜ/ⓕ
be·zi·tser/be·zi·tse·rin
oxygen *Sauerstoff* ⓜ zow·er·shtof
oyster *Auster* ⓕ ows·ter
ozone layer *Ozonschicht* ⓕ
o·tsawn·shikht

P

pacemaker (heart) *Herzschrittmacher* ⓜ
herts·shrit·ma·kher
pacifier (dummy) *Schnuller* ⓜ shnu·ler
package *Paket* ⓝ pa·kayt
packet (general) *Packung* ⓕ pa·kung
padlock *Vorhängeschloss* ⓝ
fawr·heng·e·shlos
page *Seite* ⓕ zai·te
pain *Schmerz* ⓜ shmerts
painful *schmerzhaft* shmerts·haft
painkillers *Schmerzmittel* ⓝ
shmerts·mi·tel
painter *Maler(in)* ⓜ/ⓕ
mah·ler/mah·le·rin
painting (the art) *Malerei* ⓕ mah·le·rai
paints *Farben* ⓕ pl far·ben
pair (couple) *Paar* ⓝ pahr
palace *Schloss* ⓝ shlos
pan *Pfanne* ⓕ pfa·ne

pants (trousers) *Hose* ⓕ haw·ze
panty liner *Slipeinlage* ⓕ
slip·ain·lah·ge
pantyhose *Strumpfhose* ⓕ
shtrumpf·haw·ze
pap smear *Abstrich* ⓜ ap·shtrikh
paper *Papier* ⓝ pa·peer
paperback *Taschenbuch* ⓝ
ta·shen·bookh
paperwork *Schreibarbeit* ⓕ
shraip·ar·bait
parachuting *Fallschirmspringen* ⓝ
fal·shirm·shpring·en
paragliding *Gleitschirmfliegen* ⓝ
glait·shirm·flee·gen
paraplegic *Querschnittsgelähmte* ⓜ&ⓕ
kvair·shnits·ge·laym·te
parcel *Paket* ⓝ pa·kayt
parents *Eltern* ⓝ pl el·tern
park *Park* ⓜ park
park (car) *Parkplatz* ⓜ park·plats
parliament *Parlament* ⓝ par·la·ment
parrot *Papagei* ⓜ pa·pa·gai
parsley *Petersilie* ⓕ pay·ter·zee·li·e
part *Teil* ⓝ tail
participate *sich beteiligen* zikh
be·tai·li·gen
part-time *Teilzeit-* ⓕ tail·tsait
party (fiesta/ball) *Fest* ⓝ fest
party (politics) *Partei* ⓕ par·tai
pass *Pass* ⓜ pas
passenger (bus/taxi) *Fahrgast* ⓜ
fahr·gast
passenger (plane) *Fluggast* ⓜ
flook·gast
passenger (train) *Reisende(r)* ⓜ/ⓕ
rai·zen·de
passport *(Reise)Pass* ⓜ (rai·ze·)pas
passport number *Passnummer* ⓕ
pas·nu·mer
past *Vergangenheit* ⓕ fer·gang·en·hait
pasta *Nudeln* ⓕ pl noo·deln
path *Pfad* ⓜ pfaht
patio *Terrasse* ⓕ ter·ra·se
pay *bezahlen* be·tsah·len
pay phone *Münztelefon* ⓝ
münts·te·le·fawn
payment *Zahlung* ⓕ tsah·lung
pea *Erbse* ⓕ erp·se

peace *Frieden* ⓜ free·den
peach *Pfirsich* ⓜ pfir·zikh
peak *Gipfel* ⓜ gip·fel
peanuts *Erdnüsse* ⓕ pl ert·nü·se
pear *Birne* ⓕ bir·ne
pedal *Pedal* ⓝ pe·dahl
pedestrian *Fußgänger(in)* ⓜ/ⓕ
foos·geng·er/foos·geng·e·rin
pen (ballpoint) *Kugelschreiber* ⓜ
koo·gel·shrai·ber
pencil *Bleistift* ⓜ blai·shtift
penis *Penis* ⓜ pay·nis
penknife *Taschenmesser* ⓝ
ta·shen·me·ser
pensioner *Rentner(in)* ⓜ/ⓕ
rent·ner/rent·ne·rin
people *Menschen* ⓝ pl men·shen
pepper *Pfeffer* ⓜ pfe·fer
pepper (bell) *Paprika* ⓕ pap·ri·kah
per *pro* praw
percent *Prozent* ⓝ pro·tsent
performance *Aufführung* ⓕ
owf·fü·rung
perfume *Parfüm* ⓝ par·füm
period pain
Menstruationsbeschwerden ⓕ pl
mens·tru·a·tsyawns·be·shver·den
permission *Erlaubnis* ⓕ er·lowp·nis
permit *Genehmigung* ⓕ
ge·nay·mi·gung
person *Person* ⓕ per·zawn
personal *persönlich* per·zern·likh
petition *Petition* ⓕ pe·ti·tsyawn
petrol *Benzin* ⓝ ben·tseen
petrol can *Benzinkanister* ⓜ
ben·tseen·ka·nis·ter
pharmacy *Apotheke* ⓕ a·po·tay·ke
phone book *Telefonbuch* ⓝ
te·le·fawn·bookh
phone box *Telefonzelle* ⓕ
te·le·fawn·tse·le
phonecard *Telefonkarte* ⓕ
te·le·fawn·kar·te
photo *Foto* ⓝ faw·to
photograph *Fotografie* ⓕ fo·to·gra·fee
photograph *fotografieren*
fo·to·gra·fee·ren
photographer *Fotograf(in)* ⓜ/ⓕ
fo·to·grahf/fo·to·grah·fin

photography *Fotografie* ①
   fo·to·gra·fee
phrasebook *Sprachführer* ⑩
   shprahkh·fü·rer
physics *Physik* ① fü·zeek
piano *Klavier* ⑩ kla·veer
pick *pflücken* pflü·ken
pick up *aufheben* owf·hay·ben
pickaxe *Spitzhacke* ① shpits·ha·ke
picnic *Picknick* ⑩ pik·nik
pie *Pastete* ① pas·tay·te
piece *Stück* ⑩ shtük
pig *Schwein* ⑩ shvain
pilgrimage *Pilgerfahrt* ① pil·ger·fahrt
pill *Pille* ① pi·le
the Pill *die Pille* ① dee pi·le
pillow *Kissen* ⑩ ki·sen
pillowcase *Kissenbezug* ⑩
   ki·sen·be·tsook
pineapple *Ananas* ① a·na·nas
pink *rosa* raw·za
pipe *Pfeife* ① pfai·fe
pistachio *Pistazie* ① pis·tah·tsi·e
place *Platz* ⑩ plats
place of birth *Geburtsort* ⑩
   ge·burts·ort
plain *Ebene* ① ay·be·ne
plane *Flugzeug* ⑩ flook·tsoyk
planet *Planet* ⑩ pla·nayt
plant *Pflanze* ① pflan·tse
plastic *Plastik* ⑩ plas·tik
plate *Teller* ⑩ te·ler
plateau *Hochebene* ① hawkh·ay·be·ne
platform *Bahnsteig* ⑩ bahn·shtaik
play (theatre) *Schauspiel* ⑩
   show·shpeel
play (game) *spielen* shpee·len
play (instrument) *spielen* shpee·len
please *bitte* bi·te
plenty *viel* feel
plug (bath) *Stöpsel* ⑩ shterp·sel
plug (electricity) *Stecker* ⑩ shte·ker
plum *Pflaume* ① pflow·me
plumber *Installateur(in)* ⑩/①
   in·sta·la·ter/in·sta·la·ter(·rin)
pocket *Tasche* ① ta·she
poetry *Dichtung* ① dikh·tung
point *Punkt* ⑩ pungkt
point *zeigen* tsai·gen

poisonous *giftig* gif·tikh
poker (game) *Poker* ⑩ paw·ker
police *Polizei* ① po·li·tsai
police station *Polizeirevier* ⑩
   po·li·tsai·re·veer
policy *Politik* ① po·li·teek
politician *Politiker(in)* ⑩/①
   po·lee·ti·ker/po·lee·ti·ke·rin
politics *Politik* ① po·li·teek
pollen *Pollen* ⑩ po·len
polls *Umfrage* ① um·frah·ge
pollution *Umweltverschmutzung* ①
   um·velt·fer·shmu·tsung
pony *Pony* ⑩ po·ni
pool (game) *Billard* ⑩ bil·yart
pool (swimming, indoors) *Hallenbad* ⑩
   ha·len·baht
pool (swimming, outdoors) *Freibad* ⑩
   frai·baht
poor *arm* arm
popular *beliebt* be·leept
pork *Schweinefleisch* ⑩ shvai·ne·flaish
port *Hafen* ⑩ hah·fen
possible *möglich* merk·likh
post office *Postamt* ⑩ post·amt
postage *Porto* ⑩ por·to
postcard *Postkarte* ① post·kar·te
postcode *Postleitzahl* ① post·lai·tsahl
poste restante *postlagernd*
   post·lah·gernt
poster *Plakat* ⑩ pla·kaht
pot (ceramics) *Topf* ⑩ topf
pot (dope) *Gras* ⑩ grahs
potato *Kartoffel* ① kar·to·fel
pottery *Töpferwaren* ① pl
   terp·fer·vah·ren
pound (money & weight) *Pfund* ⑩
   pfunt
poverty *Armut* ① ar·moot
power *Kraft* ① kraft
practical *praktisch* prak·tish
prawn *Garnele* ① gar·nay·le
prayer *Gebet* ⑩ ge·bayt
prefer *vorziehen* fawr·tsee·en
pregnancy test kit
   Schwangerschaftstest ⑩
   shvang·er·shafts·test
pregnant *schwanger* shvang·er
premenstrual tension
   prämenstruelle Störung ①
   pray·mens·tru·e·le shter·rung

prepare *vorbereiten* fawr·be·rai·ten
present (gift) *Geschenk* ⓝ ge·shengk
present (time) *Gegenwart* ①
  gay·gen·vart
president *Präsident(in)* ⓜ/①
  pre·zi·dent/pre·zi·den·tin
pressure *Druck* ⓜ druk
pretty *hübsch* hüpsh
prevent *verhindern* fer·hin·dern
price *Preis* ⓜ prais
priest *Priester* ⓜ prees·ter
prime minister
  Premierminister(in) ⓜ/①
  prem·yay·mi·nis·ter/
  prem·yay·mi·nis·te·rin
prime minister (in Germany &
  Austria) *Bundeskanzler(in)* ⓜ/①
  bun·des·kants·ler/bun·des·kants·le·rin
print (artwork) *Druck* ⓜ druk
print (photography) *Abzug* ⓜ ap·tsook
prison *Gefängnis* ⓝ ge·feng·nis
prisoner *Gefangene* ⓜ&① ge·fang·e·ne
private *privat* pri·vaht
produce *produzieren* pro·du·tsee·ren
profession *Beruf* ⓜ be·roof
profit *Gewinn* ⓜ ge·vin
program *Programm* ⓝ pro·gram
projector *Projektor* ⓜ pro·yek·tor
promise *versprechen* fer·shpre·khen
proposal *Vorschlag* ⓜ fawr·shlahk
prostitute *Prostituierte* ①
  pros·ti·tu·eer·te
protect *beschützen* be·shü·tsen
protected *geschützte* ge·shüts·te
protest *Protest* ⓜ pro·test
protest *protestieren* pro·tes·tee·ren
provisions *Verpflegung* ①
  fer·pflay·gung
prune *Backpflaume* ① bak·pflow·me
psychology *Psychologie* ①
  psü·kho·lo·gee
pub *Kneipe* ① knai·pe
public telephone *öffentliches Telefon* ⓝ
  er·fent·li·khes te·le·fawn
public toilet *öffentliche Toilette* ①
  er·fent·li·khe to·a·le·te
pull *ziehen* tsee·en
pump (Luft)Pumpe ① (luft·)pum·pe
pumpkin *Kürbis* ⓜ kür·bis
puncture *Reifenpanne* ① rai·fen·pa·ne

punish *bestrafen* be·shtrah·fen
pure *rein* rain
purple *lila* lee·la
push *schieben* shee·ben
put (horizontal) *legen* lay·gen
put (vertical) *stellen* shte·len

Q

qualifications *Qualifikationen* ① pl
  kva·li·fi·ka·tsyaw·nen
quality *Qualität* ① kva·li·tayt
quarantine *Quarantäne* ①
  ka·ran·tay·ne
quarrel *Streit* ⓜ shtrait
quarter *Viertel* ⓝ feer·tel
queen *Königin* ① ker·ni·gin
question *Frage* ① frah·ge
queue *Schlange* ① shlang·e
quick *schnell* shnel
quiet *ruhig* roo·ikh
quit (job) *kündigen* kün·di·gen

R

rabbit *Kaninchen* ⓝ ka·neen·khen
race (sport) *Rennen* ⓝ re·nen
racetrack *Rennbahn* ① ren·bahn
racing bike *Rennrad* ⓝ ren·raht
racism *Rassismus* ⓜ ra·sis·mus
racquet *Schläger* ⓜ shlay·ger
radiator *Kühler* ⓜ kü·ler
radio *Radio* ⓝ rah·di·o
radish *Rettich* ⓜ re·tikh
railway station *Bahnhof* ⓜ bahn·hawf
rain *Regen* ⓜ ray·gen
raincoat *Regenmantel* ⓜ
  ray·gen·man·tel
raisin *Rosine* ① ro·zee·ne
rally *Rallye* ① re·li
rape *vergewaltigen* fer·ge·val·ti·gen
rapids *Stromschnellen* ① pl
  shtrawm·shne·len
rare *selten* zel·ten
rash *Ausschlag* ⓜ ows·shlahk
raspberry *Himbeere* ① him·bair·re
rat *Ratte* ① ra·te
rate of pay *Lohn(satz)* ⓜ lawn(·zats)
raw *roh* raw

razor *Rasierer* ⓜ ra·zee·rer
razor blades *Rasierklingen* ⓕ pl ra·zeer·kling·en
read *lesen* lay·zen
reading *Lesung* ⓕ lay·zung
ready *fertig* fer·tikh
real estate agent *Makler(in)* ⓜ/ⓕ mahk·ler/mahk·le·rin
realistic *realistisch* re·a·lis·tish
reason *Grund* ⓜ grunt
receipt *Quittung* ⓕ kvi·tung
receive *erhalten* er·hal·ten
recently *vor kurzem* fawr kur·tsem
recharge *aufladen* owf·lah·den
recommend *empfehlen* emp·fay·len
recording *Aufnahme* ⓕ owf·nah·me
recyclable *wiederverwertbar* vee·der·fer·vert·bahr
recycle *recyceln* ri·sai·keln
red *rot* rawt
referee *Schiedsrichter(in)* ⓜ/ⓕ sheets·rikh·ter/sheets·rikh·te·rin
reference (work) *Zeugnis* ⓝ tsoyk·nis
referendum *Volksentscheid* ⓜ folks·ent·shait
refrigerator *Kühlschrank* ⓜ kül·shrangk
refugee *Flüchtling* ⓜ flükht·ling
refund *Rückzahlung* ⓕ rük·tsah·lung
refuse *ablehnen* ap·lay·nen
region *Region* ⓕ re·gyawn
registered mail *Einschreiben* ⓝ ain·shrai·ben
regulation *Vorschrift* ⓕ fawr·shrift
relation (family) *Verwandte* ⓜ&ⓕ fer·van·te
relationship *Beziehung* ⓕ be·tsee·ung
relax *sich entspannen* zikh ent·shpa·nen
relic (religious) *Reliquie* ⓕ re·lee·kvi·e
religion *Religion* ⓕ re·li·gyawn
religious *religiös* re·li·gyers
remote *abgelegen* ap·ge·lay·gen
remote control *Fernbedienung* ⓕ fern·be·dee·nung
rent *mieten* mee·ten
repair *reparieren* re·pa·ree·ren
repeat *wiederholen* vee·der·haw·len
republic *Republik* ⓕ re·pu·bleek
reservation *Reservierung* ⓕ re·zer·vee·rung

reserve *reservieren* re·zer·vee·ren
rest *eine Pause machen* ai·ne pow·ze ma·khen
restaurant *Restaurant* ⓝ res·to·rahng
resume (CV) *Lebenslauf* ⓜ lay·bens·lowf
retired *pensioniert* pahng·zyo·neert
return *zurückkommen* tsu·rük·ko·men
return (ticket) *Rückfahrkarte* ⓕ rük·fahr·kar·te
review (arts) *Kritik* ⓕ kri·teek
rhythm *Rhythmus* ⓜ rüt·mus
rice *Reis* ⓜ rais
rich (wealthy) *reich* raikh
ride *Ritt* ⓜ rit
ride (horse) *reiten* rai·ten
riding school *Reitschule* ⓕ rait·shoo·le
right (correct) *richtig* rikh·tikh
right (direction) *rechts* rekhts
right there *gleich dort* glaikh dort
right-wing *rechts(gerichtet)* rekhts(·ge·rikh·tet)
ring (on finger) *Ring* ⓜ ring
ring (of phone) *klingeln* kling·eln
rip-off *Abzockerei* ⓕ ap·tso·ke·rai
risk *Risiko* ⓝ ree·zi·ko
river *Fluss* ⓜ flus
road *Straße* ⓕ shtrah·se
road map *Straßenkarte* ⓕ shtrah·sen·kar·te
rob *berauben* be·row·ben
robbery *Raub* ⓜ rowp
rock *Fels* ⓜ fels
rock (music) *Rockmusik* ⓕ rok·mu·zeek
rock climbing *Klettern* ⓝ kle·tern
rock group *Rockgruppe* ⓕ rok·gru·pe
roll (bread) *Brötchen* ⓝ brert·khen
romantic *romantisch* ro·man·tish
roof *Dach* ⓝ dakh
room *Zimmer* ⓝ tsi·mer
rope *Seil* ⓝ zail
round *rund* runt
roundabout *Kreisverkehr* ⓜ krais·fer·kair
route *Route* ⓕ roo·te
rowing *Rudern* ⓝ roo·dern
rubbish *Müll* ⓜ mül
rug *Teppich* ⓜ te·pikh

rugby *Rugby* ⓝ rag·bi
ruins *Ruinen* ⓕ pl ru·ee·nen
rules *Regeln* ⓕ pl ray·geln
rum *Rum* ⓜ rum
run *laufen* low·fen
run out of *ausgehen* ows·gay·en

S

Sabbath *Sabbat* ⓜ za·bat
sad *traurig* trow·rikh
saddle *Sattel* ⓜ za·tel
safe *sicher* zi·kher
safe *Safe* ⓜ sayf
safe sex *Safe Sex* ⓜ sayf seks
safety *Sicherheit* ⓕ zi·kher·hait
sailing *Segeln* ⓝ zay·geln
saint *Heilige* ⓜ&ⓕ hai·li·ge
salad *Salat* ⓜ za·laht
salami *Salami* ⓕ za·lah·mi
salary *Gehalt* ⓝ ge·halt
sale *(Sonder)Angebot* ⓝ
    (zon·der·)an·ge·bawt
sales tax *Umsatzsteuer* ⓕ
    um·zats·shtoy·er
salmon *Lachs* ⓜ laks
salt *Salz* ⓝ zalts
same *gleiche* glai·khe
sand *Sand* ⓜ zant
sandals *Sandalen* ⓕ pl zan·dah·len
sanitary napkins *Damenbinden* ⓕ pl
    dah·men·bin·den
sardine *Sardine* ⓕ zar·dee·ne
Saturday *Samstag* ⓜ zams·tahk
sauce *Sauce/Soße* ⓕ zaw·se
sauna *Sauna* ⓕ zow·na
sausage *Wurst* ⓕ vurst
save (money) *sparen* shpah·ren
save (someone) *retten* re·ten
say *sagen* zah·gen
scarf *Schal* ⓜ shahl
scenery *Landschaft* ⓕ lant·shaft
school *Schule* ⓕ shoo·le
science *Wissenschaft* ⓕ vi·sen·shaft
scientist *Wissenschaftler(in)* ⓜ/ⓕ
    vi·sen·shaft·ler/vi·sen·shaft·le·rin
scissors *Schere* ⓕ shair·re
score *ein Tor schießen* ain tawr shee·sen
scoreboard *Anzeigetafel* ⓕ
    an·tsai·ge·tah·fel

Scotland *Schottland* ⓝ shot·lant
screen (TV/computer) *Bildschirm* ⓜ
    bilt·shirm
screwdriver *Schraubenzieher* ⓜ
    shrow·ben·tsee·er
script *Drehbuch* ⓝ dray·bookh
sculpture *Skulptur* ⓕ skulp·toor
sea *Meer* ⓝ mair
seagull *Möwe* ⓕ mer·ve
seasick *seekrank* zay·krangk
seaside *Meeresküste* ⓕ mair·res·küs·te
season *Jahreszeit* ⓕ yah·res·tsait
seat (car) *Sitz* ⓜ zits
seat (train/cinema) *Platz* ⓜ plats
seatbelt *Sicherheitsgurt* ⓜ
    zi·kher·haits·gurt
second *Sekunde* ⓕ ze·kun·de
second *zweite* tsvai·te
second-hand *gebraucht* ge·browkht
second-hand shop
    Secondhandgeschäft ⓝ
    se·kend·hend·ge·sheft
secret *Geheimnis* ⓝ ge·haim·nis
secretary *Sekretär(in)* ⓜ/ⓕ
    ze·kre·tair(·rin)
see *sehen* zay·en
self-employed *selbstständig*
    zelpst·shten·dikh
selfish *egoistisch* e·go·is·tish
self-service *Selbstbedienung* ⓕ
    zelpst·be·dee·nung
sell *verkaufen* fer·kow·fen
send *senden* zen·den
sensible *vernünftig* fer·nünf·tikh
sensual *sinnlich* zin·likh
separate *getrennt* ge·trent
serial *Serien-* zair·ri·en·
series *Serie* ⓕ zair·ri·e
serious *ernst* ernst
service charge *Bedienungszuschlag* ⓜ
    be·dee·nungks·tsoo·shlahk
service station *Tankstelle* ⓕ
    tangk·shte·le
several *einige* ai·ni·ge
sew *nähen* nay·en
sex *Sex* ⓜ seks
sexism *Sexismus* ⓜ sek·sis·mus
sexy *sexy* sek·si
shade *Schatten* ⓜ sha·ten

shadow *Schatten* ⑩ *sha*·ten
shampoo *Shampoo* ⑩ *sham*·poo
shape *Form* ① form
share (with) *teilen (mit)* *tai*·len (mit)
shave *rasieren* ra·*zee*·ren
shaving cream *Rasiercreme* ①
   ra·*zeer*·kraym
she *sie* zee
sheep *Schaf* ⑩ shahf
sheet (bed) *Bettlaken* ⑩ *bet*·lah·ken
shelf *Regal* ⑩ re·*gahl*
ship *Schiff* ⑩ shif
shirt *Hemd* ⑩ hemt
shoe shop *Schuhgeschäft* ⑩
   shoo·ge·sheft
shoes *Schuhe* ⑩ pl *shoo*·e
shoot (gun) *schießen* *shee*·sen
shop *Geschäft* ⑩ ge·*sheft*
shopping centre *Einkaufszentrum* ⑩
   ain·kowfs·tsen·trum
short *kurz* kurts
short (height) *klein* klain
shortage *Knappheit* ① *knap*·hait
shortcut *Abkürzung* ① *ap*·kür·tsung
shorts *Shorts* pl shorts
short-sleeved *kurzärmelig*
   kurts·er·me·likh
shoulder *Schulter* ① *shul*·ter
shout *schreien* *shrai*·en
show *Show* ① shoh
show *zeigen* *tsai*·gen
shower *Dusche* ① *doo*·she
shrine *Schrein* ⑩ shrain
shut (closed) *geschlossen* ge·*shlo*·sen
shut (close) *schließen* *shlee*·sen
shy *schüchtern* *shükh*·tern
sick *krank* krangk
side *Seite* ① *zai*·te
sign *Schild* ⑩ shilt
signature *Unterschrift* ① *un*·ter·shrift
signpost *Wegweiser* ⑩ *vayk*·vai·zer
silk *Seide* ① *zai*·de
silver *silbern* *zil*·bern
similar *ähnlich* *ayn*·likh
simple *einfach* *ain*·fakh
since (May) *seit (Mai)* zait (mai)
sing *singen* *zing*·en
Singapore *Singapur* ⑩ *zing*·a·poor
singer *Sänger(in)* ⑩/①
   zeng·er/*zeng*·e·rin

single (person) *Single* ⑩ singl
single (unmarried) *ledig* *lay*·dikh
single room *Einzelzimmer* ⑩
   ain·tsel·tsi·mer
singlet *Unterhemd* ⑩ *un*·ter·hemt
sister *Schwester* ① *shves*·ter
sit *sitzen* *zi*·tsen
situation *Lage* ① *lah*·ge
size *Größe* ① *grer*·se
skate *eislaufen* *ais*·low·fen
skateboarding *Skateboarden* ⑩
   skayt·bor·den
ski *skifahren* *shee*·fah·ren
skiing *Skifahren* ⑩ *shee*·fah·ren
skimmed milk *fettarme Milch* ①
   fet·ar·me milkh
skin *Haut* ① howt
skirt *Rock* ⑩ rok
sky *Himmel* ⑩ *hi*·mel
sleep *schlafen* *shlah*·fen
sleeping bag *Schlafsack* ⑩ *shlahf*·zak
sleeping car *Schlafwagen* ⑩
   shlahf·vah·gen
sleeping pills *Schlaftabletten* ① pl
   shlahf·ta·ble·ten
sleepy *schläfrig* *shlayf*·rikh
slide (film) *Dia* ⑩ *dee*·a
slippery *glatt* glat
slope *Hang* ⑩ hang
slow *langsam* *lang*·zahm
slowly *langsam* *lang*·zahm
small *klein* klain
smell *Geruch* ⑩ ge·*rookh*
smile *lächeln* *le*·kheln
smoke *rauchen* *row*·khen
snack *Snack* ⑩ snek
snail *Schnecke* ① *shne*·ke
snake *Schlange* ① *shlang*·e
snorkelling *Schnorcheln* ⑩ *shnor*·kheln
snow *Schnee* ⑩ shnay
snow pea *Zuckererbse* ① *tsu*·ker·erp·se
snowboarding *Snowboarden* ⑩
   snoh·bor·den
snowfield *Schneefeld* ⑩ *shnay*·felt
soap *Seife* ① *zai*·fe
soap opera *Seifenoper* ①
   zai·fen·aw·per
soccer *Fußball* ⑩ *foos*·bal
social welfare *Wohlfahrt* ① *vawl*·fahrt

socialist *sozialistisch* zo·tsya·*lis*·tish

socks *Socken* ① pl zo·ken

soft drink *alkoholfreies Getränk* ⓝ
al·ko·*hawl*·frai·es ge·*trengk*

sold out *ausverkauft* ows·*fer*·kowft

solid *fest* fest

some *einige* ai·ni·ge

someone *jemand* yay·mant

something *etwas* et·vas

sometimes *manchmal* mankh·mahl

son *Sohn* ⓜ zawn

song *Lied* ⓝ leet

son-in-law *Schwiegersohn* ⓜ
shvee·ger·zawn

soon *bald* balt

sore *schmerzhaft* shmerts·haft

sore throat *Halsschmerzen* ⓜ pl
hals·shmer·tsen

soup *Suppe* ① zu·pe

sour cream *Schmand* ⓜ shmant

south *Süden* ⓜ zü·den

souvenir *Souvenir* ⓝ zu·ve·*neer*

souvenir shop *Souvenirladen* ⓜ
zu·ve·*neer*·lah·den

soy milk *Sojamilch* ① zaw·ya·milkh

soy sauce *Sojasauce* ① zaw·ya·zaw·se

space *Raum* ⓜ rowm

spade *Spaten* ⓜ shpah·ten

Spain *Spanien* ⓝ shpah·ni·en

spare tyre *Reservereifen* ⓜ
re·zer·ve·rai·fen

speak *sprechen* shpre·khen

special *speziell* shpe·tsyel

specialist *Spezialist(in)* ⓜ/①
shpe·tsya·*list*/shpe·tsya·*lis*·tin

speed *Geschwindigkeit* ①
ge·shvin·dikh·kait

speed limit
Geschwindigkeits·begrenzung ①
ge·shvin·dikh·kaits·be·gren·tsung

spicy *würzig* vür·tsikh

spider *Spinne* ① shpi·ne

spinach *Spinat* ⓜ shpi·*naht*

spokes *Speichen* ① pl shpai·khen

spoon *Löffel* ⓜ ler·fel

sport *Sport* ⓜ shport

sportsperson *Sportler(in)* ⓜ/①
shport·ler/shport·le·rin

sprain *Muskelzerrung* ①
mus·kel·tser·rung

spring (coil) *Feder* ① fay·der

spring (season) *Frühling* ⓜ frü·ling

square (town) *Platz* ⓜ plats

stadium *Stadion* ⓝ shtah·di·on

stage *Stadium* ⓝ shtah·di·um

stage (theatre) *Bühne* ① bü·ne

stairway *Treppe* ① tre·pe

stamp *Briefmarke* ① breef·mar·ke

standby ticket *Standby-Ticket* ⓝ
stend·*bai*·ti·ket

standing room *Stehplatz* ⓜ shtay·plats

star sign *Sternzeichen* ⓝ
shtern·tsai·khen

star *Stern* ⓜ shtern

(four-)star *(Vier-)Sterne-* (feer·)shter·ne·

start *Beginn* ⓜ be·*gin*

start (sport) *Start* ⓜ shtart

start *anfangen* an·fang·en

state *Staat* ⓜ shtaht

station *Bahnhof* ⓜ bahn·hawf

stationer *Schreibwarenhandlung* ①
shraip·vah·ren·han·dlung

statue *Statue* ① shtah·tu·e

stay (at a hotel) *übernachten*
ü·ber·nakh·ten

stay (not leave) *bleiben* blai·ben

steak (beef) *Steak* ⓝ stayk

steal *stehlen* shtay·len

steep *steil* shtail

step (stairs) *Stufe* ① shtoo·fe

stereo *Stereoanlage* ①
shtair·re·o·an·lah·ge

stingy *geizig* gai·tsikh

stock *Vorrat* ⓜ fawr·raht

stockings *Strümpfe* ⓜ pl shtrüm·fe

stomach *Magen* ⓜ mah·gen

stomachache *Magenschmerzen* ⓜ pl
mah·gen·shmer·tsen

stone *Stein* ⓜ shtain

stoned (drugged) *stoned* stohnd

stop *Halt* ⓜ halt

stop *anhalten* an·hal·ten

storm *Sturm* ⓜ shturm

story *Geschichte* ① ge·shikh·te

stove *Herd* ⓜ hert

straight *gerade* ge·*rah*·de

strange *fremd* fremt

stranger *Fremde* ⓜ&① frem·de

strawberry *Erdbeere* ① ert·bair·re

stream *Bach* ⓜ bakh
street *Straße* ⓕ shtrah·se
street kids *Straßenkinder* ⓟ pl
  shtrah·sen·kin·der
on strike *streiken* shtrai·ken
string *Schnur* ⓕ shnoor
strong *stark* shtark
stubborn *stur* shtoor
student *Student(in)* ⓜ/ⓕ
  shtu·dent/shtu·den·tin
student card *Studentenausweis* ⓜ
  shtu·den·ten·ows·vais
studio *Studio* ⓝ shtoo·di·o
studio (art) *Atelier* ⓝ a·tel·yay
study *studieren* shtu·dee·ren
stupid *dumm* dum
style *Stil* ⓜ shteel
subtitles *Untertitel* ⓜ pl un·ter·tee·tel
suburb *Vorort* ⓜ fawr·ort
subway *U-Bahn* ⓕ oo·bahn
sugar *Zucker* ⓜ tsu·ker
suitcase *Koffer* ⓜ ko·fer
summer *Sommer* ⓜ zo·mer
sun *Sonne* ⓕ zo·ne
sunblock *Sonnencreme* ⓕ
  zo·nen·kraym
sunburn *Sonnenbrand* ⓜ zo·nen·brant
Sunday *Sonntag* ⓜ zon·tahk
sunglasses *Sonnenbrille* ⓕ
  zo·nen·bri·le
sunny *sonnig* zo·nikh
sunrise *Sonnenaufgang* ⓜ
  zo·nen·owf·gang
sunset *Sonnenuntergang* ⓜ
  zo·nen·un·ter·gang
supermarket *Supermarkt* ⓜ
  zoo·per·markt
superstition *Aberglaube* ⓜ
  ah·ber·glow·be
supporters *Anhänger* ⓜ pl an·heng·er
surf *surfen* ser·fen
surface mail *normale Post* ⓕ
  nor·mah·le post
surfboard *Surfbrett* ⓝ serf·bret
surname *Nachname* ⓜ nahkh·nah·me
surprise *Überraschung* ⓕ
  ü·ber·ra·shung
sweater *Pullover* ⓜ pu·law·ver
sweet *süß* züs

swim *schwimmen* shvi·men
swimming pool *Schwimmbad* ⓝ
  shvim·baht
swimsuit *Badeanzug* ⓜ
  bah·de·an·tsook
Switzerland *Schweiz* ⓕ shvaits
synagogue *Synagoge* ⓕ zü·na·gaw·ge
synthetic *synthetisch* zün·tay·tish
syringe *Spritze* ⓕ shpri·tse

T

table *Tisch* ⓜ tish
table tennis *Tischtennis* ⓝ tish·te·nis
tablecloth *Tischdecke* ⓕ tish·de·ke
tail *Schwanz* ⓜ shvants
tailor *Schneider(in)* ⓜ/ⓕ
  shnai·der/shnai·de·rin
take *nehmen* nay·men
take (to) *bringen* bring·en
take off *Abflug* ⓜ ap·flook
talk *sprechen* shpre·khen
tall *groß* graws
tampons *Tampons* ⓜ pl tam·pons
tanning lotion *Bräunungsmilch* ⓕ
  broy·nungks·milkh
tap *Wasserhahn* ⓜ va·ser·hahn
target *Ziel* ⓝ tseel
tasty *schmackhaft* shmak·haft
tax *Steuer* ⓕ shtoy·er
taxi *Taxi* ⓝ tak·si
taxi stand *Taxistand* ⓜ tak·si·shtant
tea *Tee* ⓜ tay
teacher *Lehrer(in)* ⓜ/ⓕ
  lair·rer/lair·re·rin
team *Mannschaft* ⓕ man·shaft
teaspoon *Teelöffel* ⓜ tay·ler·fel
technique *Technik* ⓕ tekh·nik
teeth *Zähne* ⓜ pl tsay·ne
telegram *Telegramm* ⓝ te·le·gram
telephone *Telefon* ⓝ te·le·fawn
telephone *telefonieren* te·le·fo·nee·ren
telephone book *Telefonbuch* ⓝ
  te·le·fawn·bookh
telephone centre *Telefonzentrale* ⓕ
  te·le·fawn·tsen·trah·le
telescope *Teleskop* ⓝ te·les·kawp
television *Fernseher* ⓜ fern·zay·er
tell *erzählen* er·tsay·len
temperature (fever) *Fieber* ⓝ fee·ber

temperature (weather) *Temperatur* ①
tem·pe·ra·*toor*

temple *Tempel* ⓜ *tem·pel*

ten *zehn* tsayn

tennis *Tennis* ⓝ *te·nis*

tennis court *Tennisplatz* ⓜ *te·nis·plats*

tent *Zelt* ⓝ tselt

tent pegs *Heringe* ⓜ pl hay·ring·e

terminal (transport) *Endstation* ①
ent·shta·tsyawn

terrible *schrecklich* shrek·likh

test *Test* ⓜ test

thank *danken* dang·ken

theatre *Theater* ⓝ te·ah·ter

their *ihr* eer

there *dort* dort

thermos *Thermosflasche* ①
ter·mos·fla·she

they *sie* zee

thick *dick* dik

thief *Dieb* ⓜ deep

thin *dünn* dün

think *denken* deng·ken

third *dritte* dri·te

thirsty *durstig* durs·tikh

this (month) *diesen (Monat)*
dee·zen (maw·nat)

this (one) *dieser/diese/dieses* ⓜ/①/ⓝ
dee·zer/dee·ze/dee·zes

thousand *tausend* tow·zent

throat *Hals* ⓜ hals

through *durch* durkh

thrush (condition) *Mundfäule* ①
munt·foy·le

thunder *Donner* ⓜ do·ner

Thursday *Donnerstag* ⓜ do·ners·tahk

ticket (bus/metro/train) *Fahrkarte* ①
fahr·kar·te

ticket (cinema/museum) *Eintritts-karte* ① ain·trits·kar·te

ticket (plane) *Flugticket* ⓝ flook·ti·ket

ticket collector
Fahrkartenkontrolleur/in ⓜ/①
fahr·kar·ten·kon·tro·ler/
fahr·kar·ten·kon·tro·ler·rin

ticket machine *Fahrkartenautomat* ⓜ
fahr·kar·ten·ow·to·maht

ticket office *Fahrkartenverkauf* ⓜ
fahr·kar·ten·fer·kowf

ticket office (theatre) *Theaterkasse* ①
te·ah·ter·ka·se

tides *Gezeiten* pl ge·tsai·ten

tight *eng* eng

time *Zeit* ① tsait

time difference *Zeitunterschied* ⓜ
tsait·un·ter·sheet

timetable *Fahrplan* ⓜ fahr·plahn

tin (can) *Dose* ① daw·ze

tin opener *Dosenöffner* ⓜ
daw·zen·erf·ner

tiny *winzig* vin·tsikh

tip (gratuity) *Trinkgeld* ⓝ tringk·gelt

tire *ermüden* er·mü·den

tired *müde* mü·de

tissues *Papiertaschentücher* ⓝ pl
pa·peer·ta·shen·tü·kher

toast *Toast* ⓜ tawst

toaster *Toaster* ⓜ taws·ter

tobacco *Tabak* ⓜ ta·bak

tobacconist *Tabakladen* ⓜ
ta·bak·lah·den

tobogganing *Rodeln* ⓝ raw·deln

today *heute* hoy·te

toe *Zehe* ① tsay·e

tofu *Tofu* ⓜ taw·fu

together *zusammen* tsu·za·men

toilet *Toilette* ① to·a·le·te

toilet paper *Toilettenpapier* ⓝ
to·a·le·ten·pa·peer

tomato *Tomate* ① to·mah·te

tomato sauce *Tomatensauce* ①
to·mah·ten·zaw·se

tomb *Grab* ⓝ grahp

tomorrow *morgen* mor·gen

tomorrow morning *morgen früh*
mor·gen frü

tonight *heute Abend* hoy·te ah·bent

too (also) *auch* owkh

too (many) *zu (viele)* tsoo (fee·le)

tools *Werkzeug* ⓝ verk·tsoyk

tooth *Zahn* ⓜ tsahn

toothache *Zahnschmerzen* ⓜ pl
tsahn·shmer·tsen

toothbrush *Zahnbürste* ① tsahn·bürs·te

toothpaste *Zahnpasta* ① tsahn·pas·ta

toothpick *Zahnstocher* ⓜ
tsahn·shto·kher

torch (flashlight) *Taschenlampe* ①
ta·shen·lam·pe

touch *berühren* be·rü·ren
tour *Tour* ① toor
tourist *Tourist/in* ⓜ/① tu·rist/tu·ris·tin
tourist office *Fremdenverkehrsbüro* ⓝ
 frem·den·fer·kairs·bü·raw
towards *auf ... zu* owf ... tsoo
towel *Handtuch* ⓝ hant·tookh
tower *Turm* ⓜ turm
town *Stadt* ① shtat
toxic waste *Giftmüll* ⓜ gift·mül
toy *Spielzeug* ⓝ shpeel·tsoyk
track (path) *Weg* ⓜ vayk
track (sports) *Bahn* ① bahn
trade *Handel* ⓜ han·del
traffic *Verkehr* ⓜ fer·kair
traffic lights *Ampel* ① am·pel
trail *Pfad* ⓜ pfahrt
train *Zug* ⓜ tsook
train station *Bahnhof* ⓜ bahn·hawf
tram *Straßenbahn* ① shtrah·sen·bahn
transit lounge *Transitraum* ⓜ
 tran·zeet·rowm
translate *übersetzen* ü·ber·ze·tsen
transport *Transport* ⓜ trans·port
travel *reisen* rai·zen
travel agency *Reisebüro* ⓝ
 rai·ze·bü·raw
travel sickness *Reisekrankheit* ①
 rai·ze·krangk·hait
travellers cheque *Reisescheck* ⓜ
 rai·ze·shek
tree *Baum* ⓜ bowm
trip *Reise* ① rai·ze
trousers *Hose* ① haw·ze
truck *Lastwagen* ⓜ last·vah·gen
true *wahr* vahr
trust *trauen* trow·en
try (attempt) *versuchen* fer·zoo·khen
T-shirt *T-Shirt* ⓝ tee·shert
tube (tyre) *Schlauch* ⓜ shlowkh
Tuesday *Dienstag* ⓜ deens·tahk
tuna *Thunfisch* ⓜ toon·fish
tune *Melodie* ① me·lo·dee
turkey *Truthahn* ⓜ troot·hahn
turn *abbiegen* ap·bee·gen
TV (set) *Fernseher* ⓜ fern·zay·er
TV series *Fernsehserie* ①
 fern·zay·zair·ri·e
tweezers *Pinzette* ① pin·tse·te

twice *zweimal* tsvai·mahl
twin beds *zwei Einzelbetten* ⓝ pl
 tsvai ain·tsel·be·ten
twins *Zwillinge* ⓜ pl tsvi·ling·e
type *Typ* ⓜ tüp
typical *typisch* tü·pish
tyre *Reifen* ⓜ rai·fen

U

ultrasound *Ultraschall* ⓜ ul·tra·shal
umbrella *Regenschirm* ⓜ ray·gen·shirm
uncle *Onkel* ⓜ ong·kel
uncomfortable *unbequem* un·be·kvaym
under *unter* un·ter
underground *U-Bahn* ① oo·bahn
understand *verstehen* fer·shtay·en
underwear *Unterwäsche* ①
 un·ter·ve·she
unemployed *arbeitslos* ar·baits·laws
unemployment *Arbeitslosigkeit* ①
 ar·baits·law·zikh·kait
unfair *unfair* un·fair
uniform *Uniform* ① u·ni·form
universe *Universum* ⓝ u·ni·vair·zum
university *Universität* ① u·ni·ver·zi·tayt
unleaded *bleifrei* blai·frai
unsafe *nicht sicher* nikht zi·kher
until (June) *bis (Juni)* bis (yoo·ni)
unusual *ungewöhnlich* un·ge·vern·likh
up *nach oben* nahkh aw·ben
uphill *aufwärts* owf·verts
upstairs *oben* aw·ben
urgent *dringend* dring·ent
USA *USA* ① pl oo·es·ah
useful *nützlich* nüts·likh

V

vacant *frei* frai
vacation *Ferien* pl fair·i·en
vaccination *Schutzimpfung* ①
 shuts·im·pfung
vagina *Vagina* ① va·gee·na
validate (ticket) *entwerten* ent·ver·ten
valley *Tal* ⓝ tahl
valuable *wertvoll* vert·fol
value (price) *Wert* ⓜ vert
van *Lieferwagen* ⓜ lee·fer·vah·gen

veal *Kalbfleisch* ⑩ kalp·flaish
vegetable *Gemüse* ⑪ ge·mü·ze
vegetarian *Vegetarier(in)* ⑩/⑪
    ve·ge·tah·ri·er/ve·ge·tah·ri·e·rin
vein *Vene* ⑪ vay·ne
venereal disease *Geschlechts-
    krankheit* ⑪ ge·shlekhts·krangk·hait
venue *Veranstaltungsort* ⑩
    fer·an·shtal·tungks·ort
very *sehr* zair
video tape *Videokassette* ⑪
    vee·de·o·ka·se·te
view *Aussicht* ⑪ ows·zikht
village *Dorf* ⑪ dorf
vine *Rebe* ⑪ ray·be
vinegar *Essig* ⑩ e·sikh
vineyard *Weinberg* ⑩ vain·berk
virus *Virus* ⑩ vee·rus
visa *Visum* ⑩ vee·zum
visit *besuchen* be·zoo·khen
vitamins *Vitamine* ⑪ pl vi·ta·mee·ne
vodka *Wodka* ⑩ vot·ka
voice *Stimme* ⑪ shti·me
volume (amount) *Volumen* ⑩
    vo·loo·men
volume (book) *Band* ⑩ bant
volume (loudness) *Lautstärke* ⑪
    lowt·shter·ke
vomit *brechen* bre·khen
vote *wählen* vay·len

W

wage *Lohn* ⑩ lawn
wait *warten* var·ten
waiter *Kellner(in)* ⑩/⑪
    kel·ner/kel·ne·rin
waiting room (doctor's)
    Wartezimmer ⑩ var·te·tsi·mer
waiting room (train station)
    Wartesaal ⑩ var·te·zahl
walk *gehen* gay·en
wall (outer) *Mauer* ⑪ mow·er
want *wollen* vo·len
war *Krieg* ⑩ kreek
wardrobe *Garderobe* ⑪ gar·draw·be
warm *warm* varm
warn *warnen* var·nen
wash (oneself) *sich waschen*
    zikh va·shen

wash (something) *waschen* va·shen
wash cloth (flannel) *Waschlappen* ⑩
    vash·la·pen
washing machine *Waschmaschine* ⑪
    vash·ma·shee·ne
washing powder *Waschpulver* ⑩
    vash·pul·ver
wasp *Wespe* ⑪ ves·pe
watch *Uhr* ⑪ oor
watch *beobachten* be·aw·bakh·ten
watch (TV) *fernsehen* fern·zay·en
water *Wasser* ⑩ va·ser
    tap water *Leitungswasser* ⑩
    lai·tungks·va·ser
water bottle *Wasserflasche* ⑪
    va·ser·fla·she
waterfall *Wasserfall* ⑩ va·ser·fal
watermelon *Wassermelone* ⑪
    va·ser·me·law·ne
waterproof *wasserdicht* va·ser·dikht
waterskiing *Wasserskifahren* ⑩
    va·ser·shee·fah·ren
wave *Welle* ⑪ ve·le
way *Weg* ⑩ vayk
we *wir* veer
weak *schwach* shvakh
wealthy *reich* raikh
weapon *Waffe* ⑪ va·fe
wear *tragen* trah·gen
weather *Wetter* ⑩ ve·ter
wedding *Hochzeit* ⑪ hokh·tsait
wedding cake *Hochzeitstorte* ⑪
    hokh·tsaits·tor·te
wedding present *Hochzeitsgeschenk* ⑩
    hokh·tsaits·ge·shengk
Wednesday *Mittwoch* ⑩ mit·vokh
(this) week *(diese) Woche* ⑪
    (dee·ze) vo·khe
weekend *Wochenende* ⑩
    vo·khen·en·de
weigh *wiegen* vee·gen
weight *Gewicht* ⑩ ge·vikht
welcome *willkommen* vil·ko·men
welfare *Sozialhilfe* ⑪ zo·tsyahl·hil·fe
welfare state *Sozialstaat* ⑩
    zo·tsyahl·shtaht
well *gut* goot
west *Westen* ⑩ ves·ten
wet *nass* nas

what *was* vas
wheel *Rad* ⓝ raht
wheelchair *Rollstuhl* ⓜ rol·shtool
when *(adverb)* *wann* van
when *(conjunction)* *wenn* ven
whenever *wann immer* van i·mer
where *wo* vaw
whisky *Whisky* ⓜ vis·ki
white *weiß* vais
who *wer* vair
whole *ganz* gants
why *warum* va·rum
wide *breit* brait
wife *Ehefrau* ⓕ ay·e·frow
wild *wild* vilt
win *gewinnen* ge·vi·nen
wind *Wind* ⓜ vint
window *Fenster* ⓝ fens·ter
windscreen *Windschutzscheibe* ⓕ
  vint·shuts·shai·be
windsurfing *Windsurfen* ⓝ vint·ser·fen
windy *windig* vin·dikh
wine *Wein* ⓜ vain
  red wine *Rotwein* ⓜ rawt·vain
  sparkling wine *Schaumwein* ⓜ
    showm·vain
  white wine *Weißwein* ⓜ vais·vain
wings *Flügel* ⓜ pl flü·gel
winner *Sieger(in)* ⓜ/ⓕ
  zee·ger/zee·ge·rin
winter *Winter* ⓜ vin·ter
wire *Draht* ⓜ draht
wish *wünschen* vün·shen
with *mit* mit
within *(an hour)*
  innerhalb (einer Stunde)
  i·ner·halp (ai·ner shtun·de)
without *ohne* aw·ne
woman *Frau* ⓕ frow
wonderful *wunderbar* vun·der·bahr
wood *Holz* ⓝ holts
wool *Wolle* ⓕ vo·le
word *Wort* ⓝ vort
work *Arbeit* ⓕ ar·bait
work *arbeiten* ar·bai·ten

work permit *Arbeitserlaubnis* ⓕ
  ar·baits·er·lowp·nis
workout *Training* ⓝ tray·ning
workshop *Werkstatt* ⓕ verk·shtat
world *Welt* ⓕ velt
World Cup *Weltmeisterschaft* ⓕ
  velt·mais·ter·shaft
worms *Würmer* ⓜ pl vür·mer
worried *besorgt* be·zorkt
worse *schlechter* shlekh·ter
worship *einen Gottesdienst besuchen*
  ai·nen go·tes·deenst be·zoo·khen
write *schreiben* shrai·ben
writer *Schriftsteller(in)* ⓜ/ⓕ
  shrift·shte·ler/shrift·shte·le·rin
wrong *falsch* falsh

Y

(this) year *(dieses) Jahr* ⓝ
  (dee·zes) yahr
yellow *gelb* gelp
yes *ja* yah
yesterday *gestern* ges·tern
yet *schon* shawn
not yet *noch nicht* nokh nikht
yoga *Joga* ⓝ yaw·ga
yogurt *Joghurt* ⓜ yaw·gurt
you sg inf *du* doo
you sg&pl pol *Sie* zee
young *jung* yung
your sg inf *dein* dain
your sg&pl pol *Ihr* eer
youth hostel *Jugendherberge* ⓕ
  yoo·gent·her·ber·ge

Z

zero *null* nul
zipper *Reißverschluss* ⓜ rais·fer·shlus
zodiac *Sternzeichen* ⓝ shtern·tsai·khen
zoo *Zoo* ⓜ tsaw
zucchini *Zucchini* ⓕ tsu·kee·ni

german–english
deutsch–englisch

Nouns in the dictionary, and adjectives affected by gender, have their gender indicated by ⓕ, ⓜ or ⓝ. If it's a plural noun, you'll also see pl. Where a word that could be either a noun or a verb has no gender indicated, it's a verb.

A

abbiegen *ap*·bee·gen *turn*
Abend ⓜ *ah*·bent *evening*
Abendessen ⓝ *ah*·bent·e·sen *dinner*
aber *ah*·ber *but*
Aberglaube ⓜ *ah*·ber·glow·be *superstition*
abfahren *ap*·fah·ren *leave (depart)*
Abfahrt ⓕ *ap*·fahrt *departure*
Abfall ⓜ *ap*·fal *garbage*
Abfertigungsschalter ⓜ *ap*·fer·ti·gungks·shal·ter *check-in (desk)*
Abflug ⓜ *ap*·flook *take off*
Abführmittel ⓝ *ap*·für·mi·tel *laxatives*
abgelegen *ap*·ge·lay·gen *remote*
Abgeordnete ⓜ&ⓕ *ap*·ge·ord·ne·te *member of parliament*
abgeschlossen *ap*·ge·shlo·sen *locked*
abhängig *ap*·heng·ikh *addicted*
Abholzung ⓕ *ap*·hol·tsung *deforestation*
Abkürzung ⓕ *ap*·kür·tsung *shortcut*
ablehnen *ap*·lay·nen *refuse*
Abschleppdienst ⓜ *ap*·shlep·deenst *breakdown service*
abseits *ap*·zaits *offside*
Abstrich ⓜ *ap*·shtrikh *pap smear*
Abtreibung ⓕ *ap*·trai·bung *abortion*
abwärts *ap*·verts *downhill*
Abzockerei ⓕ *ap*·tso·ke·rai *rip-off*
Abzug ⓜ *ap*·tsook *print (photography)*
Adapter ⓜ a·*dap*·ter *adaptor*
Adressanhänger ⓜ a·*dres*·an·heng·er *luggage tag*
Adresse ⓕ a·*dre*·se *address*
Aerobics pl e·*ro*·biks *aerobics*
Aerogramm ⓝ air·ro·gram *aerogram*
Afrika ⓝ a·*fri*·kah *Africa*
Aftershave ⓕ *ahf*·ter·shayf *aftershave*
ähnlich *ayn*·likh *similar*
AIDS ⓜ aydz *AIDS*

Aktentasche ⓕ *ak*·ten·ta·she *briefcase*
Aktivist(in) ⓜ/ⓕ ak·ti·*vist*/ak·ti·*vis*·tin *activist*
Aktuelles ⓝ ak·tu·e·les *current affairs*
Akupunktur ⓕ a·ku·pungk·*toor* *acupuncture*
Alkohol ⓜ *al*·ko·hawl *alcohol*
alkoholfreies Getränk ⓝ al·ko·*hawl*·frai·es ge·*trengk* *soft drink*
Alkoholiker(in) ⓜ/ⓕ al·ko·*haw*·li·ker/al·ko·*haw*·li·ke·rin *alcoholic*
alkoholisch al·ko·*haw*·lish *alcoholic*
alle a·le *all*
Allee ⓕ a·*lay* *avenue*
allein a·*lain* *alone*
Allergie ⓕ a·lair·*gee* *allergy*
alles a·les *everything*
allgemein al·ge·*main* *general*
alltäglich al·*tayk*·likh *every day*
alt alt *old* • *ancient*
Altar ⓜ al·*tahr* *altar*
Alter ⓝ al·ter *age*
Amateur(in) ⓜ/ⓕ a·ma·*ter*(·rin) *amateur*
Ameise ⓕ *ah*·mai·ze *ant*
Ampel ⓕ am·pel *traffic lights*
sich amüsieren zikh a·mü·*zee*·ren *enjoy (oneself)*
an an *at* • *to*
Anarchist(in) ⓜ/ⓕ a·nar·*khist*/a·nar·*khis*·tin *anarchist*
anbaggern an·ba·gern *chat up*
andere an·de·re *other* • *different*
anfangen an·fang·en *start*
Anführer ⓜ an·fü·rer *leader*
Angel ⓕ ang·el *fishing rod*
Angestellte ⓜ&ⓕ an·ge·shtel·te *employee*
Angst (haben) angkst (*hah*·ben) *(to be) afraid*
anhalten an·hal·ten *stop*

Anhänger ⓜ pl an·heng·er *supporters*
ankommen an·ko·men *arrive*
Ankunft ⓕ an·kunft *arrivals*
ansehen an·zay·en *look at*
(an)statt an·shtat *instead of*
Anti-Atom- an·ti·a·tawm- *antinuclear*
Antibiotika ⓝ pl an·ti·bi·aw·ti·ka *antibiotics*
Antiquariat ⓝ an·ti·kva·ri·aht *second-hand bookshop*
Antiquität ⓕ an·ti·kvi·tayt *antique*
Antiseptikum ⓝ an·ti·zep·ti·kum *antiseptic*
Antwort ⓕ ant·vort *answer*
antworten ant·vor·ten *answer*
Anzahlung ⓕ an·tsah·lung *deposit*
Anzeige ⓕ an·tsai·ge *advertisement*
Anzeigetafel ⓕ an·tsai·ge·tah·fel *scoreboard*
Apfel ⓜ ap·fel *apple*
Apfelmost ⓜ ap·fel·most *cider*
Apotheke ⓕ a·po·tay·ke *chemist • pharmacy*
Aprikose ⓕ a·pri·kaw·ze *apricot*
Arbeit ⓕ ar·bait *work*
arbeiten ar·bai·ten *work*
Arbeiter(in) ⓜ/ⓕ ar·bai·ter/ar·bai·te·rin *worker • labourer*
Arbeitgeber ⓜ ar·bait·gay·ber *employer*
Arbeitserlaubnis ⓕ ar·baits·er·lowp·nis *work permit*
arbeitslos ar·baits·laws *unemployed*
Arbeitslosengeld ⓝ ar·baits·law·zen·gelt *dole • unemployment benefit*
Arbeitslosigkeit ⓕ ar·baits·law·zikh·kait *unemployment*
Arbeitsstelle ⓕ ar·baits·shte·le *job*
archäologisch ar·khe·o·law·gish *archaeological*
Architektur ⓕ ar·khi·tek·toor *architecture*
Arm ⓜ arm *arm*
arm arm *poor*
Armut ⓕ ar·moot *poverty*
Arzt ⓜ artst *doctor (medical)*
Ärztin ⓕ erts·tin *doctor (medical)*
Aschenbecher ⓜ a·shen·be·kher *ashtray*
Asien ⓝ ah·zi·en *Asia*
Asthma ⓝ ast·ma *asthma*

Asylant(in) ⓜ/ⓕ a·zü·lant/a·zü·lan·tin *asylum seeker*
Atelier ⓝ a·tel·yay *studio (art)*
atmen aht·men *breathe*
Atmosphäre ⓕ at·mos·fair·re *atmosphere*
Atomenergie ⓕ a·tawm·e·ner·gee *nuclear energy*
Atommüll ⓜ a·tawm·mül *nuclear waste*
Aubergine ⓕ aw·ber·zhee·ne *eggplant • aubergine*
auch owkh *too • also*
auch nicht owkh nikht *neither*
auf owf *on • at*
auf ... zu owf ... tsoo *towards*
Aufführung ⓕ owf·fü·rung *performance*
aufheben owf·hay·ben *pick up (object)*
Aufnahme ⓕ owf·nah·me *recording*
aufpassen owf·pa·sen *mind (object) • pay attention*
Auftritt ⓜ owf·trit *gig*
aufwärts owf·verts *uphill*
Auge ⓝ ow·ge *eye*
Augenblick ⓜ ow·gen·blik *moment*
Augentropfen ⓜ pl ow·gen·trop·fen *eye drops*
aus ows *from • out*
aus (Baumwolle) ows (bawm·vo·le) *made of (cotton)*
Ausbeutung ⓕ ows·boy·tung *exploitation*
Ausgang ⓜ ows·gang *exit*
ausgebucht ows·ge·bookht *booked out*
ausgehen ows·gay·en *go out • run out of*
mit jemandem ausgehen mit yay·man·dem ows·gay·en *date someone*
ausgeschlossen ows·ge·shlo·sen *excluded*
ausgezeichnet ows·ge·tsaikh·net *excellent*
Auskunft ⓕ ows·kunft *information*
im Ausland im ows·lant *abroad*
ausländisch ows·len·dish *foreign*
Auspuff ⓜ ows·puf *exhaust (car)*
Ausrüstung ⓕ ows·rüs·tung *equipment*
Ausschlag ⓜ ows·shlahk *rash*

außer ow·ser *apart from • besides*
Aussicht ① ows·zikht *view*
Aussichtspunkt ⑩ ows·zikhts·pungkt
 lookout
Ausstellung ① ows·shte·lung *exhibition*
austeilen ows·tai·len *deal (cards)*
Auster ① ows·ter *oyster*
Australien ⑩ ows·trah·li·en *Australia*
ausverkauft ows·fer·kowft *sold out*
Ausweis ⑩ ows·vais *identification*
Auto ⑩ ow·to *car*
Autobahn ① ow·to·bahn
 motorway (tollway)
Autokennzeichen ⑩
 ow·to·ken·tsai·khen
 licence plate number
automatisch ow·to·mah·tish *automatic*
Autor(in) ⑩/① ow·tor/ow·taw·rin
 author
Autoverleih ⑩ ow·to·fer·lai *car hire*
Avokado ① a·vo·kah·do *avocado*
Axt ① akst *axe*

B

Baby ⑩ bay·bi *baby*
Babynahrung ① bay·bi·nah·rung
 baby food
Babypuder ⑩ bay·bi·poo·der
 baby powder
Babysitter ⑩ bay·bi·si·ter *babysitter*
Bach ⑩ bakh *stream*
Bäckerei ① be·ke·rai *bakery*
Backpflaume ① bak·pflow·me *prune*
Bad ⑩ baht *bath*
Badeanzug ⑩ bah·de·an·tsook *swimsuit*
Badetuch ⑩ bah·de·tookh *bath towel*
Badezimmer ⑩ bah·de·tsi·mer
 bathroom
Bahn ① bahn *track (sports) • railway*
Bahnhof ⑩ bahn·hawf *railway station*
Bahnsteig ⑩ bahn·shtaik *platform*
bald balt *soon*
Balkon ⑩ bal·kawn *balcony*
Ball ⑩ bal *ball*
Ballett ⑩ ba·let *ballet*
Banane ① ba·nah·ne *banana*
Band ① bent *band (music)*
Band ⑩ bant *volume (book)*

Bank ① bangk *bank*
Bankauszug ⑩ bangk·ows·tsook
 bankdraft
Bankkonto ⑩ bangk·kon·to *bank
 account*
Bär ⑩ bair *bear*
Bargeld ⑩ bahr·gelt *cash*
Batterie ① ba·te·ree *battery*
bauen bow·en *build*
Bauer ⑩ bow·er *farmer*
Bäuerin ① boy·e·rin *farmer*
Bauernhof ⑩ bow·ern·hawf *farm*
Baum ⑩ bowm *tree*
Baumwolle ① bowm·vo·le *cotton*
Bedienungszuschlag ⑩ be·dee·nungks·
 tsoo·shlahk *service·charge*
bedrohte be·draw·te *endangered*
beenden be·en·den *finish*
Beginn ⑩ be·gin *beginning*
beginnen be·gi·nen *begin*
Begleiter(in) ⑩/① be·glai·ter/
 be·glai·te·rin *companion*
Begräbnis ⑩ be·grayp·nis *funeral*
behindert be·hin·dert *disabled*
bei bai *at*
Beichte ① baikh·te
 confession (religious)
beide bai·de *both*
Bein ⑩ bain *leg (body)*
Beispiel ⑩ bai·shpeel *example*
Bekleidungsgeschäft ⑩
 be·klai·dungks·ge·sheft
 clothing store
Belästigung ① be·les·ti·gung
 harassment
Belichtungsmesser ⑩
 be·likh·tungks·me·ser *light meter*
beliebt be·leept *popular*
Benzin ⑩ ben·tseen *gas/petrol*
Benzinkanister ⑩ ben·tseen·ka·nis·ter
 petrol can
beobachten be·aw·bakh·ten *watch*
bequem be·kvaym *comfortable*
berauben be·row·ben *rob*
Berg ⑩ berk *mountain*
Berghütte ① berk·hü·te *mountain hut*
Bergsteigen ⑩ berk·shtai·gen
 mountaineering
Bergweg ⑩ berk·vayk *mountain path*

Beruf ⓜ be·*roof* occupation • profession
berühmt be·*rümt* famous
berühren be·*rü·*ren touch
beschäftigt be·*shef·*tikht busy (person)
beschützen be·*shü·*tsen protect
sich beschweren zikh be·*shvair·*ren complain
besetzt be·*zetst* busy (phone)
Besitzer(in) ⓜ/ⓕ be·*zi·*tser/be·*zi·*tse·rin owner
besorgt be·*zorkt* worried
besser be·*ser* better
bestätigen be·*shtay·*ti·gen confirm (reservation)
beste bes·te best
bestechen be·*shte·*khen bribe
Besteck ⓝ be·*shtek* cutlery
besteigen be·*shtai·*gen board (plane, ship)
bestellen be·*shte·*len order
Bestellung ⓕ be·*shte·*lung order (restaurant)
bestrafen be·*shtrah·*fen punish
besuchen be·*zoo·*khen visit
Betäubung ⓕ be·*toy·*bung anaesthetic
sich beteiligen zikh be·*tai·*li·gen participate
Betrag ⓜ be·*trahk* amount
Betrüger(in) ⓜ/ⓕ be·*trü·*ger/ be·*trü·*ge·rin cheat
betrunken be·*trung·*ken drunk
Bett ⓝ bet *bed*
Bettlaken ⓝ bet·*lah·*ken sheet (bed)
Bettler(in) ⓜ/ⓕ bet·*ler/*bet·*le·*rin beggar
Bettwäsche ⓕ bet·*ve·*she linen (bed)
Bettzeug ⓝ bet·*tsoyk* bedding
Beutelmelone ⓕ boy·*tel·*me·law·ne cantaloupe
bezahlen be·*tsah·*len pay
Beziehung ⓕ be·*tsee·*ung relationship
BH ⓜ bay·*hah* bra
Bibel ⓕ bee·bel bible
Bibliothek ⓕ bi·bli·o·*tayk* library
Biene ⓕ bee·ne bee
Bier ⓝ beer beer
Bildschirm ⓜ bilt·*shirm* screen (TV, computer)
Billard ⓝ bil·*yart* pool (game)

billig bi·likh cheap
Birne ⓕ bir·ne pear
bis (Juni) bis (yoo·ni) until (June)
bis zu ... bis tsoo ... as far as ...
Biss ⓜ bis bite (animal)
ein bisschen ain bis·khen a little
bitte bi·te please
um etwas bitten um et·vas bi·ten ask for something
bitter bi·ter bitter
Blase ⓕ blah·ze blister
Blasenentzündung ⓕ blah·zen·en·tsün·dung cystitis
Blatt ⓝ blat leaf
blau blow blue
bleiben blai·ben stay (remain)
bleifrei blai·frai unleaded
Bleistift ⓜ blai·shtift pencil
blind blint blind
Blinddarm ⓜ blint·darm appendix
Blindenhund ⓜ blin·den·hunt guide dog
Blindenschrift ⓕ blin·den·shrift Braille
Blinker ⓜ bling·ker indicator
Blitz ⓜ blits lightning • flash
blockiert blo·keert blocked
Blume ⓕ bloo·me flower
Blumenhändler ⓜ bloo·men·hen·dler florist
Blumenkohl ⓜ bloo·men·kawl cauliflower
Blut ⓝ bloot blood
Blutdruck ⓜ bloot·druk blood pressure
Blutgruppe ⓕ bloot·gru·pe blood group
Bluttest ⓜ bloot·test blood test
Boden ⓜ baw·den floor
Bohne ⓕ baw·ne bean
Bonbon ⓝ bong·bong candy
Boot ⓝ bawt boat
an Bord an bort aboard
Bordkarte ⓕ bort·kar·te boarding pass
Botanischer Garten ⓜ bo·tah·ni·sher gar·ten botanic garden
Botschaft ⓕ bawt·shaft embassy
Botschafter(in) ⓜ/ⓕ bawt·shaf·ter/ bawt·shaf·te·rin ambassador
Boxen ⓝ bok·sen boxing
braten brah·ten fry

Bratpfanne ⓕ *braht·pfa·ne frying pan*
brauchen *brow·khen need*
braun *brown brown*
brechen *bre·khen vomit*
breit *brait wide*
Bremsen ⓕ pl *brem·zen brakes*
Bremsflüssigkeit ⓕ *brems·flü·sikh·kait brake fluid*
Brennholz ⓝ *bren·holts firewood*
Brennstoff ⓜ *bren·shtof fuel*
Brett ⓝ *bret board (plank)*
Brief ⓜ *breef letter*
Briefkasten ⓜ *breef·kas·ten mailbox*
Briefmarke ⓕ *breef·mar·ke stamp*
Briefumschlag ⓜ *breef·um·shlahk envelope*
brillant *bril·yant brilliant*
Brille ⓕ *bri·le glasses (spectacles)*
bringen *bring·en bring • take (something somewhere)*
Brokkoli ⓜ pl *bro·ko·li broccoli*
Bronchitis ⓕ *bron·khee·tis bronchitis*
Broschüre ⓕ *bro·shü·re brochure*
Brot ⓝ *brawt bread*
Brötchen ⓝ *brert·khen bread roll*
Brücke ⓕ *brü·ke bridge*
Bruder ⓜ *broo·der brother*
Brunnen ⓜ *bru·nen fountain*
Brust ⓕ *brust breast*
Brustkorb ⓜ *brust·korp chest*
Buch ⓝ *bookh book*
buchen *boo·khen book (reserve)*
Buchhalter(in) ⓜ/ⓕ *bookh·hal·ter/ bookh·hal·te·rin accountant*
Buchhandlung ⓕ *bookh·han·dlung bookshop*
Buddhist(in) ⓜ/ⓕ *bu·dist/bu·dis·tin Buddhist*
Buffet ⓝ *bü·fay buffet*
bügeln *bü·geln iron (clothes)*
Bühne ⓕ *bü·ne stage (theatre)*
Bundeskanzler(in) ⓜ/ⓕ *bun·des·kants·ler/bun·des·kants·le·rin prime minister (in Germany & Austria)*
Burg ⓕ *burk castle*
Bürgermeister(in) ⓜ/ⓕ *bür·ger·mais·ter/bür·ger·mais·te·rin mayor*
Bürgerrechte ⓝ pl *bür·ger·rekh·te civil rights*

Büro ⓝ *bü·raw office*
Büroangestellte ⓜ&ⓕ *bü·raw·an·ge·shtel·te office worker*
Bus ⓜ *bus bus (city)*
Busbahnhof ⓜ *bus·bahn·hawf bus station*
Bushaltestelle ⓕ *bus·hal·te·shte·le bus stop*
Butter ⓕ *bu·ter butter*

C

Café ⓝ *ka·fay cafe*
Campingplatz ⓜ *kem·ping·plats camping ground*
Cashewnuss ⓕ *kesh·yoo·nus cashew*
CD ⓕ *tsay·day CD*
Celsius ⓜ *tsel·zi·us centigrade*
Chancengleichheit ⓕ *shahng·sen·glaikh·hait equal opportunity*
charmant *shar·mant charming*
Chef(in) ⓜ/ⓕ *shef/she·fin boss*
chemische Reinigung ⓕ *khay·mi·she rai·ni·gung dry-cleaner*
Chili(sauce) ⓕ *chi·li(·zaw·se) chilli (sauce)*
Christ(in) ⓜ/ⓕ *krist/kris·tin Christian*
Computerspiel ⓝ *kom·pyoo·ter·shpeel computer game*
Coupon ⓜ *ku·pong coupon*
Couscous ⓜ *kus·kus couscous*
Cousin(e) ⓜ/ⓕ *ku·zen/ku·zee·ne cousin*
Cracker ⓜ *kre·ker cracker*
Cricket ⓝ *kri·ket cricket*
Curry(pulver) ⓝ *ker·ri(·pul·ver) curry (powder)*

D

Dach ⓝ *dakh roof*
Dachboden ⓜ *dakh·baw·den attic*
Dachs ⓜ *daks badger*
Damenbinden ⓕ pl *dah·men·bin·den sanitary napkins*
Dämmerung ⓕ *de·me·rung dawn • dusk*
danken *dang·ken thank*
Datum ⓝ *dah·tum date (day)*

Decke ① de·ke *blanket*
dein dain *your* sg inf
Demokratie ① de·mo·kra·*tee* *democracy*
Demonstration ① de·mon·stra·*tsyawn* *demonstration*
denken *deng*·ken *think*
Denkmal ⑩ dengk·mahl *monument*
Deo ① day·o *deodorant*
Detail ⑩ de·tai *detail*
Deutsch ⑩ doytsh *German*
Deutschland ⑩ doytsh·lant *Germany*
Dia ⑩ dee·a *slide (film)*
Diabetis ⑩ di·a·*bay*·tis *diabetes*
Diät ① di·ayt *diet*
Dichtung ① dikh·tung *poetry*
dick dik *thick • fat*
Dieb ⑩ deep *thief*
Dienstag ⑩ deens·tahk *Tuesday*
dieser *dee*·zer *this (one)*
direkt di·rekt *direct*
Diskette ① dis·ke·te *disk (computer)*
Disko(thek) ① dis·ko(·*tayk*) *disco*
Diskriminierung ① dis·kri·mi·*nee*·rung *discrimination*
Doktor(in) ⑩/① dok·tor/dok·*taw*·rin *doctor (title)*
Dokumentation ① do·ku·men·ta·*tsyawn* *documentary*
Dollar ⑩ do·lahr *dollar*
Dolmetscher(in) ⑩/① *dol*·met·sher/ *dol*·met·she·rin *interpreter*
Dom ⑩ dawm *cathedral*
Donner ⑩ do·ner *thunder*
Donnerstag ⑩ do·ners·tahk *Thursday*
Dope ⑩ dawp/dohp *dope (drugs)*
Doppelbett ⑩ do·pel·bet *double bed*
doppelt do·pelt *double*
Doppelzimmer ⑩ do·pel·tsi·mer *double room*
Dorf ⑩ dorf *village*
dort dort *there*
Dose ① daw·ze *can (tin)*
Dosenöffner ⑩ daw·zen·erf·ner *can opener*
Dozent(in) ⑩/① do·*tsent*/do·*tsen*·tin *lecturer*
Drachenfliegen ⑩ dra·khen·flee·gen *hang-gliding*

Draht ⑩ draht *wire*
draußen *drow*·sen *outside*
dringend *dring*·ent *urgent*
dritte *dri*·te *third*
Droge ① *draw*·ge *drug*
Drogenabhängigkeit ① *draw*·gen·ap· heng·ikh·kait *drug addiction*
Drogenhändler ⑩ *draw*·gen·hen·dler *drug dealer*
Druck ⑩ druk *pressure • print (artwork)*
Drüsenfieber ① *drü*·zen·fee·ber *glandular fever*
du doo *you* sg inf
dumm dum *stupid*
dunkel *dung*·kel *dark*
dünn dün *thin*
durch durkh *through*
Durchfall ⑩ durkh·fal *diarrhoea*
Durchwahl ① durkh·vahl *direct-dial*
durstig durs·tikh *thirsty*
Dusche ① doo·she *shower*
Dutzend ⑩ du·tsent *dozen*

E

Ebene ① ay·be·ne *plain*
Echse ① ek·se *lizard*
Ecke ① e·ke *corner*
egoistisch e·go·is·tish *selfish*
Ehe ① ay·e *marriage*
Ehefrau ① ay·e·frow *wife*
Ehemann ⑩ ay·e·man *husband*
ehrlich air·likh *honest*
Ei ⑩ ai *egg*
Eierstockzyste ① ai·er·shtok·tsüs·te *ovarian cyst*
eifersüchtig ai·fer·zükh·tikh *jealous*
in Eile in ai·le *in a hurry*
Eimer ⑩ ai·mer *bucket*
ein(s) ain(s) *one*
einfach ain·fakh *simple*
einfache Fahrkarte ① ain·fa·khe fahr·kar·te *one-way ticket*
einige ai·ni·ge *some • several*
einkaufen gehen ain·kow·fen gay·en *go shopping*
Einkaufszentrum ⑩ ain·kowfs·tsen·trum *shopping centre*
Einkommensteuer ① ain·ko·men·shtoy·er *income tax*

einladen *ain*·lah·den *invite*
einlassen *ain*·la·sen
    admit (allow to enter)
einlösen *ain*·ler·zen *cash (a cheque)*
einmal *ain*·mahl *once*
Einschreiben ⓝ *ain*·shrai·ben *registered mail*
eintreten *ain*·tray·ten *enter*
Eintrittsgeld ⓝ *ain*·trits·gelt
    cover charge
Eintrittskarte ⓕ *ain*·trits·kar·te
    (admission) ticket
Eintrittspreis ⓜ *ain*·trits·prais *admission price*
einzeln aufgeführt *ain*·tseln *owf*·ge·fürt
    itemised
Einzelzimmer ⓝ *ain*·tsel·tsi·mer
    single room
Eis ⓝ *ais* *ice*
Eiscreme ⓕ *ais*·kraym *ice cream*
Eisdiele ⓕ *ais*·dee·le *ice cream parlour*
Eisenwarengeschäft ⓝ *ai*·zen·vah·ren·ge·sheft *hardware store*
Eishockey ⓝ *ais*·ho·ki *ice hockey*
eislaufen *ais*·low·fen *ice skating*
Eispickel ⓜ *ais*·pi·kel *ice axe*
Ekzem ⓝ *ek*·tsaym *eczema*
Elektrizität ⓕ e·lek·tri·tsi·*tayt* *electricity*
Elektrogeschäft ⓝ e·lek·tro·ge·sheft
    electrical store
Eltern ⓜ pl *el*·tern *parents*
emotional e·mo·tsyo·*nahl* *emotional*
empfehlen emp·*fay*·len *recommend*
Empfindlichkeit ⓕ emp·*fint*·likh·kait
    film speed • sensitivity
(am) Ende (am) *en*·de *(at the) end*
Endstation ⓕ ent·shta·tsyawn *terminal*
Energie ⓕ e·ner·*gee* *energy*
eng eng *tight*
Englisch ⓝ *eng*·lish *English*
Enkelkind ⓝ *eng*·kel·kint *grandchild*
Ente ⓕ *en*·te *duck*
entscheiden ent·*shai*·den *decide*
sich entspannen zikh ent·*shpa*·nen *relax*
entwerfen ent·*ver*·fen *design*
entwerten ent·*ver*·ten *validate (ticket)*
Entzündung ⓕ en·*tsün*·dung
    infection • inflammation
Epilepsie ⓕ e·pi·lep·*see* *epilepsy*

er air *he*
erbrechen er·*bre*·khen *vomit*
Erbse ⓕ *erp*·se *pea*
Erdbeben ⓝ *ert*·bay·ben *earthquake*
Erdbeere ⓕ *ert*·bair·re *strawberry*
Erde ⓕ *er*·de *Earth*
Erdnuss ⓕ *ert*·nus *peanut • ground nut*
Erfahrung ⓕ er·*fah*·rung *experience*
erhalten er·*hal*·ten *receive*
erkältet sein er·*kel*·tet zain *have a cold*
Erlaubnis ⓕ er·*lowp*·nis *permission*
ermüden er·*mü*·den *tire*
ernst ernst *serious*
erstaunlich er·*shtown*·likh *amazing*
erste *ers*·te *first*
Erwachsene ⓜ&ⓕ er·*vak*·se·ne *adult*
erzählen er·*tsay*·len *tell*
Erziehung ⓕ er·*tsee*·ung *education*
Essen ⓝ *e*·sen *food*
essen *e*·sen *eat*
Essig ⓜ *e*·sikh *vinegar*
etwas *et*·vas *something • anything*
Euro ⓜ *oy*·ro *euro*
Europa ⓝ oy·*raw*·pa *Europe*
Euthanasie ⓕ oy·ta·na·*zee* *euthanasia*
Express- eks·*pres*· *express*
Expresspost ⓕ eks·*pres*·post
    express mail

F

Fabrik ⓕ fa·*breek* *factory*
fahren *fah*·ren *travel by vehicle*
Fahrgast ⓜ *fahr*·gast
    passenger (bus/taxi)
Fahrkarte ⓕ *fahr*·kar·te *ticket*
Fahrkartenautomat ⓜ *fahr*·kar·ten·ow·to·maht *ticket machine*
Fahrkartenkontrolleur(in) ⓜ/ⓕ *fahr*·kar·ten·kon·tro·ler·(rin) *ticket collector*
Fahrkartenverkauf ⓜ *fahr*·kar·ten·fer·kowf *ticket office*
Fahrplan ⓜ *fahr*·plahn *timetable*
Fahrrad ⓝ *fahr*·raht *bicycle*
Fahrradkette ⓕ *fahr*·raht·ke·te
    bicycle chain
Fahrzeugpapiere ⓝ pl
    fahr·tsoyk·pa·pee·re *car owner's title
    (document)*
Fallschirmspringen ⓝ
    fal·shirm·shpring·en *parachuting*

falsch falsh *false* • *wrong*
Familie ① fa·*mee*·li·e *family*
Familienname ⓜ fa·*mee*·li·en·nah·me *family name*
Familienstand ⓜ fa·*mee*·li·en·shtant *marital status*
Fan ⓜ fen *fan (sports)*
Farbe ① *far*·be *colour*
Farben ① pl *far*·ben *paints*
fast fast *almost*
Fastenzeit ① *fas*·ten·tsait *Lent*
faul fowl *lazy*
Fax ⓝ faks *fax*
Fechten ⓝ *fekh*·ten *fencing (sports)*
Feder ① *fay*·der *spring (coil)*
Fehler ⓜ *fay*·ler *mistake*
fehlerhaft fay·ler·haft *faulty*
Fehlgeburt ① *fayl*·ge·burt *miscarriage*
Feier ① *fai*·er *celebration*
Feige ① *fai*·ge *fig*
Feinkostgeschäft ⓝ *fain*·kost·ge·sheft *delicatessen*
Feld ⓝ felt *field*
Feldfrucht ① *felt*·frukht *crop*
Fels ⓜ fels *rock*
Fenster ⓝ *fens*·ter *window*
Ferien pl *fair*·ri·en *holidays/vacation*
Fern- fern· *long-distance*
Fernbedienung ① *fern*·be·dee·nung *remote control*
Fernbus ⓜ *fern*·bus *bus (intercity)*
Fernglas ⓝ *fern*·glahs *binoculars*
fernsehen *fern*·zay·en *watch TV*
Fernseher ⓜ *fern*·zay·er *TV set*
Fernsehserie ① *fern*·zay·zair·ri·e *TV series*
fertig *fer*·tikh *ready* • *finished*
Fest ⓝ fest *festival* • *party*
fest fest *solid*
fettarme Milch ① *fet*·ar·me milkh *skimmed milk*
feucht foykht *damp*
Feuchtigkeitscreme ①
foykh·tikh·kaits·kraym *moisturiser*
Feuer ⓝ *foy*·er *fire*
Feuerzeug ⓝ *foy*·er·tsoyk *cigarette lighter*
Fieber ⓝ *fee*·ber *fever*
Filet ⓝ fi·*lay* *fillet*

Film ⓜ film *movie (cinema)* • *film (for camera)*
finden *fin*·den *find*
Finger ⓜ *fing*·er *finger*
Firma ① *fir*·ma *company*
Fisch ⓜ fish *fish*
Fischen ⓝ *fi*·shen *fishing*
Fitness-Studio ⓝ *fit*·nes·shtoo·di·o *gym*
flach flakh *flat*
Flagge ① *fla*·ge *flag*
Flasche ① *fla*·she *bottle*
Flaschenöffner ⓜ *fla*·shen·erf·ner *bottle opener*
Fleisch ⓝ flaish *meat*
Fliege ① *flee*·ge *fly*
fliegen *flee*·gen *fly*
Flitterwochen pl *fli*·ter·vo·khen *honeymoon*
Floh ⓜ flaw *flea*
Flohmarkt ⓜ *flaw*·markt *flea-market*
Flüchtling ⓜ *flükht*·ling *refugee*
Flug ⓜ flook *flight*
Flügel ⓜ pl *flü*·gel *wings*
Fluggast ⓜ *flook*·gast *passenger (plane)*
Flughafen ⓜ *flook*·hah·fen *airport*
Flughafengebühr ①
flook·hah·fen·ge·bür *airport tax*
Fluglinie ① *flook*·lee·ni·e *airline*
Flugticket ⓝ *flook*·ti·ket *plane ticket*
Flugzeug ⓝ *flook*·tsoyk *aeroplane*
Fluss ⓜ flus *river*
folgen *fol*·gen *follow*
Forderung ① *for*·de·rung *demand*
Form ① form *shape*
formell for·*mel* *formal*
Foto ⓝ *faw*·to *photo*
Fotogeschäft ⓝ *faw*·to·ge·sheft *camera shop*
Fotograf(in) ⓜ/① fo·to·*grahf*/ fo·to·*grah*·fin *photographer*
Fotografie ① fo·to·gra·*fee* *photograph* • *photography*
fotografieren fo·to·gra·*fee*·ren *take a photograph*
Foul ⓝ fowl *foul*
Foyer ⓝ fo·a·*yay* *foyer*
Frage ① *frah*·ge *question*
eine Frage stellen *ai*·ne *frah*·ge *shte*·len *ask a question*

Frankreich ⓝ frangk·raikh France
Frau ⓕ frow woman
frei frai free (not bound) • vacant
Freibad ⓝ frai·baht
  (outdoor) swimming pool
Freigepäck ⓝ frai·ge·pek baggage
  allowance
Freitag ⓜ frai·tahk Friday
fremd fremt strange
Fremde ⓜ&ⓕ frem·de stranger
Fremdenverkehrsbüro ⓝ frem·den·fer·
  kairs·bü·raw tourist office
Freund ⓜ froynt
  male friend • boyfriend
Freundin ⓕ froyn·din
  female friend • girlfriend
freundlich froynt·likh friendly
Frieden ⓜ free·den peace
Friedhof ⓜ freet·hawf cemetery
frisch frish fresh (not stale)
Frischkäse ⓜ frish·kay·ze cream cheese
Friseur(in) ⓜ/ⓕ fri·zer/fri·zer·rin
  hairdresser
Frosch ⓜ frosh frog
Frost ⓜ frost frost
Frucht ⓕ frukht fruit
früh frü early
Frühling ⓜ frü·ling spring (season)
Frühstück ⓝ frü·shtük breakfast
Frühstücksflocke ⓕ frü·shtüks·flo·ke
  breakfast cereal
Frühstücksspeck ⓜ frü·shtüks·shpek
  bacon
fühlen fü·len feel
Führer ⓜ fü·rer (tour) guide •
  guidebook
Führerschein ⓜ fü·rer·shain
  driving licence
Führung ⓕ fü·rung guided tour
füllen fü·len fill
Fundbüro ⓝ funt·bü·raw
  lost property office
für für for
Fuß ⓜ foos foot
Fußball ⓜ foos·bal football • soccer
Fußgänger(in) ⓜ/ⓕ foos·geng·er/
  foos·geng·e·rin pedestrian
füttern fü·tern feed

G

Gabel ⓕ gah·bel fork
Gang ⓜ gang aisle
Gänge ⓜ pl geng·e gears
ganz gants whole
Garage ⓕ ga·rah·zhe
  garage (car shelter)
Garderobe ⓕ gar·draw·be wardrobe •
  cloakroom
Garnele ⓕ gar·nay·le prawn
Garten ⓜ gar·ten garden
Gas ⓝ gahs gas (for cooking)
Gasflasche ⓕ gahs·fla·she gas cylinder
Gaskartusche ⓕ gahs·kar·tu·she
  gas cartridge
Gastfreundschaft ⓕ gast·froynt·shaft
  hospitality
Gebäude ⓝ ge·boy·de building
geben gay·ben give
Gebet ⓝ ge·bayt prayer
Gebirgszug ⓜ ge·birks·tsook
  mountain range
gebraucht ge·browkht second-hand
Geburtsdatum ⓝ ge·burts·dah·tum date
  of birth
Geburtsort ⓜ ge·burts·ort
  place of birth
Geburtstag ⓜ ge·burts·tahk birthday
Geburtsurkunde ⓕ ge·burts·oor·kun·de
  birth certificate
gefährlich ge·fair·likh dangerous
Gefangene ⓜ&ⓕ ge·fang·e·ne prisoner
Gefängnis ⓝ ge·feng·nis prison
gefiltert ge·fil·tert filtered
gefrieren ge·free·ren freeze
Gefühle ⓝ pl ge·fü·le feelings
gegen gay·gen against
gegenüber gay·gen·ü·ber opposite
Gegenwart ⓕ gay·gen·vart
  present (time)
Gehacktes ⓝ ge·hak·tes mince
Gehalt ⓝ ge·halt salary
Geheimnis ⓝ ge·haim·nis secret
gehen gay·en walk
Gehweg ⓜ gay·vayk footpath
Geisteswissenschaften ⓕ pl
  gais·tes·vi·sen·shaf·ten humanities

geizig *gai*-tsikh *stingy*
gelangweilt ge-*lang*-vailt *bored*
gelb gelp *yellow*
Geld ⑩ gelt *money*
Geldautomat ⑩ *gelt*-ow-to-maht
  automatic teller machine (ATM)
Geldbuße ① *gelt*-boo-se
  fine (payment)
Geldschein ⑩ *gelt*-shain *banknote*
Geldwechsel ⑩ *gelt*-vek-sel
  currency exchange
Gelegenheitsarbeit ①
  ge-*lay*-gen-haits-ar-bait *casual work*
Gemüse ⑩ ge-*mü*-ze *vegetable*
Genehmigung ① ge-*nay*-mi-gung
  permit
genug ge-*nook* *enough*
Gepäck ⑩ ge-*pek* *luggage*
Gepäckaufbewahrung ①
  ge-*pek*-owf-be-vah-rung *left luggage*
Gepäckausgabe ① ge-*pek*-ows-gah-be
  luggage claim
gerade ge-*rah*-de *straight (direction)*
Gerechtigkeit ① ge-*rekh*-tikh-kait *justice*
Gericht ⑩ ge-*rikht* *court (legal)*
Geruch ⑩ ge-*rookh* *smell*
Geschäft ⑩ ge-*sheft* *shop • business*
Geschäftsfrau ① ge-*shefts*-frow
  businesswoman
Geschäftsmann ⑩ ge-*shefts*-man
  businessman
Geschäftsreise ① ge-*shefts*-rai-ze
  business trip
Geschenk ⑩ ge-*shengk* *present (gift)*
Geschichte ① ge-*shikh*-te *story*
Geschlechtskrankheit ①
  ge-*shlekhts*-krangk-hait *venereal disease*
geschlossen ge-*shlo*-sen *closed*
geschützte (Tierarten) ① pl ge-*shüts*-te
  (teer-ar-ten) *protected (species)*
Geschwindigkeit ① ge-*shvin*-dikh-kait
  speed
Geschwindigkeitsbegrenzung ①
  ge-*shvin*-dikh-kaits-be-gren-tsung
  speed limit
Gesetz ⑩ ge-*zets* *law*
Gesetzgebung ① ge-*zets*-gay-bung
  legislation
Gesicht ⑩ ge-*zikht* *face*

gestern ges-tern *yesterday*
Gesundheit ① ge-*zunt*-hait *health*
Getränk ⑩ ge-*trengk* *drink*
Getränkehandel ⑩ ge-*treng*-ke-han-del
  liquor store
getrennt ge-*trent* *separate (distinct)*
Gewebe ⑩ ge-*vay*-be *fabric*
Gewicht ⑩ ge-*vikht* *weight*
Gewinn ⑩ ge-*vin* *profit*
gewinnen ge-*vi*-nen *win*
Gewürznelke ① ge-*vürts*-nel-ke
  clove (spice)
Gezeiten pl ge-*tsai*-ten *tides*
giftig *gif*-tikh *poisonous*
Giftmüll ⑩ *gift*-mül *toxic waste*
Gin ⑩ dzhin *gin*
Gipfel ⑩ *gip*-fel *peak*
Gitarre ① gi-*ta*-re *guitar*
Glas ⑩ glahs *glass • jar*
glatt glat *slippery*
gleich dort glaikh dort *right (exactly) there*
gleiche *glai*-khe *same*
Gleichheit ① *glaikh*-hait *equality*
Gleis ⑩ glais *platform*
Gleitschirmfliegen ⑩
  glait-shirm-flee-gen *paragliding*
Gletscher ⑩ *glet*-sher *glacier*
Glück ⑩ glük *luck • happiness*
glücklich *glük*-likh *lucky • happy*
Glückwunsch ⑩ *glük*-vunsh
  congratulations
Glühbirne ① *glü*-bir-ne *light bulb*
Gold ⑩ golt *gold*
Golfplatz ⑩ *golf*-plats *golf course*
Gott ⑩ got *god (general)*
Gottesdienst ⑩ go-*tes*-deenst
  church service
Grab ⑩ grahp *grave • tomb*
Grad ⑩ graht *degree*
grafische Kunst ① *grah*-fi-she kunst
  graphic art
Gramm ⑩ gram *gram*
Gras ⑩ grahs *grass • pot (dope)*
gratis *grah*-tis *free (gratis)*
grau grow *grey*
Grenze ① *gren*-tse *border*
Grippe ① *gri*-pe *influenza*
groß grows *big • great • tall*

Größe ① grer·se *size (general)*
Großeltern ⊙ pl graws·el·tern *grandparents*
Großmutter ① graws·mu·ter *grandmother*
Großvater ⊙ graws·fah·ter *grandfather*
grün grün *green*
Grund ⊙ grunt *reason*
Gurke ① gur·ke *cucumber*
Gürtel ⊙ gür·tel *belt*
gut goot *good • well*
gutaussehend goot·ows·zay·ent *handsome*
Gymnastik ① güm·nas·tik *gymnastics*
Gynäkologe ⊙ gü·ne·ko·law·ge *gynaecologist*
Gynäkologin ① gü·ne·ko·law·gin *gynaecologist*

H

Haar ⊙ hahr *hair*
Haarbürste ① hahr·bürs·te *hairbrush*
haben hah·ben *have*
Hafen ⊙ hah·fen *port • harbour*
Hafer(flocken) ⊙ pl hah·fer(·flo·ken) *oats*
Hähnchenschenkel ⊙ hayn·khen·sheng·kel *chicken drumstick*
Halal- ha·lal· *halal*
Hälfte ① helf·te *half*
Hallenbad ⊙ ha·len·baht *(indoor) swimming pool*
hallo ha·lo/ha·law *hello*
halluzinieren ha·lu·tsi·nee·ren *hallucinate*
Hals ⊙ hals *throat*
Halskette ① hals·ke·te *necklace*
Halsschmerzen pl hals·shmer·tsen *sore throat*
Halt ⊙ halt *stop*
Hammer ⊙ ha·mer *hammer*
Hamster ⊙ hams·ter *hamster*
Hand ① hant *hand*
Handel ⊙ han·del *trade*
handgemacht hant·ge·makht *handmade*
Handschuh ⊙ hant·shoo *glove*
Handtasche ① hant·ta·she *handbag*
Handtuch ⊙ han·tookh *towel*

Handwerk ⊙ hant·verk *crafts*
Handy ⊙ hen·di *mobile phone*
Hang ⊙ hang *slope*
Hängematte ① heng·e·ma·te *hammock*
hart hart *hard (not soft)*
Haschee ⊙ ha·shay *hash*
Haupt- howpt· *main*
Hauptplatz ⊙ howpt·plats *main square*
Haus ⊙ hows *house*
Hausarbeit ① hows·ar·bait *housework*
nach Hause nahkh how·ze *(go) home*
Hausfrau ① hows·frow *homemaker*
Hausmann ⊙ hows·man *homemaker*
Haut ① howt *skin*
heilig hai·likh *holy*
Heiligabend ⊙ hai·likh·ah·bent *Christmas Eve*
Heilige ⊙&① hai·li·ge *saint*
Heim ⊙ haim *home*
Heimweh haben haim·vay hah·ben *to be homesick*
heiraten hai·rah·ten *marry*
heiß hais *hot*
Heizgerät ⊙ haits·ge·rayt *heater*
helfen hel·fen *help*
hell hel *light (weight)*
Helm ⊙ helm *helmet*
Hemd ⊙ hemt *shirt*
Herausgeber(in) ⊙/① he·rows·gay·ber/he·rows·gay·be·rin *editor*
Herbst ⊙ herpst *autumn • fall*
Herd ⊙ hert *stove*
Hering ⊙ hay·ring *herring*
Heringe ⊙ pl hay·ring·e *tent pegs*
Heroin ⊙ he·ro·een *heroin*
Herz ⊙ herts *heart*
Herzleiden ⊙ herts·lai·den *heart condition*
Herzschrittmacher ⊙ herts·shrit·ma·kher *pacemaker (heart)*
Heuschnupfen ⊙ hoy·shnup·fen *hay fever*
heute hoy·te *today*
heute Abend hoy·te ah·bent *tonight*
hier heer *here*
Hilfe ① hil·fe *help*
Himbeere ① him·bair·re *raspberry*
Himmel ⊙ hi·mel *sky*
Hindu ⊙&① hin·du *Hindu*

hinten *hin*·ten *at the back*
hinter *hin*·ter *behind*
hinüber hi·*nü*·ber *across (to)*
historisch his·*taw*·rish *historical*
Hitze ① *hi*·tse *heat*
HIV-positiv hah-ee-fow-*paw*·zi·teef *HIV positive*
hoch hawkh *high (up)*
Hochebene ① *hawkh*·ay·be·ne *plateau*
Hochzeit ① *hokh*·tsait *wedding*
Hochzeitsgeschenk ⑪ *hokh*·tsaits·ge·shengk *wedding present*
Hochzeitstorte ① *hokh*·tsaits·tor·te *wedding cake*
Hockey ⑪ *ho*·ki *hockey*
Höhe ① *he*·re *altitude*
Höhle ① *her*·le *cave*
Holz ⑪ holts *wood*
homöopathisches Mittel ⑪ haw·mer·o·*pah*·ti·shes *mi*·tel *homeopathic medicine*
homosexuell haw·mo·zek·su·*el* *homosexual*
Honig ⑪ *haw*·nikh *honey*
hören *her*·ren *hear • listen*
Hörgerät ⑪ *her*·ge·rayt *hearing aid*
Horoskop ⑪ ho·ros·*kawp* *horoscope*
Hose ① *haw*·ze *trousers/pants*
Hotel ⑪ ho·*tel* *hotel*
hübsch hüpsh *pretty*
Hüfttasche ① *hüft*·ta·she *bumbag*
Hügel ⑪ *hü*·gel *hill*
Huhn ⑪ hoon *chicken*
Hühnerbrust ① *hü*·ner·brust *chicken breast*
Hülsenfrucht ① *hül*·zen·frukht *legume*
Hund ⑪ hunt *dog*
hundert *hun*·dert *hundred*
hungrig *hung*·rikh *hungry*
husten *hoos*·ten *cough*
Hustensaft ⑪ *hoos*·ten·zaft *cough medicine*
Hut ⑪ hoot *hat*
Hütte ① *hü*·te *hut*
Hüttenkäse ⑪ *hü*·ten·kay·ze *cottage cheese*

I

ich ikh *I*
Idee ① i·*day* *idea*
Idiot ⑪ i·di·*awt* *idiot*

ihr eer *her • their*
Ihr eer *your (polite)*
illegal i·le·*gahl* *illegal*
immer *i*·mer *always • forever*
Immigration ① i·mi·gra·*tsyawn* *immigration*
in in *in • at*
inbegriffen *in*·be·gri·fen *included*
Indien *in*·di·en *India*
Industrie ① in·dus·*tree* *industry*
Informationstechnologie ① in·for·ma·*tsyawns*·tekh·no·lo·gee *IT*
Ingenieuer(in) ⑪/① in·zhe·*nyer*(·rin) *engineer*
Ingenieurwesen ⑪ in·zhe·*nyer*·vay·zen *engineering*
Ingwer ⑪ *ing*·ver *ginger*
Injektion ① in·yek·*tsyawn* *injection (medical)*
injizieren in·yi·*tsee*·ren *inject*
innen *i*·nen *inside*
Innenstadt ① *i*·nen·shtat *city centre*
innerhalb (einer Stunde) *i*·ner·halp (*ai*·ner shtun·de) *within (an hour)*
Insekt ⑪ in·*zekt* *insect*
Insektenschutzmittel ⑪ in·*zek*·ten·shuts·mi·tel *insect repellant*
Insel ① *in*·zel *island*
Installateur(in) ⑪/① in·sta·la·*ter*/ in·sta·la·*ter*·rin *plumber*
interessant in·tre·*sant* *interesting*
international in·ter·na·tsyo·*nahl* *international*
Internet ⑪ *in*·ter·net *Internet*
Interview ⑪ *in*·ter·vyoo *interview*
Intrauterinpessar ⑪ in·tra·u·te·reen·pe·*sahr* *IUD*
irgendein ir·gent·*ain* *any*
irgendetwas ir·gent·*et*·vas *anything*
irgendwo ir·gent·*vaw* *anywhere*
Irland ① *ir*·lant *Ireland*

J

ja yah *yes*
Jacke ① *ya*·ke *jacket*
Jagd ① yahkt *hunting*
Jahr ⑪ yahr *year*
Jahreszeit ① *yah*·res·tsait *season*

I

Japan ⓝ *yah·pahn Japan*
Jeans ⓟ pl *dzheens jeans*
jeder *yay·der everyone*
jeder ⓜ *yay·der each • every*
jemand *yay·mant someone*
Jetlag ⓜ *dzhet·leg jet lag*
jetzt *yetst now*
Jockey ⓜ *dzho·ki jockey*
Joga ⓝ *yaw·ga yoga*
Joggen ⓝ *dzho·gen jogging*
Joghurt ⓜ *yaw·gurt yogurt*
Journalist(in) ⓜ/ⓕ *zhur·na·list/*
  zhur·na·lis·tin journalist
Juckreiz ⓜ *yuk·raits itch*
jüdisch *yü·dish Jewish*
Jugendherberge ⓕ *yoo·gent·her·ber·ge*
  youth hostel
jung *yung young*
Junge ⓜ *yung·e boy*
Jura ⓝ *yoo·ra law (subject)*

K

Kabel ⓝ *kah·bel cable*
Kaffee ⓜ *ka·fay coffee*
Kakao ⓜ *ka·kow cocoa*
Kakerlake ⓕ *kah·ker·lah·ke cockroach*
Kalbfleisch ⓝ *kalp·flaish veal*
Kalender ⓜ *ka·len·der calendar*
kalt *kalt cold*
Kamera ⓕ *ka·me·ra camera*
Kamm ⓜ *kam comb*
Kampf ⓜ *kampf fight*
Kampfsport ⓜ *kampf·shport*
  martial arts
Kanada ⓝ *ka·na·dah Canada*
Kanarienvogel ⓜ *ka·nah·ri·en·faw·gel*
  canary
Kaninchen ⓝ *ka·neen·khen rabbit*
Kantine ⓕ *kan·tee·ne canteen*
Kapelle ⓕ *ka·pe·le*
  chapel • band (music)
Kapitalismus ⓜ *ka·pi·ta·lis·mus*
  capitalism
kaputt *ka·put broken*
Karte ⓕ *kar·te map • ticket*
Karten ⓕ pl *kar·ten cards*
Kartoffel ⓕ *kar·to·fel potato*
Karton ⓜ *kar·tong box • carton*
Karwoche ⓕ *kahr·vo·khe Holy Week*

Käse ⓜ *kay·ze cheese*
Kasino ⓝ *ka·zee·no casino*
Kasse ⓕ *ka·se cash register • checkout •*
  ticket counter
Kassette ⓕ *ka·se·te cassette*
Kassierer(in) ⓜ/ⓕ *ka·see·rer/*
  ka·see·re·rin cashier
Katholik(in) ⓜ/ⓕ *ka·to·leek/*
  ka·to·lee·kin Catholic
Kätzchen ⓝ *kets·khen kitten*
Katze ⓕ *ka·tse cat*
kaufen *kow·fen buy*
Kaugummi ⓝ *kow·gu·mi chewing gum*
Kaviar ⓜ *kah·vi·ahr caviar*
Keilriemen ⓜ *kail·ree·men fanbelt*
keine *kai·ne none*
Keks ⓜ *kayks biscuit • cookie*
Keller ⓜ *ke·ler cellar*
Kellner(in) ⓜ/ⓕ *kel·ner/kel·ne·rin*
  waiter
kennen *ke·nen know (a person)*
Keramik ⓕ *ke·rah·mik ceramic*
Kerze ⓕ *ker·tse candle*
Kessel ⓜ *ke·sel kettle*
Ketchup ⓜ *ket·chap ketchup*
Kette ⓕ *ke·te chain*
Kichererbse ⓕ *ki·kher·erp·se chickpea*
Kiefer ⓜ *kee·fer jaw*
Kilogramm ⓝ *kee·lo·gram kilogram*
Kilometer ⓜ *ki·lo·may·ter kilometre*
Kind ⓝ *kint child*
Kinder ⓟ pl *kin·der children*
Kinderbetreuung ⓕ *kin·der·be·troy·ung*
  childminding
Kindergarten ⓜ *kin·der·gar·ten*
  kindergarten
Kinderkrippe ⓕ *kin·der·kri·pe creche*
Kindersitz ⓜ *kin·der·zits child seat*
Kino ⓝ *kee·no cinema*
Kiosk ⓜ *kee·osk convenience store*
Kirche ⓕ *kir·khe church*
Kissen ⓝ *ki·sen pillow*
Kissenbezug ⓜ *ki·sen·be·tsook*
  pillowcase
Kiwifrucht ⓕ *kee·vi·frukht kiwifruit*
Klasse ⓕ *kla·se class*
klassisch *kla·sish classical*
Klavier ⓝ *kla·veer piano*
Kleid ⓝ *klait dress*

Kleidung ① *klai*-dung *clothing*
klein klain *little • small• short* (height)
Kleingeld ⑩ *klain*-gelt *loose change*
klettern *kle*-tern *climb*
Klettern ⑩ *kle*-tern *rock climbing*
Klima ⑩ *klee*-ma *climate*
Klimaanlage ① *klee*-ma-an-lah-ge *air-conditioning*
klingeln *kling*-eln *ring* (of phone)
Klippe ① *kli*-pe *cliff*
Kloster ⑩ *klaws*-ter *convent • monastery*
Knappheit ① *knap*-hait *shortage*
Kneipe ① *knai*-pe *pub*
Knie ⑩ *knee knee*
Knoblauch ⑩ *knawp*-lowkh *garlic*
Knöchel ⑩ *kner*-khel *ankle*
Knochen ⑩ *kno*-khen *bone*
Knopf ⑩ knopf *button*
Knoten ⑩ *knaw*-ten *lump* (health)
Koch ⑩ kokh *chef • cook*
kochen *ko*-khen *cook*
Kocher ⑩ *ko*-kher *camping stove*
Köchin ① *ker*-khin *chef • cook*
Köder ⑩ *ker*-der *bait*
Koffer ⑩ *ko*-fer *suitcase*
Kofferraum ⑩ *ko*-fer-rowm *boot • trunk*
Kohl ⑩ kawl *cabbage*
Kokain ⑩ ko-ka-*een cocaine*
Kollege ⑩ ko-*lay*-ge *colleague*
Kollegin ① ko-*lay*-gin *colleague*
kommen *ko*-men *come*
Kommunion ① ko-mun-*yawn communion*
Komödie ① ko-*mer*-di-e *comedy*
Kompass ⑩ *kom*-pas *compass*
Konditorei ① kon-dee-to-*rai cake shop*
Kondom ⑩ kon-*dawm condom*
König ⑩ *ker*-nikh *king*
Königin ① *ker*-ni-gin *queen*
können *ker*-nen *be able to • have permission to*
konservativ kon-zer-va-*teef conservative*
Konsulat ⑩ kon-zu-*laht consulate*
Kontaktlinsen ① pl kon-*takt*-lin-zen *contact lenses*
Kontostand ⑩ *kon*-to-shtant *balance* (account)
Kontrollstelle ① kon-*trol*-shte-le *checkpoint*

Konzert ⑩ kon-*tsert concert*
Konzerthalle ① kon-*tsert*-ha-le *concert hall*
Kopf ⑩ kopf *head*
Kopfsalat ⑩ *kopf*-za-laht *lettuce*
Kopfschmerzen pl *kopf*-shmer-tsen *headache*
Kopfschmerztablette ① *kopf*-shmerts-ta-ble-te *aspirin*
Korb ⑩ korp *basket*
Körper ⑩ *ker*-per *body*
korrupt ko-*rupt corrupt*
koscher *kaw*-sher *kosher*
kosten *kos*-ten *cost*
köstlich *kerst*-likh *delicious*
Kraft ① kraft *power*
Krampf ⑩ krampf *cramp*
krank krangk *sick*
Krankenhaus ⑩ *krang*-ken-hows *hospital*
Krankenpfleger ⑩ *krang*-ken-pflay-ger *nurse*
Krankenschwester ① *krang*-ken-shves-ter *nurse*
Krankenwagen ⑩ *krang*-ken-vah-gen *ambulance*
Krankheit ① *krangk*-hait *disease*
Kräuter pl *kroy*-ter *herbs*
Krebs ⑩ krayps *cancer*
Kreditkarte ① kre-*deet*-kar-te *credit card*
Kreisverkehr ⑩ *krais*-fer-kair *roundabout*
Kreuz ⑩ kroyts *cross* (religious)
Krieg ⑩ kreek *war*
Kritik ① kri-*teek review* (arts)
Küche ① *kü*-khe *kitchen*
Kuchen ⑩ *koo*-khen *cake*
Kuckucksuhr ① *ku*-kuks-oor *cuckoo clock*
Kugelschreiber ⑩ *koo*-gel-shrai-ber *pen* (ballpoint)
Kuh ① koo *cow*
Kühler ⑩ *kü*-ler *radiator*
Kühlschrank ⑩ *kül*-shrangk *refrigerator*
sich kümmern um zikh *kü*-mern um *look after*
Kunde ⑩ *kun*-de *client*
kündigen *kün*-di-gen *resign*
Kundin ① *kun*-din *client*

Kunst ① kunst *art*
Kunstgalerie ① kunst·ga·le·ree *art gallery*
Kunstgewerbe ⑩ kunst·ge·ver·be *arts & crafts*
Kunsthandwerk ⑩ kunst·hant·verk *handicrafts*
Künstler(in) ⑩/① künst·ler/künst·le·rin *artist*
Kunstsammlung ① kunst·zam·lung *art collection*
Kunstwerk ⑩ kunst·verk *work of art*
Kupplung ① kup·lung *clutch (car)*
Kürbis ⑩ kür·bis *pumpkin*
kurz kurts *short*
kurzärmelig kurts·er·me·likh *short-sleeved*
Kuss ⑩ kus *kiss*
küssen kü·sen *kiss*
Küste ① küs·te *coast*

L

lächeln le·kheln *smile*
lachen la·khen *laugh*
Lachs ⑩ laks *salmon*
Lage ① lah·ge *situation*
Lager ⑩ lah·ger *lager*
Lamm ⑩ lam *lamb*
Land ⑩ lant *country • countryside*
Landschaft ① lant·shaft *scenery*
Landwirtschaft ① lant·virt·shaft *agriculture*
lang lang *long*
langärmelig lang·er·me·likh *long-sleeved*
langsam lang·zahm *slow • slowly*
langweilig lang·vai·likh *boring*
Laptop ⑩ lep·top *laptop*
Lastwagen ⑩ last·vah·gen *truck*
Lauch ⑩ lowkh *leek*
laufen low·fen *run*
Läuse ① pl loy·ze *lice*
laut lowt *loud • noisy*
Lautstärke ① lowt·shter·ke *volume (loudness)*
Lawine ① la·vee·ne *avalanche*
leben lay·ben *to live*
Leben ⑩ lay·ben *life*

Lebenslauf ⑩ lay·bens·lowf *resume • CV*
Lebensmittelhändler ⑩ lay·bens·mi·tel·hen·dler *greengrocer*
Lebensmittelladen ⑩ lay·bens·mi·tel·lah·den *grocery store*
Lebensmittelvergiftung ① lay·bens·mi·tel·fer·gif·tung *food poisoning*
Leber ① lay·ber *liver*
Leder ⑩ lay·der *leather*
ledig lay·dikh *single (of person)*
leer lair *empty*
legen lay·gen *put (horizontal)*
Lehrer(in) ⑩/① lair·rer/lair·re·rin *teacher • instructor*
leicht laikht *easy*
Leichtathletik ① laikht·at·lay·tik *athletics*
leihen lai·en *borrow*
Leinen ⑩ lai·nen *linen (fabric)*
Leitungswasser ⑩ lai·tungks·va·ser *tap water*
Lenker ⑩ leng·ker *handlebar*
lernen ler·nen *learn*
Lesbierin ① les·bi·e·rin *lesbian*
lesen lay·zen *read*
letzte lets·te *last*
Licht ⑩ likht *light*
lieben lee·ben *love*
liebevoll lee·be·fol *caring*
Liebhaber(in) ⑩/① leep·hah·ber/leep·hah·be·rin *lover*
Lied ⑩ leet *song*
liefern lee·fern *deliver*
Lieferwagen ⑩ lee·fer·vah·gen *van*
liegen lee·gen *lie (not stand)*
Lift ⑩ lift *lift • elevator*
lila lee·la *purple*
Limonade ① li·mo·nah·de *lemonade*
Limone ① li·maw·ne *lime*
Linie ① lee·ni·e *line*
links lingks *left (direction)*
linksgerichtet lingks·ge·rikh·tet *left-wing*
Linse ① lin·ze *lentil*
Lippen ① pl li·pen *lips*
Lippenbalsam ⑩ li·pen·bal·zahm *lip balm*
Lippenstift ⑩ li·pen·shtift *lipstick*

Liter ⓝ *lee-*ter *litre*
Löffel ⓜ *ler-*fel *spoon*
Lohn ⓜ *lawn wage*
Lohnsatz ⓜ *lawn-*zats *rate of pay*
Lokal ⓝ *lo-kahl bar*
Luft ⓕ *luft air*
Luftkrankheit ⓕ *luft-*krangk-hait
  airsickness
Luftpost ⓕ *luft-*post *airmail*
Luftpumpe ⓕ *luft-*pum-pe *pump*
Luftverschmutzung ⓕ
  *luft-*fer-shmu-tsung *air pollution*
Lügner(in) ⓜ/ⓕ *lüg-*ner/*lüg-*ne-rin *liar*
Lungen(in) ⓟ pl *lung-*en *lungs*
lustig *lus-*tikh *funny*
luxuriös *luk-*su-ri-ers *luxury*

M

machen *ma-*khen *make*
Mädchen ⓝ *mayt-*khen *girl*
Magen ⓜ *mah-*gen *stomach*
Magen-Darm-Katarrh ⓜ
  *mah-*gen-darm-ka-tar *gastroenteritis*
Magenschmerzen ⓜ pl
  *mah-*gen-shmer-tsen *stomachache*
Magenverstimmung ⓕ
  *mah-*gen-fer-shti-mung *indigestion*
Majonnaise ⓕ *ma-*yo-nay-ze
  mayonnaise
Makler(in) ⓜ/ⓕ *mahk-*ler/*mahk-*le-rin
  real estate agent
Maler(in) ⓜ/ⓕ *mah-*ler/*mah-*le-rin
  painter
Malerei ⓕ *mah-*le-rai *painting (the art)*
Mama ⓕ *ma-*ma *mum* • *mom*
Mammogramm ⓝ *ma-*mo-gram
  mammogram
manchmal *mankh-*mahl *sometimes*
Mandarine ⓕ *man-*da-ree-ne *mandarin*
Mandel ⓕ *man-*del *almond*
Mann ⓜ *man man*
Mannschaft ⓕ *man-*shaft *team*
Mantel ⓜ *man-*tel *overcoat* • *cloak*
Margarine ⓕ *mar-*ga-ree-ne *margarine*
Marihuana ⓕ *ma-ri-*hu-ah-na *marijuana*
Markt ⓜ *markt market*
Marktplatz ⓜ *markt-*plats
  market square
Marmelade ⓕ *mar-*me-lah-de *jam*

Maschine ⓕ *ma-*shee-ne *machine*
Masern pl *mah-*zern *measles*
Massage ⓕ *ma-*sah-zhe *massage*
Masseur(in) ⓜ/ⓕ *ma-*ser(-rin) *masseur/
  masseuse*
Material ⓝ *ma-*te-ri-ahl *material*
Matratze ⓕ *ma-*tra-tse *mattress*
Matte ⓕ *ma-*te *mat*
Mauer ⓕ *mow-*er *wall (outer)*
Maurer(in) ⓜ/ⓕ *mow-*rer/*mow-*re-rin
  bricklayer
Maus ⓕ *mows mouse*
Mechaniker(in) ⓜ/ⓕ *me-*khah-ni-ker/
  *me-*khah-ni-ke-rin *mechanic*
Medien pl *may-*di-en *media*
Meditation ⓕ *me-*di-ta-tsyawn
  meditation
Medizin ⓕ *me-*di-tseen *medicine*
Meer ⓝ *mair sea*
Meeresküste ⓕ *mair-*res-küs-te *seaside*
Meerrettich ⓜ *mair-*re-tikh *horseradish*
Mehl ⓝ *mayl flour*
mehr *mair more*
nicht mehr *nikht mair not any more*
mein *main mine* • *my*
Meinung ⓕ *mai-*nung *opinion*
Meisterschaften ⓕ pl *mais-*ter-shaf-ten
  championships
Melodie ⓕ *me-*lo-dee *tune*
Melone ⓕ *me-*law-ne *melon*
Mensch ⓜ *mensh person*
Menschen ⓜ pl *men-*shen *people*
Menschenrechte ⓝ pl *men-*shen-rekh-te
  human rights
menschlich *mensh-*likh *human*
Menstruation ⓕ *mens-*tru-a-tsyawn
  menstruation
Menstruationsbeschwerden ⓟ pl *mens-*
  tru-a-tsyawns-be-shver-den *period pain*
Messe ⓕ *me-*se *mass (Catholic)* • *trade
  fair*
Messer ⓝ *me-*ser *knife*
Metall ⓝ *me-*tal *metal*
Meter ⓜ *may-*ter *metre*
Metzgerei ⓕ *mets-*ge-rai
  butcher's shop
mieten *mee-*ten *rent* • *hire*
Mietvertrag ⓜ *meet-*fer-trahk *lease*
Migräne ⓕ *mi-*gray-ne *migraine*

Mikrowelle ① *mee*·kro·ve·le *microwave*
Milch ① *milkh milk*
Milchprodukte ⑩ pl *milkh*·pro·duk·te
dairy products
Militär ⑩ mi·li·*tair military*
Millimeter ⑩ mi·li·*may*·ter *millimetre*
Million ① mi·*lyawn million*
Mineralwasser ⑩ mi·ne·*rahl*·va·ser
mineral water
Minute ① mi·*noo*·te *minute*
mischen *mi*·shen *mix*
mit mit *with*
Mitglied ⑩ *mit*·gleet *member*
Mittag ⑩ *mi*·tahk *noon*
Mittagessen ⑩ *mi*·tahk·e·sen *lunch*
Mitteilung ① *mi*·tai·lung *message*
Mitternacht ① *mi*·ter·nakht *midnight*
Mittwoch ⑩ *mit*·vokh *Wednesday*
Möbel ⑩ pl *mer*·bel *furniture*
Modem ⑩ *maw*·dem *modem*
mögen *mer*·gen *to like*
möglich *merk*·likh *possible*
Mohrrübe ① *mawr*·rü·be *carrot*
Monat ⑩ *maw*·nat *month*
Montag ⑩ *mawn*·tahk *Monday*
Morgen ⑩ *mor*·gen
morning (6am – 10am)
morgen *mor*·gen *tomorrow*
morgen früh *mor*·gen frü
tomorrow morning
Moschee ① mo·*shay mosque*
Moskitospirale ① mos·ke·to·shpi·rah·le
mosquito coil
Moslem ⑩ *mos*·lem *Muslim*
Moslime ① mos·*lee*·me *Muslim*
Motor ⑩ *maw*·tor/mo·*tawr engine*
Motorboot ⑩ *maw*·tor·bawt *motorboat*
Motorrad ⑩ *maw*·tor·raht *motorcycle*
Möwe ① *mer*·ve *seagull*
müde *mü*·de *tired*
Müll ⑩ mül *rubbish*
Mülleimer ⑩ *mül*·ai·mer *rubbish bin*
Mund ⑩ munt *mouth*
Mundfäule ① *munt*·foy·le
thrush (medical condition)
Münzen ① pl *mün*·tsen *coins*
Muschel ① *mu*·shel *mussel*
Museum ⑩ mu·*zay*·um *museum*
Musik ① mu·*zeek music*

Musiker(in) ⑩/① *moo*·zi·ker/
moo·zi·ke·rin *musician*
Muskel ⑩ *mus*·kel *muscle*
Muskelzerrung ① *mus*·kel·tser·rung
sprain
Müsli ⑩ *müs*·li *muesli*
mutig *moo*·tikh *brave*
Mutter ① *mu*·ter *mother*

N

nach nahkh *after • towards*
Nachkomme ⑩ *nahkh*·ko·me
descendant
Nachmittag ⑩ *nahkh*·mi·tahk *afternoon*
Nachname ⑩ *nahkh*·nah·me *surname*
Nachrichten pl *nahkh*·rikh·ten *news*
nächste *naykhs*·te *next • nearest*
Nacht ① nakht *night*
Nadel ① *nah*·del *sewing needle •*
syringe
Nagelknipser ⑩ pl *nah*·gel·knip·ser
nail clippers
nahe *nah*·e *close (nearby)*
in der Nähe in dair *nay*·e *nearby*
nähen *nay*·en *sew*
Name ⑩ *nah*·me *name*
Nase ① *nah*·ze *nose*
nass nas *wet*
Natur ① na·*toor nature*
Naturheilkunde ① na·*toor*·hail·kun·de
naturopathy
Naturreservat ⑩ na·*toor*·re·zer·vaht
nature reserve
neben *nay*·ben *next to*
neblig *nay*·blikh *foggy*
Neffe ⑩ *ne*·fe *nephew*
nehmen *nay*·men *take*
nein nain *no*
nett net *nice • kind*
Netz ⑩ nets *net*
neu noy *new*
Neujahrstag ⑩ *noy*·yahrs·tahk
New Year's Day
Neuseeland ⑩ *noy*·zay·lant
New Zealand
nicht nikht *not*
Nichte ① *nikh*·te *niece*
Nichtraucher- *nikht*·row·kher·
non-smoking

nichts nikhts *nothing*
nie nee *never*
Niederlande pl nee·der·lan·de *Netherlands*
niedrig nee·drikh *low*
noch nicht nokh nikht *not yet*
Nonne ① no·ne *nun*
Norden ⑩ nor·den *north*
normal nor·mahl *ordinary*
normale Post ① nor·mah·le post *surface mail*
Notfall ⑩ nawt·fal *emergency*
Notizbuch ⑥ no·teets·bookh *notebook*
notwendig nawt·ven·dikh *necessary*
Nudeln pl noo·deln *noodles • pasta*
null nul *zero*
Nummer ① nu·mer *number*
nur noor *only*
Nuss ① nus *nut*
nützlich nüts·likh *useful*

O

obdachlos op·dakh·laws *homeless*
oben aw·ben *upstairs*
Objektiv ⑥ op·yek·teef *lens (camera)*
Obsternte ① awpst·ern·te *fruit picking*
oder aw·der *or*
Ofen ⑩ aw·fen *oven*
offen o·fen *open*
offensichtlich o·fen·zikht·likh *obvious*
öffentlich er·fent·likh *public*
öffnen erf·nen *open*
Öffnungszeiten ① pl erf·nungks·tsai·ten *opening hours*
oft oft *often*
ohne aw·ne *without*
Ohr ⑥ awr *ear*
Ohrenstöpsel ⑥ aw·ren·shterp·sel *earplugs*
Ohrringe ⑥ pl awr·ring·e *earrings*
Öl ⑥ erl *oil*
Olive ① o·lee·ve *olive*
Olivenöl ⑥ o·lee·ven·erl *olive oil*
Olympische Spiele ⑥ pl o·lüm·pi·she shpee·le *Olympic Games*
Oma ① aw·ma *grandmother*
Onkel ⑩ ong·kel *uncle*
Opa ⑩ aw·pa *grandfather*

Oper ① aw·per *opera*
Operation ① o·pe·ra·tsyawn *operation*
Opernhaus ⑥ aw·pern·hows *opera house*
Optiker(in) ⑩/① op·ti·ker/op·ti·ke·rin *optician*
orange o·rahngzh *orange (colour)*
Orange ① o·rahng·zhe *orange*
Orangenmarmelade ① o·rahng·zhen·m ar·me·lah·de *marmalade*
Orangensaft ⑩ o·rahng·zhen·zaft *orange juice*
Orchester ⑥ or·kes·ter *orchestra*
organisieren or·ga·ni·zee·ren *organise*
Orgasmus ⑩ or·gas·mus *orgasm*
Orgel ① or·gel *organ (church)*
Original- o·ri·gi·nahl· *original (not copied)*
örtlich ert·likh *local*
Osten ⑩ os·ten *east*
der Nahe Osten ⑩ dair nah·e os·ten *Middle East*
Ostern ⑥ aws·tern *Easter*
Österreich ⑥ ers·ter·raikh *Austria*
Ozean ⑩ aw·tse·ahn *ocean*
Ozonschicht ① o·tsawn·shikht *ozone layer*

P

Paar ⑥ pahr *pair (couple)*
ein paar ain pahr *a few*
Packung ① pa·kung *packet (general)*
Paket ⑥ pa·kayt *package • parcel*
Pampelmuse ① pam·pel·moo·ze *grapefruit*
eine Panne haben ai·ne pa·ne hah·ben *break down*
Papa ⑩ pa·pa *dad*
Papagei ⑥ pa·pa·gai *parrot*
Papier ⑥ pa·peer *paper*
Papiertaschentücher ⑥ pl pa·peer·ta·shen·tü·kher *tissues*
Paprika ① pap·ri·kah *paprika • capsicum • bell pepper*
Parfüm ⑥ par·füm *perfume*
Park ⑩ park *park*
Parkplatz ⑩ park·plats *carpark*
Parlament ⑥ par·la·ment *parliament*

Partei ① par·*tai party (politics)*
Pass ⓜ pas *pass • passport*
Passnummer ① *pas·nu·mer
passport number*
Pause ① *pow·ze intermission*
eine Pause machen ai·ne *pow·ze
ma·khen rest*
Pedal ⓝ pe·*dahl pedal*
Penis ⓜ *pay·nis penis*
Pension ① pahng·*zyawn boarding
house • bed & breakfast*
pensioniert pahng·zyo·*neert retired*
Person ① per·*zawn person*
Personalausweis ⓜ
per·zo·*nahl·ows·vais
identification card*
persönlich per·*zern·likh personal*
Petersilie ① pay·ter·zee·li·e *parsley*
Petition ① pe·ti·*tsyawn petition*
Pfad ⓜ pfaht *path • trail*
Pfanne ① *pfa·ne pan*
Pfeffer ⓜ *pfe·fer pepper*
Pfefferminzbonbons ⓝ pl
pfe·fer·*mints·bong·bongs mints*
Pfeife ① *pfai·fe pipe*
Pferd ⓝ pfert *horse*
Pfirsich ⓜ *pfir·zikh peach*
Pflanze ① *pflan·tse plant*
Pflaster ⓝ *pflas·ter Band-aids*
Pflaume ① *pflow·me plum*
pflücken *pflü·ken pick (flowers)*
Pfund ⓝ pfunt *pound (weight)*
Phantasie ① fan·ta·*zee imagination*
Physik ① fü·*zeek physics*
Picknick ⓝ *pik·nik picnic*
Pilgerfahrt ① *pil·ger·fahrt pilgrimage*
Pille ① *pi·le pill*
die Pille ① dee *pi·le the Pill*
Pilz ⓜ pilts *mushroom*
Pinzette ① pin·*tse·te tweezers*
PKW-Zulassung ①
*pay·kah·vay·tsoo·la·sung
car registration*
Plakat ⓝ pla·*kaht poster*
Planet ⓜ pla·*nayt planet*
Plastik ① *plas·tik plastic*
Platz ⓜ plats *place • seat (train,
cinema) • square (town) •
court (tennis)*

Platz am Gang plats am gang
aisle seat
Poker ⓝ *paw·ker poker (game)*
Politik ① po·li·*teek politics • policy*
Politiker(in) ⓜ/① po·*lee·ti·ker/
po·*lee·ti·ke·rin politician*
Polizei ① po·li·*tsai police*
Polizeirevier ⓝ po·li·*tsai·re·veer
police station*
Pollen ⓜ *po·len pollen*
Pony ⓝ *po·ni pony*
Porto ⓝ *por·to postage*
Post ① post *mail*
Postamt ⓝ *post·amt post office*
Postkarte ① *post·kar·te postcard*
postlagernd *post·lah·gernt
poste restante*
Postleitzahl ① *post·lai·tsahl postcode*
praktisch *prak·tish practical*
prämenstruelle Störung ①
*pray·mens·tru·e·le shter·rung
premenstrual tension*
Präsident(in) ⓜ/① pre·zi·*dent/
pre·zi·*den·tin president*
Preis ⓜ prais *price*
Premierminister(in) ⓜ/①
prem·*yay·mi·nis·ter/
prem·*yay·mi·nis·te·rin prime minister*
Priester ⓜ *prees·ter priest*
privat pri·*vaht private*
Privatklinik ① pri·*vaht·klee·nik
private hospital*
pro praw *per*
produzieren pro·du·*tsee·ren produce*
Programm ⓝ pro·*gram program*
Projektor ⓜ pro·*yek·tor projector*
Prosa ① *praw·za fiction*
Prostituierte ① pros·ti·tu·*eer·te
prostitute*
Protest ⓜ pro·*test protest*
protestieren pro·tes·*tee·ren protest*
Prozent ⓝ pro·*tsent percent*
prüfen *prü·fen check*
Psychologie ① psü·kho·lo·*gee
psychology*
Pullover ⓜ pu·*law·ver jumper • sweater*
Pumpe ① *pum·pe pump*
Punkt ⓜ pungkt *point*
Puppe ① *pu·pe doll*

Q

Qualifikationen ① pl
kva·li·fi·ka·tsyaw·nen *qualifications*
Qualität ① kva·li·*tayt* quality
Quarantäne ① ka·ran·*tay*·ne *quarantine*
Querschnittsgelähmte ⓜ&①
kvair·shnits·ge·laym·te *paraplegic*
Quittung ① *kvi*·tung *receipt*

R

Rabatt ⓜ ra·*bat* discount
Rad ⓝ raht *wheel*
radfahren raht·fah·ren *cycle*
Radfahrer(in) ⓜ/① raht·fah·rer/
raht·fah·re·rin *cyclist*
Radio ⓝ rah·di·o *radio*
Radsport ⓜ raht·shport *cycling*
Radweg ⓜ raht·vayk *bike path*
Rahmen ⓜ rah·men *frame*
Rallye ① *ra*·li *rally*
Rasiercreme ① ra·zeer·kraym
shaving cream
rasieren ra·zee·ren *shave*
Rasierer ⓜ ra·zee·rer *razor*
Rasierklingen ① pl ra·zeer·kling·en
razor blades
Rassismus ⓜ ra·sis·mus *racism*
Rat ⓜ raht *advice*
raten rah·ten *advise • guess*
Ratte ① *ra*·te *rat*
Raub ⓜ rowp *robbery*
rauchen row·khen *smoke*
Raum ⓜ rowm *space*
realistisch re·a·*lis*·tish *realistic*
Rebe ① ray·be *vine*
Rechnung ① rekh·nung *bill • check*
rechts rekhts *right (direction)*
rechtsgerichtet rekhts·ge·rikh·tet *right-wing*
Rechtsanwalt ⓜ rekhts·an·valt *lawyer*
Rechtsanwältin ① rekhts·an·vel·tin
lawyer
recyceln ri·sai·keln *recycle*
Regal ⓝ re·gahl *shelf*
Regeln ① pl ray·geln *rules*
Regen ⓜ ray·gen *rain*

Regenmantel ⓜ ray·gen·man·tel
raincoat
Regenschirm ⓜ ray·gen·shirm *umbrella*
Regierung ① re·gee·rung *government*
Region ① re·gyawn *region*
Regisseur(in) ⓜ/① re·zhi·*ser*/
re·zhi·*ser*·rin *director*
reich raikh *wealthy*
Reifen ⓜ rai·fen *tyre*
Reifenpanne ① rai·fen·pa·ne *puncture*
rein rain *pure*
Reinigung ① rai·ni·gung *cleaning*
Reis ⓜ rais *rice*
Reise ① rai·ze *journey • trip*
Reisebüro ⓝ rai·ze·bü·raw
travel agency
Reiseführer ⓜ rai·ze·fü·rer *guidebook*
Reisekrankheit ① rai·ze·krangk·hait
travel sickness
reisen rai·zen *travel*
Reisende ⓜ/① rai·zen·de
passenger (train)
Reisepass ⓜ rai·ze·pas *passport*
Reiseroute ① rai·ze·roo·te *itinerary*
Reisescheck ⓜ rai·ze·shek
travellers cheque
Reiseziel ⓝ rai·ze·tseel *destination*
Reißverschluss ⓜ rais·fer·shlus *zipper*
Reiten ⓝ rai·ten *horse riding*
reiten rai·ten *ride (horse)*
Reitweg ⓜ rait·vayk *bridle path*
Religion ① re·li·gyawn *religion*
religiös re·li·gyers *religious*
Reliquie ① re·lee·kvi·e *relic (religious)*
Rennbahn ① ren·bahn *racetrack*
rennen re·nen *run*
Rennen ⓝ re·nen *race (sport)*
Rennrad ⓝ ren·raht *racing bike*
Rentner(in) ⓜ/① rent·ner/rent·ne·rin
pensioner
reparieren re·pa·ree·ren *repair*
Republik ① re·pu·bleek *republic*
Reservereifen ⓜ re·zer·ve·rai·fen
spare tyre
reservieren re·zer·vee·ren *reserve*
Reservierung ① re·zer·vee·rung
reservation
Restaurant ⓝ res·to·rahng *restaurant*
retten re·ten *save (someone)*

Rettich ⓜ re·tikh *radish*
R-Gespräch ⓝ air·ge·shpraykh
  collect call • reverse-charge call
Rhythmus ⓜ rüt·mus *rhythm*
Richter(in) ⓜ/ⓕ rikh·ter/rikh·te·rin
  judge
richtig rikh·tikh *right (correct)*
riesig ree·zikh *huge*
Rindfleisch ⓝ rint·flaish *beef*
Ring ⓜ ring *ring (on finger)*
Risiko ⓝ ree·zi·ko *risk*
Ritt ⓜ rit *ride*
Rock ⓜ rok *skirt*
Rockgruppe ⓕ rok·gru·pe *rock group*
Rockmusik ⓕ rok·mu·zeek
  rock (music)
Rodeln ⓝ raw·deln *tobogganing*
Roggenbrot ⓝ ro·gen·brawt *rye bread*
roh raw *raw*
Rollschuhfahren ⓝ rol·shoo·fah·ren
  in-line skating
Rollstuhl ⓜ rol·shtool *wheelchair*
Rolltreppe ⓕ rol·tre·pe *escalator*
romantisch ro·man·tish *romantic*
rosa raw·za *pink*
Rosenkohl ⓜ raw·zen·kawl
  Brussels sprouts
Rosine ⓕ ro·zee·ne *raisin*
rot rawt *red*
Rotwein ⓜ rawt·vain *red wine*
Route ⓕ roo·te *route*
Rücken ⓜ rü·ken *back (body)*
Rückfahrkarte ⓕ rük·fahr·kar·te *return
  (ticket)*
Rucksack ⓜ ruk·zak *backpack •
  knapsack*
Rückzahlung ⓕ rük·tsah·lung *refund*
Rudern ⓝ roo·dern *rowing*
Rugby ⓝ rag·bi *rugby*
ruhig roo·ikh *quiet*
Ruinen ⓕ pl ru·ee·nen *ruins*
Rum ⓜ rum *rum*
rund runt *round*

S

Sabbat ⓜ za·bat *Sabbath*
Safe ⓜ sayf *safe*
Safe Sex ⓜ sayf seks *safe sex*

Saft ⓜ zaft *juice*
sagen zah·gen *say*
Sahne ⓕ zah·ne *cream*
Salami ⓕ za·lah·mi *salami*
Salat ⓜ za·laht *salad*
Salz ⓝ zalts *salt*
Samstag ⓜ zams·tahk *Saturday*
Sand ⓜ zant *sand*
Sandalen ⓕ pl zan·dah·len *sandals*
Sänger(in) ⓜ/ⓕ zeng·er/zeng·e·rin
  singer
Sardine ⓕ zar·dee·ne *sardine*
Sattel ⓜ za·tel *saddle*
sauber zow·ber *clean*
Sauce ⓕ zaw·se *sauce*
Sauerstoff ⓜ zow·er·shtof *oxygen*
Sauerteigbrot ⓝ zow·er·taik·brawt
  sourdough bread
Sauna ⓕ zow·na *sauna*
Schach ⓝ shakh *chess*
Schaf ⓝ shahf *sheep*
Schaffner(in) ⓜ/ⓕ shaf·ner/shaf·ne·rin
  conductor
Schal ⓜ shahl *scarf*
Schatten ⓜ sha·ten *shade • shadow*
einen Schaufensterbummel machen
  ai·nen show·fens·ter·bu·mel ma·khen
  go window-shopping
Schaumwein ⓜ showm·vain *sparkling
  wine*
Schauspiel ⓝ show·shpeel
  play (theatre) • drama
Schauspieler(in) ⓜ/ⓕ show·shpee·ler/
  show·shpee·le·rin *actor*
Scheck ⓜ shek *cheque (bank)*
einen Scheck einlösen ai·nen shek
  ain·ler·zen *cash a cheque*
Scheckkarte ⓕ shek·kar·te *cheque card*
Scheinwerfer ⓜ pl shain·ver·fer
  headlights
Schere ⓕ shair·re *scissors*
schieben shee·ben *push*
Schiedsrichter(in) ⓜ/ⓕ sheets·rikh·ter/
  sheets·rikh·te·rin *referee*
schießen shee·sen *shoot (gun)*
Schiff ⓝ shif *ship*
Schild ⓝ shilt *sign*
Schinken ⓜ shing·ken *ham*
schlafen shlah·fen *sleep*

schläfrig *shlayf*·rikh *sleepy*
Schlafsack ⓜ *shlahf*·zak *sleeping bag*
Schlaftabletten ① pl *shlahf*·ta·ble·ten
  sleeping pills
Schlafwagen ⓜ *shlahf*·vah·gen *sleeping
  car*
Schlafzimmer ⓝ *shlahf*·tsi·mer *bedroom*
Schläger ⓜ *shlay*·ger *racquet*
Schlamm ⓜ *shlam mud*
Schlange ① *shlang*·e *queue • snake*
Schlauch ⓜ *shlowkh tube (tyre)*
schlecht *shlekht bad • off (of food)*
schlechter *shlekh*·ter *worse*
schließen *shlee*·sen *close (shut)*
Schließfächer ⓝ pl *shlees*·fe·kher
  luggage lockers
Schloss ⓝ *shlos lock • palace*
Schlucht ① *shlukht gorge*
Schlüssel ⓜ *shlü*·sel *key*
schmackhaft *shmak*·haft *tasty*
Schmalz ⓝ *shmalts lard*
Schmand ⓜ *shmant sour cream*
Schmerz ⓜ *shmerts pain*
schmerzhaft *shmerts*·haft *sore • painful*
Schmerzmittel ⓝ *shmerts*·mi·tel
  painkillers
Schmetterling ⓜ *shme*·ter·ling *butterfly*
Schmiermittel ⓝ *shmeer*·mi·tel *lubricant*
Schminke ① *shming*·ke *make-up*
Schmuck ⓜ *shmuk jewellery*
schmutzig *shmu*·tsikh *dirty*
Schnecke ① *shne*·ke *snail*
Schnee ⓜ *shnay snow*
Schneefeld ⓝ *shnay*·felt *snowfield*
schneiden *shnai*·den *cut*
Schneider(in) ⓜ/① *shnai*·der/
  shnai·de·rin *tailor*
schnell *shnel quick*
Schnorcheln ⓝ *shnor*·kheln *snorkelling*
Schnuller ⓜ *shnu*·ler *dummy • pacifier*
Schnur ① *shnoor string*
Schokolade ① *sho*·ko·lah·de *chocolate*
schon *shawn yet • already*
schön *shern beautiful*
Schönheitssalon ⓜ *shern*·haits·za·long
  beauty salon
Schottland ⓝ *shot*·lant *Scotland*
Schramme ① *shra*·me *bruise*
Schrank ⓜ *shrangk cupboard*

Schraubenzieher ⓜ *shrow*·ben·tsee·er
  screwdriver
schrecklich *shrek*·likh *terrible*
Schreibarbeit ① *shraip*·ar·bait
  paperwork
schreiben *shrai*·ben *write*
Schreibwarenhandlung ①
  shraip·vah·ren·han·dlung *stationer*
schreien *shrai*·en *shout*
Schrein ⓜ *shrain shrine*
Schreiner(in) ⓜ/① *shrai*·ner/*shrai*·ne·rin
  carpenter
Schriftsteller(in) ⓜ/① *shrift*·shte·ler/
  shrift·shte·le·rin *writer*
schüchtern *shükh*·tern *shy*
Schuhe ⓜ pl *shoo*·e *shoes*
Schuld ① *shult (someone's) fault*
schulden *shul*·den *owe*
schuldig *shul*·dikh *guilty*
Schule ① *shoo*·le *school*
Schulter ① *shul*·ter *shoulder*
Schüssel ① *shü*·sel *bowl*
Schutzimpfung ① *shuts*·im·pfung
  vaccination
schwach *shvakh weak*
schwanger *shvang*·er *pregnant*
Schwangerschaftserbrechen ⓝ
  shvang·er·shafts·er·bre·khen
  morning sickness
Schwangerschaftstest ⓜ
  shvang·er·shafts·test
  pregnancy test kit
Schwanz ⓜ *shvants tail*
schwarz *shvarts black*
schwarzer Pfeffer ⓜ *shvar*·tser *pfe*·fer
  black pepper
schwarzweiß *shvarts*·vais *B&W (film)*
Schwein ⓝ *shvain pig*
Schweinefleisch ⓝ *shvai*·ne·flaish *pork*
Schweiz ① *shvaits Switzerland*
schwer *shvair difficult (task) • heavy*
Schwester ① *shves*·ter *sister*
Schwiegermutter ① *shvee*·ger·mu·ter
  mother-in-law
Schwiegersohn ⓜ *shvee*·ger·zawn
  son-in-law
Schwiegertochter ① *shvee*·ger·tokh·ter
  daughter-in-law
Schwiegervater ⓜ *shvee*·ger·fah·ter
  father-in-law

schwierig *shvee*·rikh *difficult*
Schwimmbad ⑩ *shvim*·baht *swimming pool*
schwimmen *shvi*·men *swim*
Schwimmweste ① *shvim*·ves·te *lifejacket*
schwindelig *shvin*·de·likh *dizzy*
schwul *shvool* *gay*
schwül *shvül* *muggy*
Secondhandgeschäft ⑩ se·kend·*hend*·ge·sheft *second-hand shop*
See ⑩ *zay* *lake*
seekrank *zay*·krangk *seasick*
Segeln ⑩ *zay*·geln *sailing*
segnen *zayg*·nen *bless*
sehen *zay*·en *see* • *look*
sehr *zair* *very*
Seide ① *zai*·de *silk*
Seife ① *zai*·fe *soap*
Seifenoper ① *zai*·fen·aw·per *soap opera*
Seil ⑩ *zail* *rope*
Seilbahn ① *zail*·bahn *cable car*
sein *zain* *his*
sein *zain* *be*
seit (Mai) *zait* (mai) *since (May)*
Seite ① *zai*·te *side* • *page*
Sekretär(in) ⑩/① ze·kre·*tair*/ze·kre·*tair*·rin *secretary*
Sekundarschule ① ze·kun·*dahr*·shoo·le *high school*
Sekunde ① ze·*kun*·de *second*
Selbstbedienung ① *zelpst*·be·dee·nung *self-service*
selbstständig *zelpst*·shten·dikh *self-employed*
selten *zel*·ten *rare*
senden *zen*·den *send*
Senf ⑩ *zenf* *mustard*
Serie ① *zair*·ri·e *series*
Serviette ① zer·*vye*·te *napkin*
Sessellift ⑩ *ze*·se·lift *chairlift (skiing)*
Sex ⑩ *seks* *sex*
Sexismus ⑩ *sek*·sis·mus *sexism*
sexy *sek*·si *sexy*
Shampoo ⑩ *sham*·poo *shampoo*
Shorts pl *shorts* *shorts* • *boxer shorts*
Show ① *shoh* *show*
sicher *zi*·kher *safe*
Sicherheit ① *zi*·kher·hait *safety*

Sicherheitsgurt ⑩ *zi*·kher·haits·gurt *seatbelt*
Sicherung ① *zi*·khe·rung *fuse*
sie *zee* *she* • *they*
Sie *zee* *you* sg&pl pol
Sieger(in) ⑩/① *zee*·ger/*zee*·ge·rin *winner*
silbern *zil*·bern *silver*
Silvester ⑩ *zil*·ves·ter *New Year's Eve*
Singapur ⑩ *zing*·a·poor *Singapore*
singen *zing*·en *sing*
Single ① *singl* *single (of person)*
sinnlich *zin*·likh *sensual*
Sitz ⑩ *zits* *seat (car)*
sitzen *zi*·tsen *sit*
Skateboarden ⑩ *skayt*·bor·den *skateboarding*
Skibrille ① *shee*·bri·le *goggles (skiing)*
skifahren *shee*·fah·ren *ski*
Skulptur ① *skulp*·toor *sculpture*
Slipeinlage ① *slip*·ain·lah·ge *panty liner*
Snack ⑩ *snek* *snack*
Snowboarden ⑩ *snoh*·bor·den *snowboarding*
Socken ⑩ pl *zo*·ken *socks*
sofort *zo*·fort *immediately*
Sohn ⑩ *zawn* *son*
Sojamilch ① *zaw*·ya·milkh *soy milk*
Sojasauce ① *zaw*·ya·zaw·se *soy sauce*
Sommer ⑩ *zo*·mer *summer*
Sonne ① *zo*·ne *sun*
Sonnenaufgang ⑩ *zo*·nen·owf·gang *sun...*
Sonnenbrand ⑩ *zo*·nen·brant *sunburn*
Sonnenbrille ① *zo*·nen·bri·le *sunglasses*
Sonnencreme ① *zo*·nen·kraym *sunblock*
Sonnenuntergang ⑩ *zo*·nen·un·ter·gang *sunset*
sonnig *zo*·nikh *sunny*
Sonntag ⑩ *zon*·tahk *Sunday*
Soße ① *zaw*·se *sauce*
Souvenir ⑩ *zu*·ve·*neer* *souvenir*
Souvenirladen ⑩ *zu*·ve·*neer*·lah·den *souvenir shop*
Sozialhilfe ① *zo*·tsyahl·hil·fe *welfare*
sozialistisch zo·tsya·*lis*·tish *socialist*

Sozialstaat ⓜ zo·*tsyahl*·shtaht welfare state
Spanien ⓝ *shpah*·ni·en Spain
sparen *shpah*·ren save (money)
Spargel ⓜ *shpar*·gel asparagus
Spaß ⓜ shpahs fun
Spaß haben shpahs *hah*·ben have fun
spät shpayt late
Spaten ⓜ *shpah*·ten spade
Speichen ⓝ pl *shpai*·khen spokes
Speisekarte ① *shpai*·ze·kar·te menu
Speisewagen ⓜ *shpai*·ze·vah·gen dining car
Spezialist(in) ⓜ/① shpe·tsya·*list*/ shpe·tsya·*lis*·tin specialist
speziell shpe·*tsyel* special
Spiegel ⓜ *shpee*·gel mirror
Spiel ⓜ shpeel match (sport)
spielen *shpee*·len play (game) • play (instrument)
Spielzeug ⓝ *shpeel*·tsoyk toy
Spinat ⓜ shpi·*naht* spinach
Spinne ① *shpi*·ne spider
Spitze ① *shpi*·tse lace
Spitzhacke ① *shpits*·ha·ke pickaxe
Spitzname ⓜ *shpits*·nah·me nickname
Sport ⓜ shport sport
Sportler(in) ⓜ/① *shport*·ler/*shport*·le·rin sportsperson
Sprache ① *shprah*·khe language
Sprachführer ⓜ *shprahkh*·fü·rer phrasebook
sprechen *shpre*·khen speak
springen *shpring*·en jump
Spritze ① *shpri*·tse syringe
Spülung ① *shpü*·lung conditioner
Staat ⓜ shtaht state
Staatsangehörigkeit ① *shtahts*·an·ge·her·rikh·kait nationality
Staatsbürgerschaft ① *shtahts*·bür·ger·shaft citizenship
Stadion ⓝ *shtah*·di·on stadium
Stadium ⓝ *shtah*·di·um stage
Stadt ① shtat city • town
Standby-Ticket ⓝ *stend*·bai·ti·ket stand-by ticket
stark shtark strong
Start ⓜ shtart start (sport)

statt shtat instead of
Statue ① *shtah*·tu·e statue
Steak ⓝ stayk steak (beef)
Stechmücke ① *shtekh*·mü·ke mosquito
Stecker ⓜ *shte*·ker plug (electricity)
stehlen *shtay*·len steal
Stehplatz ⓜ *shtay*·plats standing room
steil shtail steep
Stein ⓜ shtain stone
stellen *shte*·len put (vertical)
sterben *shter*·ben die
Stereoanlage ① *shtair*·re·o·an·lah·ge stereo
Sterne ⓜ pl *shter*·ne stars
Sternzeichen ⓝ *shtern*·tsai·khen star sign • zodiac
Steuer ① *shtoy*·er tax
Stich ⓜ shtikh bite (insect)
Stickerei ① shti·ke·*rai* embroidery
Stiefel ⓜ *shtee*·fel boot (footwear)
Stil ⓜ shteel style
stilles Wasser ⓝ *shti*·les va·ser still water
Stimme ① *shti*·me voice
Stock ⓜ shtok floor (storey)
stoned shtohnd stoned (drugged)
stoppen *shto*·pen stop
Stöpsel ⓜ *shterp*·sel plug (bath)
stornieren shtor·*nee*·ren cancel
Strand ⓜ shtrant beach
Straße ① *shtrah*·se street • road
Straßenbahn ① *shtrah*·sen·bahn tram
Straßenkarte ① *shtrah*·sen·kar·te road map
Straßenkinder ⓝ pl *shtrah*·sen·kin·der street kids
Straßenmusiker(in) ⓜ/① *shtrah*·sen·moo·zi·ker/ *shtrah*·sen·moo·zi·ke·rin busker
Streichhölzer ⓝ pl *shtraikh*·herl·tser matches
streiken *shtrai*·ken (to be) on strike
Streit ⓜ shtrait quarrel
streiten *shtrai*·ten argue
Strom ⓜ shtrawm current (electricity)
Stromschnellen ① pl *shtrawm*·shne·len rapids
Strümpfe ⓜ pl *shtrümp*·fe stockings

Strumpfhose ① *shtrumpf·haw·ze*
pantyhose
Stück ⑥ *shtük piece*
Student(in) ⑩/① *shtu·dent/shtu·den·tin*
student
Studentenausweis ⑩
shtu·den·ten·ows·vais student card
studieren *shtu·dee·ren study*
Studio ⑥ *shtoo·di·o studio*
Stufe ① *shtoo·fe step (stairs)*
Stuhl ⑩ *shtool chair*
stumm *shtum mute*
stur *shtoor stubborn*
Sturm ⑩ *shturm storm*
suchen nach *zoo·khen nahkh look for*
Süchtige ⑩/① *zükh·ti·ge addict*
Süden ⑩ *zü·den south*
Supermarkt ⑩ *zoo·per·markt*
supermarket
Suppe ① *zu·pe soup*
Surfbrett ⑥ *serf·bret surfboard*
surfen *ser·fen surf*
süß *züs sweet/candy*
Süßigkeiten ① pl *zü·sikh·kai·ten lollies*
Synagoge ① *zü·na·gaw·ge synagogue*
synthetisch *zün·tay·tish synthetic*

T

Tabak ⑩ *ta·bak tobacco*
Tabakladen ⑩ *ta·bak·lah·den*
tobacconist
Tag ⑩ *tahk day*
Tagebuch ⑥ *tah·ge·bookh diary*
(journal)
täglich *tayk·likh daily*
Tal ⑥ *tahl valley*
Tampons ⑩ pl *tam·pons tampons*
Tankstelle ① *tangk·shte·le*
service station
Tante ① *tan·te aunt*
tanzen *tan·tsen dance*
Tasche ① *ta·she bag • pocket*
Taschenbuch ⑥ *ta·shen·bookh*
paperback
Taschenlampe ① *ta·shen·lam·pe*
torch • flashlight
Taschenmesser ⑥ *ta·shen·me·ser*
penknife

Taschenrechner ⑩ *ta·shen·rekh·ner*
calculator
Tasse ① *ta·se cup*
Tastatur ① *tas·ta·toor keyboard*
taub *towp deaf*
Tauchen ⑥ *tow·khen diving*
Taufe ① *tow·fe baptism • christening*
tausend *tow·zent thousand*
Taxi ⑥ *tak·si taxi*
Taxistand ⑩ *tak·si·shtant taxi stand*
Technik ① *tekh·nik technique*
Tee ⑩ *tay tea*
Teelöffel ⑩ *tay·ler·fel teaspoon*
Teil ⑥ *tail part*
teilen *tai·len share*
Teilzeit ① *tail·tsait part-time*
Telefon ⑥ *te·le·fawn telephone*
Telefonauskunft ① *te·le·fawn·ows·kunft*
directory enquiries
Telefonbuch ⑥ *le·le·fawn·bookh phone*
book
telefonieren *te·le·fo·nee·ren phone*
Telefonkarte ① *te·le·fawn·kar·te*
phone card
Telefonzelle ① *te·le·fawn·tse·le*
phone box
Telefonzentrale ① *te·le·fawn·*
tsen·trah·le telephone centre
Telegramm ⑥ *te·le·gram telegram*
Teleskop ⑥ *te·les·kawp telescope*
Teller ⑩ *te·ler plate*
Tempel ⑩ *tem·pel temple*
Temperatur ① *tem·pe·ra·toor*
temperature (weather)
Tennis ⑥ *te·nis tennis*
Tennisplatz ⑩ *te·nis·plats tennis court*
Teppich ⑩ *te·pikh rug*
Termin ⑩ *ter·meen appointment*
Terminkalender ⑩ *ter·meen·ka·len·der*
diary (for appointments)
Terrasse ① *te·ra·se patio*
Test ⑩ *test test*
teuer *toy·er expensive*
Theater ⑥ *te·ah·ter theatre*
Theaterkasse ① *te·ah·ter·ka·se*
ticket office (theatre)
Theke ① *tay·ke counter (at bar)*
Thermosflasche ① *ter·mos·fla·she*
thermos

Thunfisch ⓜ *toon*·fish *tuna*
tief teef *deep*
Tier ⓝ teer *animal*
Tisch ⓜ tish *table*
Tischdecke ⓕ *tish*·de·ke *tablecloth*
Tischtennis ⓝ *tish*·te·nis *table tennis*
Toast ⓜ tawst *toast*
Toaster ⓜ *taws*·ter *toaster*
Tochter ⓕ *tokh*·ter *daughter*
Tofu ⓜ *taw*·fu *tofu*
Toilette ⓕ to·a·*le*·te *toilet*
Toilettenpapier ⓝ to·a·*le*·ten·pa·peer *toilet paper*
toll tol *terrific*
Tomate ⓕ to·*mah*·te *tomato*
Tomatensauce ⓕ to·*mah*·ten·zaw·se *tomato sauce*
Topf ⓜ topf *pot (ceramics)*
Töpferwaren ⓟⓛ *terp*·fer·vah·ren *pottery*
Tor ⓝ tawr *gate • goal*
Torhüterin ⓕ *tawr*·hü·te·rin *goalkeeper*
Torwart ⓜ *tawr*·vart *goalkeeper*
ein Tor schießen ain *tawr* shee·sen *score a goal*
tot tawt *dead*
töten *ter*·ten *kill*
Tour ⓕ toor *tour*
Tourist(in) ⓜ/ⓕ tu·*rist*/tu·*ris*·tin *tourist*
Touristenklasse ⓕ tu·*ris*·ten·kla·se *economy class*
tragen *trah*·gen *carry • wear*
Training ⓝ *tray*·ning *workout*
trampen *trem*·pen *hitchhike*
Transitraum ⓜ tran·*zeet*·rowm *transit lounge*
Transport ⓜ trans·*port* *transport*
trauen *trow*·en *trust*
träumen *troy*·men *dream*
traurig *trow*·rikh *sad*
treffen *tre*·fen *meet*
Treppe ⓕ *tre*·pe *stairway*
treten *tray*·ten *kick*
trinken *tringk*·en *drink*
Trinkgeld ⓝ *tringk*·gelt *tip (gratuity)*
trocken *tro*·ken *dry*
Trockenobst ⓝ *tro*·ken·awpst *dried fruit*
trocknen *trok*·nen *dry (clothes)*
Truthahn ⓜ *troot*·hahn *turkey*

T-Shirt ⓝ tee·shert *T-shirt*
tun toon *do*
Tür ⓕ tür *door*
Turm ⓜ turm *tower*
Türsteher ⓜ *tür*·shtay·er *bouncer (club heavy)*
Tüte ⓕ *tü*·te *carton (milk)*
Typ ⓜ tüp *type*
typisch *tü*·pish *typical*

U

U-Bahn ⓕ *oo*·bahn *subway (underground)*
U-Bahnhof ⓜ *oo*·bahn·hawf *metro station*
Übelkeit ⓕ *ü*·bel·kait *nausea*
über *ü*·ber *about • above • over*
Überbrückungskabel ⓝ *ü*·ber·*brü*·kungks·kah·bel *jumper leads*
Überdosis ⓕ *ü*·ber·daw·zis *overdose*
überfüllt ü·ber·*fült* *crowded*
Übergepäck ⓝ *ü*·ber·ge·pek *excess baggage*
übermorgen *ü*·ber·mor·gen *day after tomorrow*
übernachten ü·ber·*nakh*·ten *stay (at a hotel)*
Überraschung ⓕ ü·ber·*ra*·shung *surprise*
Überschwemmung ⓕ ü·ber·*shve*·mung *flooding*
übersetzen ü·ber·*ze*·tsen *translate*
Uhr ⓕ oor *clock • watch*
Ultraschall ⓜ *ul*·tra·shal *ultrasound*
umarmen um·*ar*·men *hug*
Umfrage ⓕ *um*·frah·ge *polls*
Umkleideraum ⓜ *um*·klai·de·rowm *changing room*
Umsatzsteuer ⓕ *um*·zats·shtoy·er *sales tax*
umsteigen *um*·shtai·gen *change (trains)*
Umtausch ⓜ *um*·towsh *exchange*
Umwelt ⓕ *um*·velt *environment*
Umweltverschmutzung ⓕ *um*·velt·fer·shmu·tsung *pollution*
unbequem *un*·be·kvaym *uncomfortable*
und unt *and*

unfair un·fair *unfair*
Unfall ⓜ un·fal *accident*
ungefähr un·ge·fair *approximately*
ungewöhnlich un·ge·vern·likh *unusual*
Ungleichheit ⓕ un·glaikh·hait *inequality*
Uniform ⓕ u·ni·form *uniform*
Universität ⓕ u·ni·ver·zi·tayt *university*
Universum ⓜ u·ni·vair·zum *universe*
unmöglich un·merk·likh *impossible*
unschuldig un·shul·dikh *innocent*
unser un·zer *our*
unten un·ten *down • at the bottom*
unter un·ter *among • below • under*
Unterhemd ⓝ un·ter·hemt *singlet*
Unterkunft ⓕ un·ter·kunft *accommodation*
Unterschrift ⓕ un·ter·shrift *signature*
Untertitel ⓜ pl un·ter·tee·tel *subtitles*
Unterwäsche ⓕ un·ter·ve·she *underwear*
Urlaub ⓜ oor·lowp *holiday*

V

Vagina ⓕ va·gee·na *vagina*
Vater ⓜ fah·ter *father*
Vegetarier(in) ⓜ/ⓕ ve·ge·tah·ri·er/ve·ge·tah·ri·e·rin *vegetarian*
Vene ⓕ vay·ne *vein*
Ventilator ⓜ ven·ti·lah·tor *fan (machine)*
Verabredung ⓕ fer·ap·ray·dung *date (appointment)*
Veranstaltungskalender ⓜ fer·an·shtal·tungks·ka·len·der *entertainment guide*
Veranstaltungsort ⓜ fer·an·shtal·tungks·ort *venue*
Verband ⓜ fer·bant *bandage*
Verbandskasten ⓜ fer·bants·kas·ten *first-aid kit*
Verbindung ⓕ fer·bin·dung *connection*
verbrennen fer·bre·nen *burn*
verdienen fer·dee·nen *earn*
Vergangenheit ⓕ fer·gang·en·hait *past*
Vergaser ⓜ fer·gah·zer *carburettor*
vergessen fer·ge·sen *forget*
vergewaltigen fer·ge·val·ti·gen *rape*

Verhaftung ⓕ fer·haf·tung *arrest*
verhindern fer·hin·dern *prevent*
Verhütungsmittel ⓝ fer·hü·tungks·mi·tel *contraceptives*
verkaufen fer·kow·fen *sell*
Verkehr ⓜ fer·kair *traffic*
Verlängerung ⓕ fer·leng·e·rung *extension (visa)*
verlegen fer·lay·gen *embarrassed*
verletzen fer·le·tsen *hurt*
Verletzung ⓕ fer·le·tsung *injury*
verlieren fer·lee·ren *lose*
Verlobte ⓜ&ⓕ fer·lawp·te *fiance • fiancee*
Verlobung ⓕ fer·law·bung *engagement (marriage)*
verloren fer·law·ren *lost*
Vermieter(in) ⓜ/ⓕ fer·mee·ter/fer·mee·te·rin *landlord/landlady*
vermissen fer·mi·sen *miss (feel absence of)*
Vermittlung ⓕ fer·mit·lung *operator*
vernünftig fer·nünf·tikh *sensible*
verpassen fer·pa·sen *miss (the bus)*
Verpflegung ⓕ fer·pflay·gung *provisions*
verrückt fer·rükt *crazy*
Versicherung ⓕ fer·zi·khe·rung *insurance*
Verspätung ⓕ fer·shpay·tung *delay*
versprechen fer·shpre·khen *promise*
verstehen fer·shtay·en *understand*
Verstopfung ⓕ fer·shtop·fung *constipation*
versuchen fer·zoo·khen *try (attempt)*
Vertrag ⓜ fer·trahk *contract*
Verwaltung ⓕ fer·val·tung *administration*
Verwandte ⓜ&ⓕ fer·van·te *relation (family)*
verzeihen fer·tsai·en *forgive*
Videokassette ⓕ vee·de·o·ka·se·te *video tape*
viel feel a *lot (of) • plenty*
viele fee·le *many*
vielleicht fi·laikht *maybe*
Viertel ⓝ feer·tel *quarter*
vierzehn Tage ⓜ pl feer·tsayn tah·ge *fortnight*

W

Virus ⓜ vee·rus *virus (health)* • *virus (computer)*
Visum ⓝ vee·zum *visa*
Vitamine ⓕ pl vi·ta·mee·ne *vitamins*
Vogel ⓜ faw·gel *bird*
Volksentscheid ⓜ folks·ent·shait *referendum*
voll fol *full*
Vollkornbrot ⓝ fol·korn·brawt *wholemeal bread*
Vollkornreis ⓜ fol·korn·rais *brown rice*
Vollzeit ⓕ fol·tsait *full-time*
Volumen ⓝ vo·loo·men *volume*
von fon *from*
vor fawr *in front of* • *before*
vor kurzem fawr kur·tsem *recently*
vor uns fawr uns *ahead*
vorbereiten fawr·be·rai·ten *prepare*
vorgestern fawr·ges·tern *day before yesterday*
Vorhängeschloss ⓝ fawr·heng·e·shlos *padlock*
Vormittag ⓜ fawr·mi·tahk *morning (10am – 12pm)*
Vorname ⓜ fawr·nah·me *Christian/given name*
Vorort ⓜ fawr·ort *suburb*
Vorrat ⓜ fawr·raht *stock*
vorsichtig fawr·zikh·tikh *careful*
Vorwahl ⓕ fawr·vahl *area code*
vorziehen fawr·tsee·en *prefer*

W

wachsen vak·sen *grow*
sich waschen zikh va·shen *wash (oneself)*
Waffe ⓕ va·fe *weapon*
Wagen ⓜ vah·gen *carriage (train)*
wählen vay·len *choose* • *vote*
Wahlen ⓕ pl vah·len *elections*
Wählton ⓜ vayl·tawn *dial tone*
wahr vahr *true*
während vair·rent *during*
Währung ⓕ vair·rung *currency*
Wald ⓜ valt *forest*
wandern van·dern *hike*
Wanderstiefel ⓜ pl van·der·shtee·fel *hiking boots*

Wanderweg ⓜ van·der·vayk *hiking route*
wann van *when*
wann immer van i·mer *whenever*
Warenhaus ⓝ vah·ren·hows *department store*
warm varm *warm*
warnen var·nen *warn*
warten var·ten *wait*
Wartesaal ⓜ var·te·zahl *waiting room (train station)*
Wartezimmer ⓝ var·te·tsi·mer *waiting room (doctor's)*
warum va·rum *why*
was vas *what*
Wäscheleine ⓕ ve·she·lai·ne *clothesline*
waschen va·shen *wash (something)*
Wäscherei ⓕ ve·she·rai *laundrette*
Waschküche ⓕ vash·kü·khe *laundry (room)*
Waschlappen ⓜ vash·la·pen *wash cloth (flannel)*
Waschmaschine ⓕ vash·ma·shee·ne *washing machine*
Waschpulver ⓝ vash·pul·ver *washing powder*
Wasser ⓝ va·ser *water*
wasserdicht va·ser·dikht *waterproof*
Wasserfall ⓜ va·ser·fal *waterfall*
Wasserflasche ⓕ va·ser·fla·she *water bottle*
Wasserhahn ⓜ va·ser·hahn *faucet* • *tap*
Wassermelone ⓕ va·ser·me·law·ne *watermelon*
Wasserskifahren ⓝ va·ser·shee·fah·ren *waterskiing*
Watte-Pads pl va·te·pedz *cotton balls*
Wechselgeld ⓝ vek·sel·gelt *change (coins)*
Wechselkurs ⓜ vek·sel·kurs *exchange rate*
wechseln vek·seln *exchange (money)*
Wecker ⓜ ve·ker *alarm clock*
Weg ⓜ vayk *track (path)* • *way*
wegen vay·gen *because of*
Wegweiser ⓜ vayk·vai·zer *signpost*
sich weh tun zikh vay toon *hurt (yourself)*

Wehrdienst ⓜ *vair·deenst*
military service
Weihnachten ⓝ *vai·nakh·ten Christmas*
Weihnachtsbaum ⓜ *vai·nakhts·bowm*
Christmas tree
Weihnachtsfeiertag ⓜ
vai·nakhts·fai·er·tahk Christmas Day
weil vail *because*
Wein ⓜ *vain wine*
Weinberg ⓜ *vain·berk vineyard*
Weinbrand ⓜ *vain·brant brandy*
Weintrauben ⓕ pl *vain·trow·ben grapes*
weiß vais *white*
Weißbrot ⓝ *vais·brawt white bread*
weißer Pfeffer ⓜ *vai·ser pfe·fer*
white pepper
weißer Reis ⓜ *vai·ser rais white rice*
Weißwein ⓜ *vais·vain white wine*
weit vait *far*
Welle ⓕ *ve·le wave*
Welt ⓕ *velt world*
Weltmeisterschaft ⓕ *velt·mais·ter·shaft*
World Cup
wenig *vay·nikh (a) little*
wenige *vay·ni·ge few*
weniger *vay·ni·ger less*
wenn ven *when • if*
wer vair *who*
Werkstatt ⓕ *verk·shtat*
garage (car repair)
Werkzeug ⓝ *verk·tsoyk tools*
Wert ⓜ *vert value (price)*
wertvoll *vert·fol valuable*
Wespe ⓕ *ves·pe wasp*
Westen ⓜ *ves·ten west*
Wette ⓕ *ve·te bet*
Wetter ⓝ *ve·ter weather*
Whisky ⓜ *vis·ki whisky*
wichtig *vikh·tikh important*
wie vee *how*
wie viel vee feel *how much*
wieder *vee·der again*
wiederverwertbar *vee·der·fer·vert·bahr*
recyclable
wiegen *vee·gen weigh*
wild vilt *wild*
willkommen *vil·ko·men welcome*
Wind ⓜ *vint wind*
Windel ⓕ *vin·del nappy (diaper)*
Windeldermatitis ⓕ
vin·del·der·ma·tee·tis nappy rash

windig *vin·dikh windy*
Windschutzscheibe ⓕ *vint·shuts·shai·be*
windscreen
Windsurfen ⓝ *vint·ser·fen windsurfing*
Winter ⓜ *vin·ter winter*
winzig *vin·tsikh tiny*
wir veer *we*
wissen *vi·sen know (something)*
Wissenschaft ⓕ *vi·sen·shaft science*
Wissenschaftler(in) ⓜ/ⓕ *vi·sen·shaft·ler/*
vi·sen·shaft·le·rin scientist
Witz ⓜ *vits joke*
wo vaw *where*
Wochenende ⓝ *vo·khen·en·de*
weekend
Wodka ⓜ *vot·ka vodka*
Wohlfahrt ⓕ *vawl·fahrt social welfare*
wohnen *vaw·nen reside*
Wohnung ⓕ *vaw·nung*
apartment (flat)
Wohnwagen ⓜ *vawn·vah·gen caravan*
Wolke ⓕ *vol·ke cloud*
wolkig *vol·kikh cloudy*
Wolle ⓕ *vo·le wool*
wollen *vo·len want*
Wort ⓝ *vort word*
Wörterbuch ⓝ *ver·ter·bookh dictionary*
wunderbar *vun·der·bahr wonderful*
wünschen *vün·shen wish*
Würfel ⓜ *vür·fel dice*
Würmer ⓜ pl *vür·mer worms*
Wurst ⓕ *vurst sausage*
würzig *vür·tsikh spicy*
Wüste ⓕ *vüs·te desert*
wütend *vü·tent angry*

Z

Zahl ⓕ *tsahl number*
zählen *tsay·len count*
Zahlung ⓕ *tsah·lung payment*
Zahn ⓜ *tsahn tooth*
Zahnarzt ⓜ *tsahn·artst dentist*
Zahnärztin ⓕ *tsahn·erts·tin dentist*
Zahnbürste ⓕ *tsahn·bürs·te toothbrush*
Zähne ⓝ pl *tsay·ne teeth*
Zahnfleisch ⓝ *tsahn·flaish gum (mouth)*
Zahnpasta ⓕ *tsahn·pas·ta toothpaste*

Zahnschmerzen pl *tsahn*-shmer-tsen
toothache

Zahnseide ⓕ *tsahn*-zai-de *dental floss*

Zahnstocher ⓜ *tsahn*-shto-kher
toothpick

Zauberer(in) ⓜ/ⓕ *tsow*-be-rer/
tsow-be-re-rin *magician*

Zaun ⓜ *tsown* fence

Zehe ⓕ *tsay*-e toe • clove (of garlic)

zehn tsayn ten

zeigen *tsai*-gen show • point

Zeit ⓕ tsait time

Zeitschrift ⓕ *tsait*-shrift magazine

Zeitung ⓕ *tsai*-tung newspaper

Zeitungshändler ⓜ *tsai*-tungks-hen-dler
newsagency

Zeitungskiosk ⓜ *tsai*-tungks-kee-osk
newsstand

Zeitunterschied ⓜ *tsait*-un-ter-sheet
time difference

Zelt ⓝ tselt tent

zelten *tsel*-ten camp

Zeltplatz ⓜ tselt-plats campsite

Zentimeter ⓜ tsen-ti-*may*-ter centimetre

Zentralheizung ⓕ tsen-*trahl*-hai-tsung
central heating

Zentrum ⓝ *tsen*-trum centre

zerbrechen tser-*bre*-khen break

zerbrechlich tser-*brekh*-likh fragile

Zertifikat ⓝ tser-ti-fi-*kaht* certificate

Zeugnis ⓝ *tsoyk*-nis reference (work)

Ziege ⓕ *tsee*-ge goat

ziehen *tsee*-en pull

Ziel ⓝ tseel target • finish (sport)

Zigarette ⓕ tsi-ga-*re*-te cigarette

Zigarre ⓕ tsi-*gar*-re cigar

Zimmer ⓝ *tsi*-mer room

Zimmernummer ⓕ *tsi*-mer-nu-mer
room number

Zirkus ⓜ *tsir*-kus circus

Zitrone ⓕ tsi-*traw*-ne lemon

Zoll ⓜ tsol customs

Zoo ⓜ tsaw zoo

zu tsoo too • at

zu Hause tsoo how-ze (at) home

Zucchini ⓕ tsu-*kee*-ni
zucchini • courgette

Zucker ⓜ *tsu*-ker sugar

Zuckererbse ⓕ *tsu*-ker-erp-se snow pea

Zufall ⓜ *tsoo*-fal chance

Zug ⓜ tsook train

zugeben *tsoo*-gay-ben
admit (accept as true)

Zukunft ⓕ *tsoo*-kunft future

Zulassung ⓕ *tsoo*-la-sung
car registration

zum Beispiel tsum *bai*-shpeel
for example

Zündung ⓕ *tsün*-dung ignition

zurück tsu-*rük* back (return)

zurückkommen tsu-*rük*-ko-men return

zusammen tsu-*za*-men together

Zusammenstoß ⓜ tsu-*za*-men-staws
crash

zustimmen *tsoo*-shti-men agree

Zutat ⓕ *tsoo*-taht ingredient

zweimal *tsvai*-mahl twice

zweite *tsvai*-te second

Zwerchfell ⓝ *tsverkh*-fel diaphragm

Zwiebel ⓕ *tsvee*-bel onion

Zwillinge ⓜ pl *tsvi*-ling-e twins

zwischen *tsvi*-shen between

INDEX